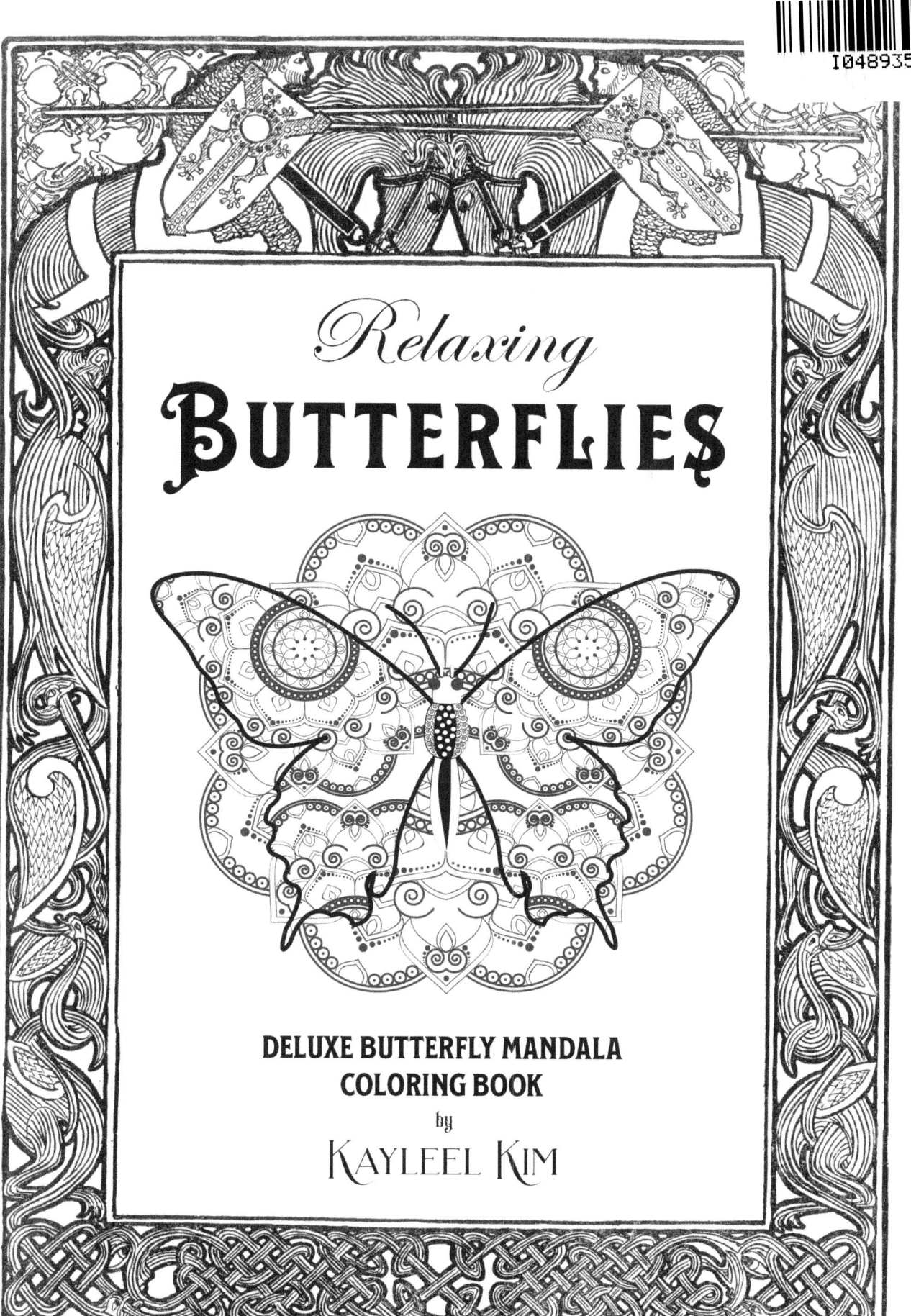

# *Relaxing*
# BUTTERFLIES

### DELUXE BUTTERFLY MANDALA COLORING BOOK

by

## KAYLEEL KIM

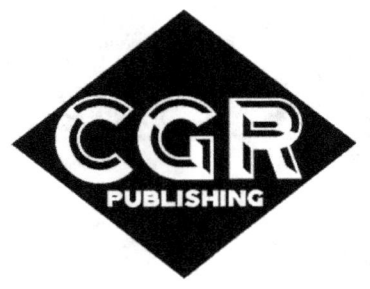

# Relaxing Butterflies:
## Deluxe Butterfly Mandala Coloring Book

by Kayleel Kim

More books at
**CGRpublishing.com**

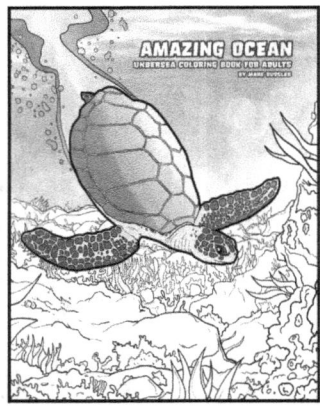

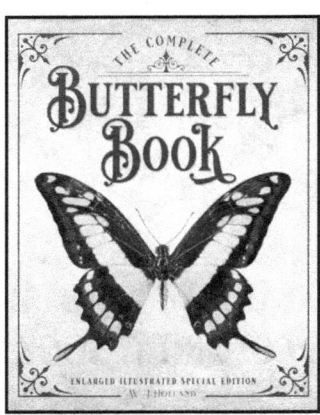

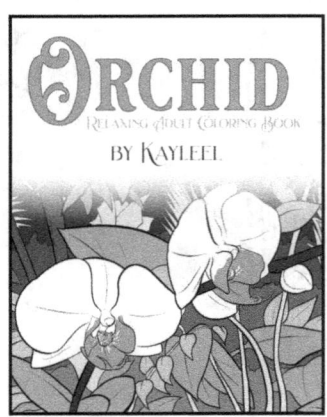

Amazing Ocean: Undersea
Coloring Book for Adults

The Complete Butterfly Book:
Enlarged Illustrated Special Edition

Orchid Relaxing Adult Coloring
Book by Kayleel

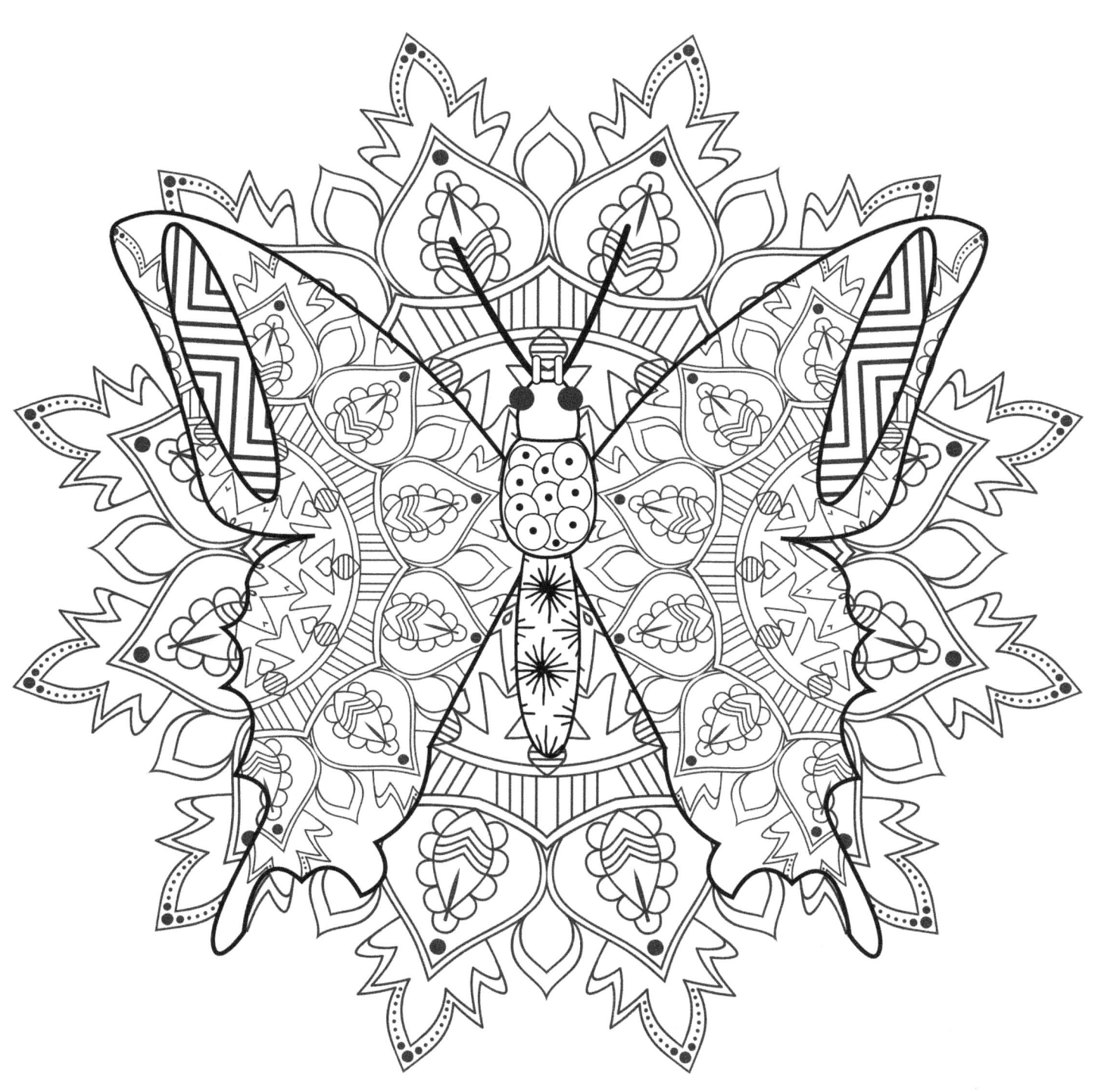

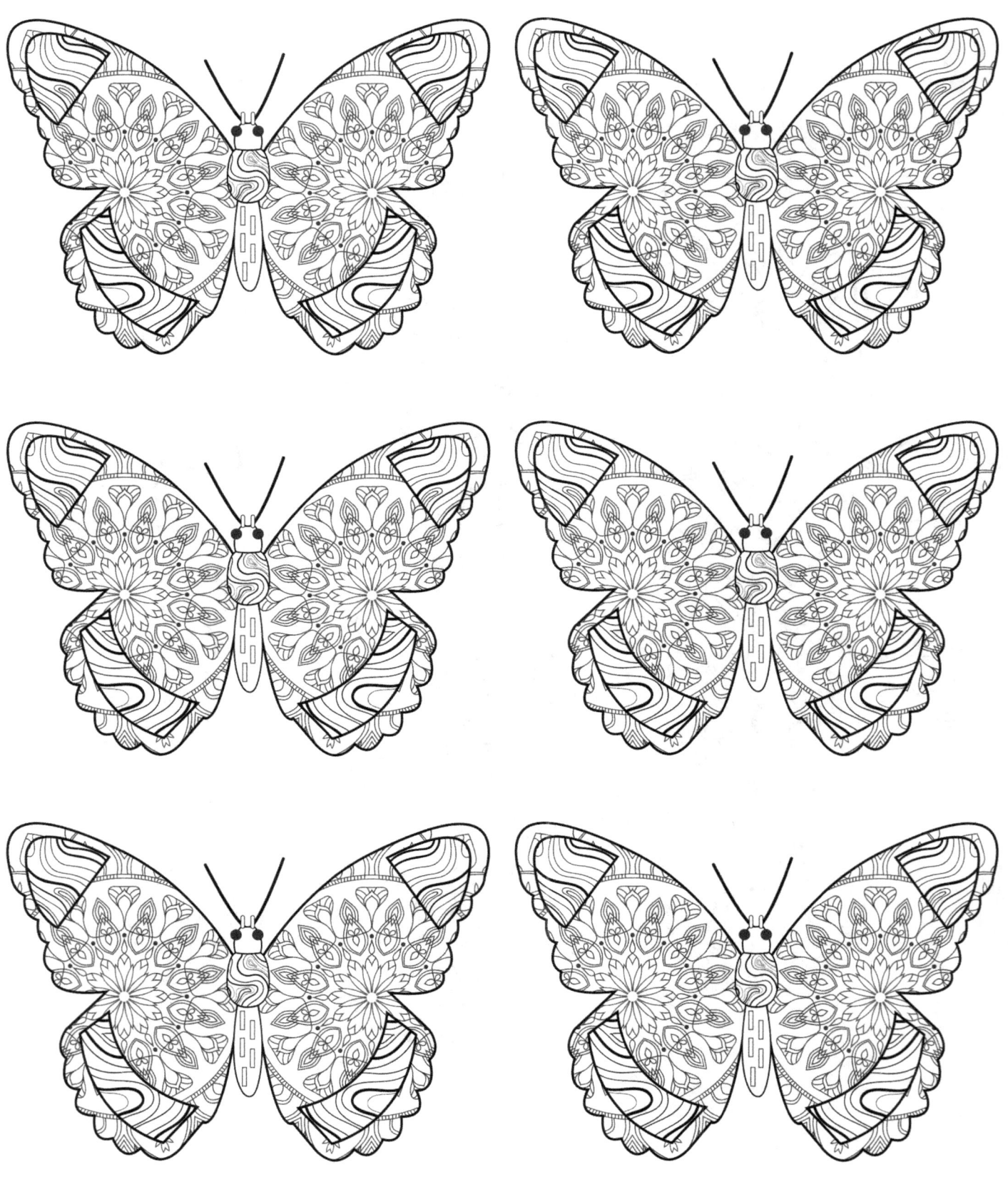

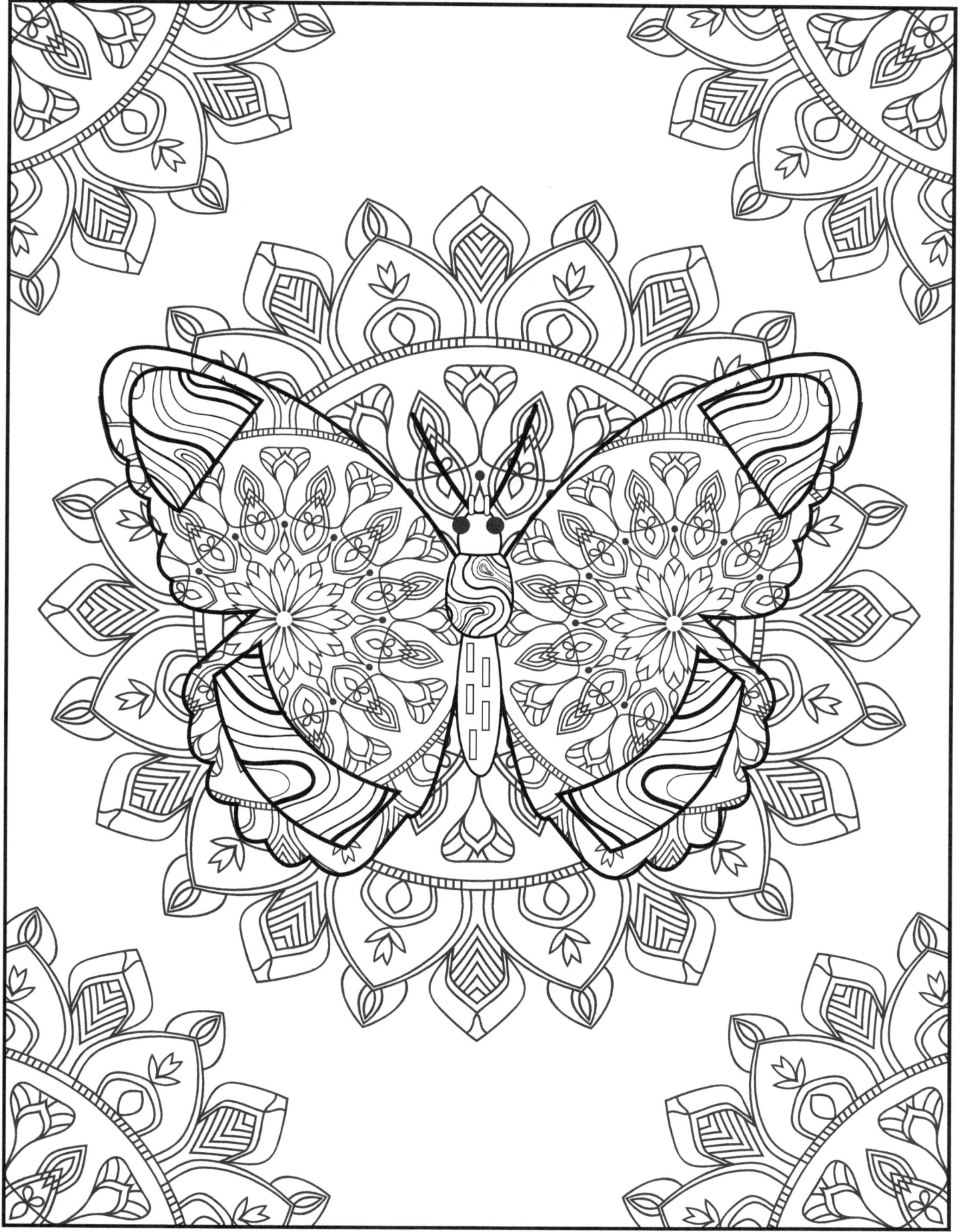

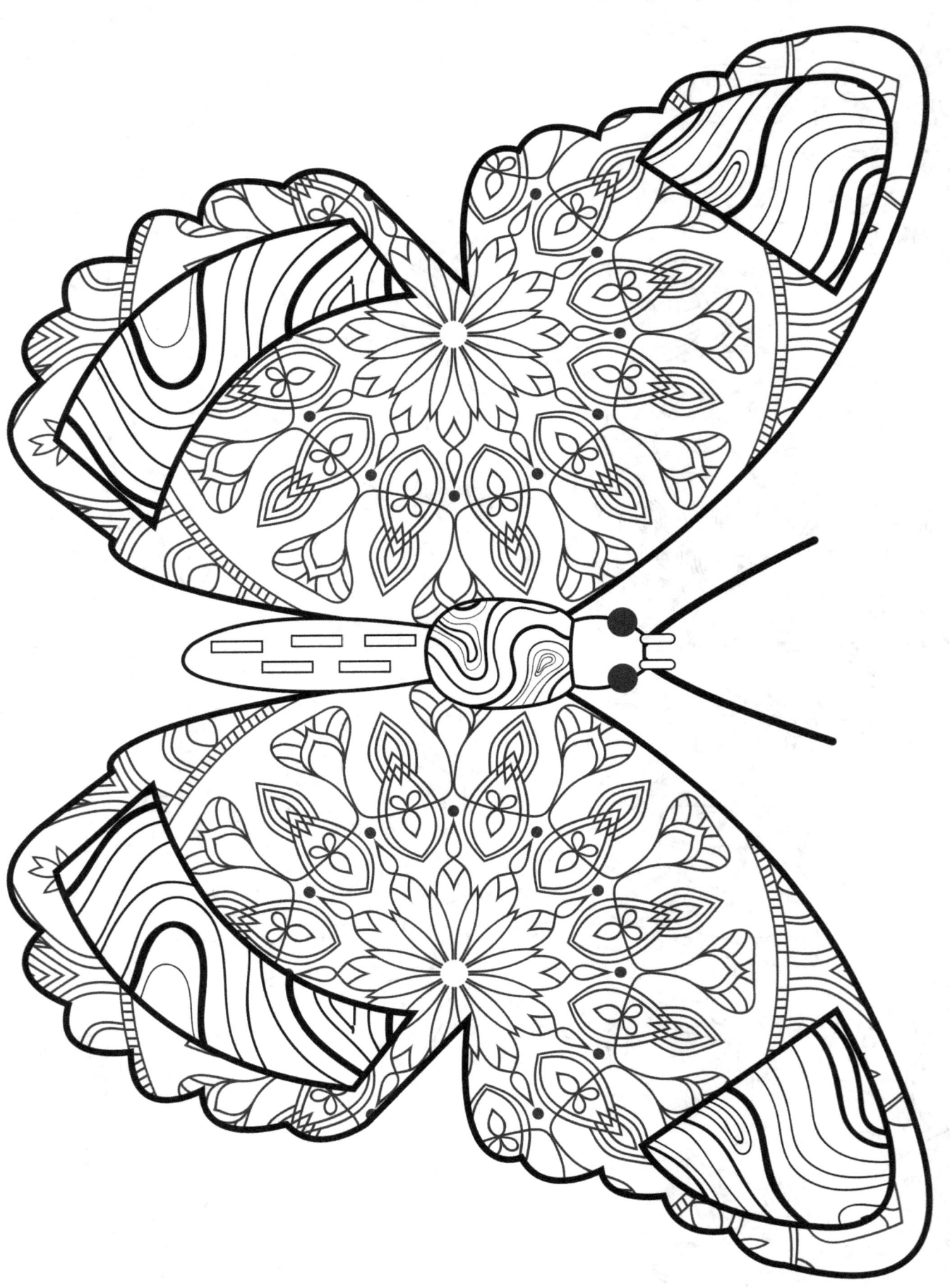

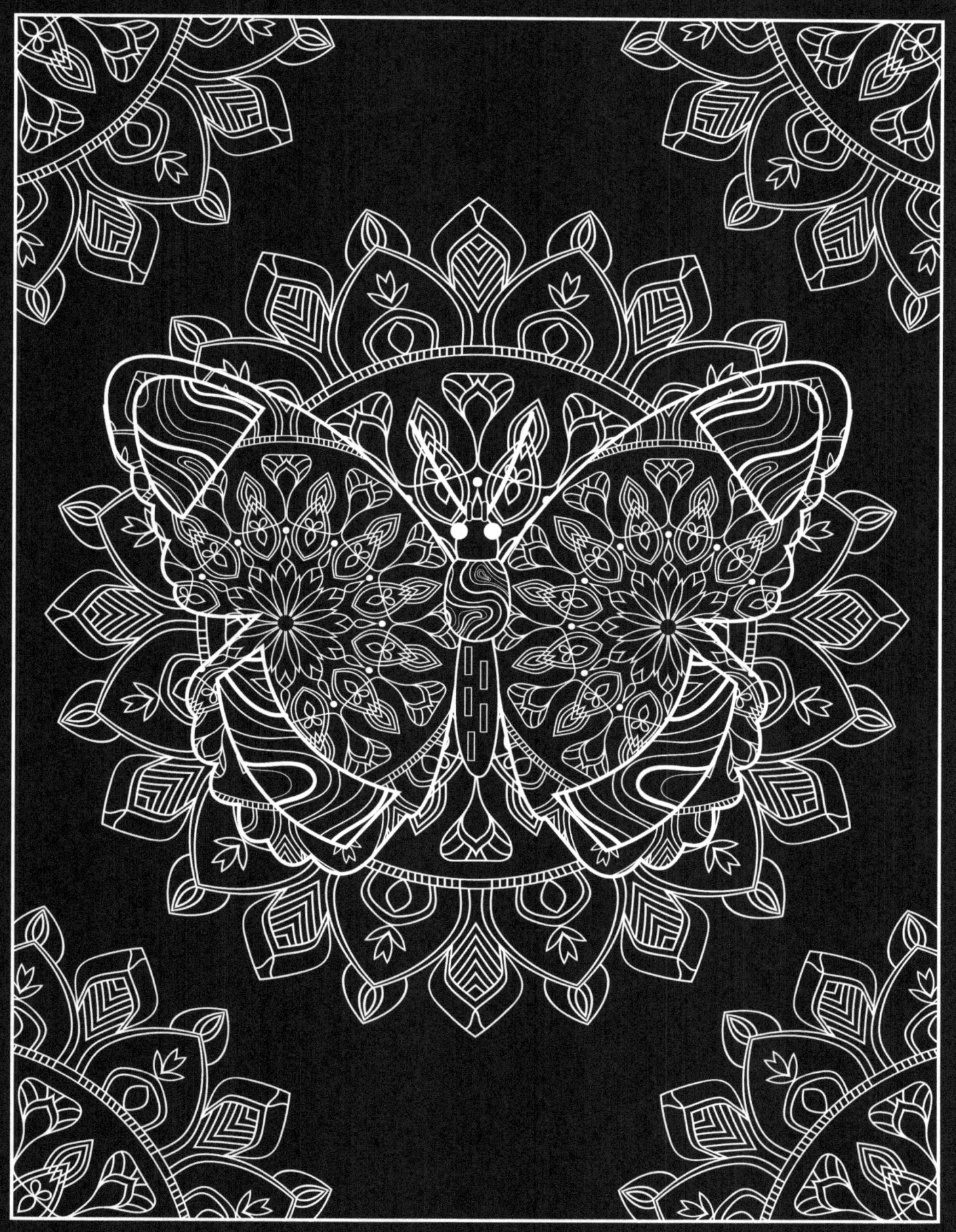

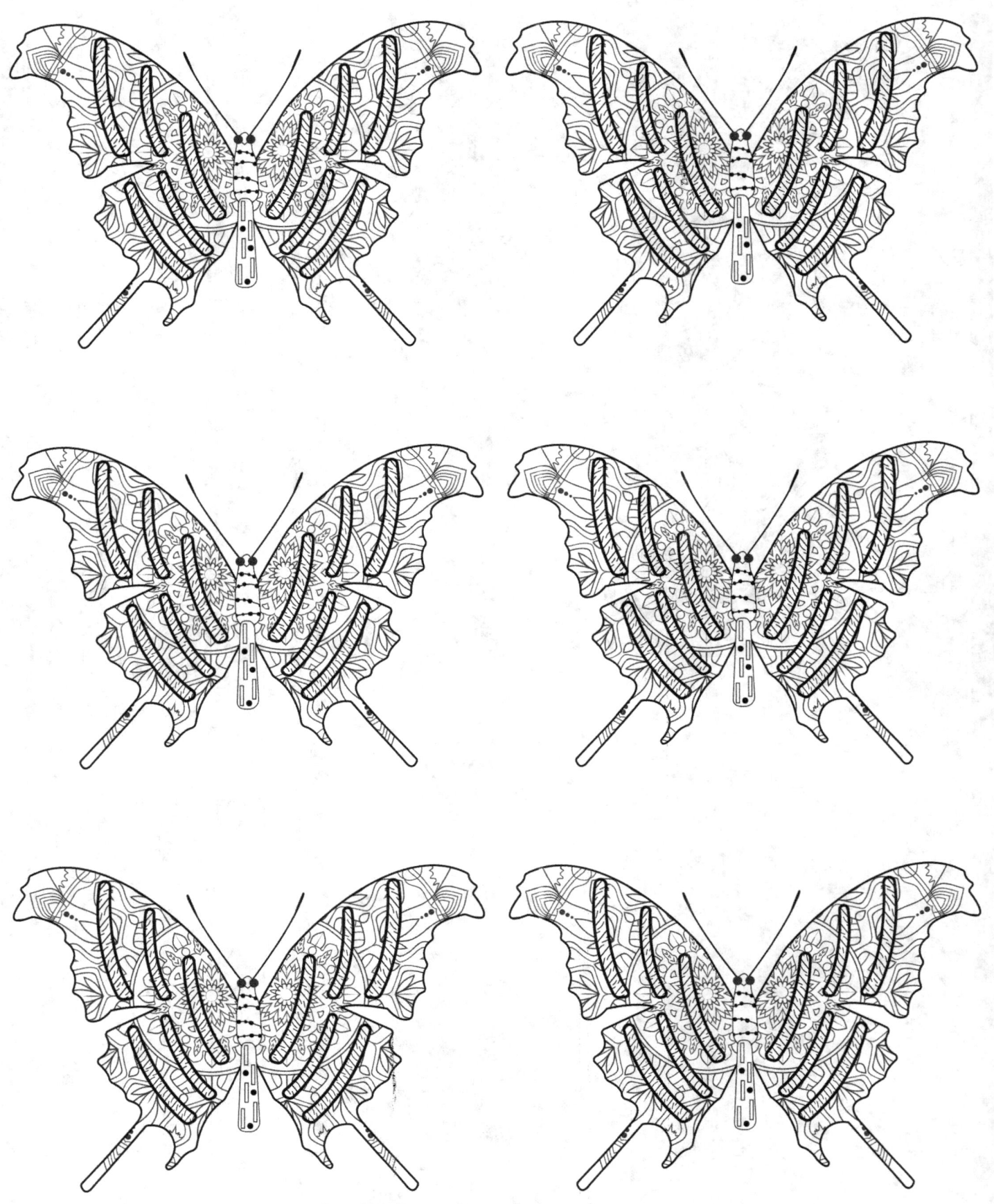

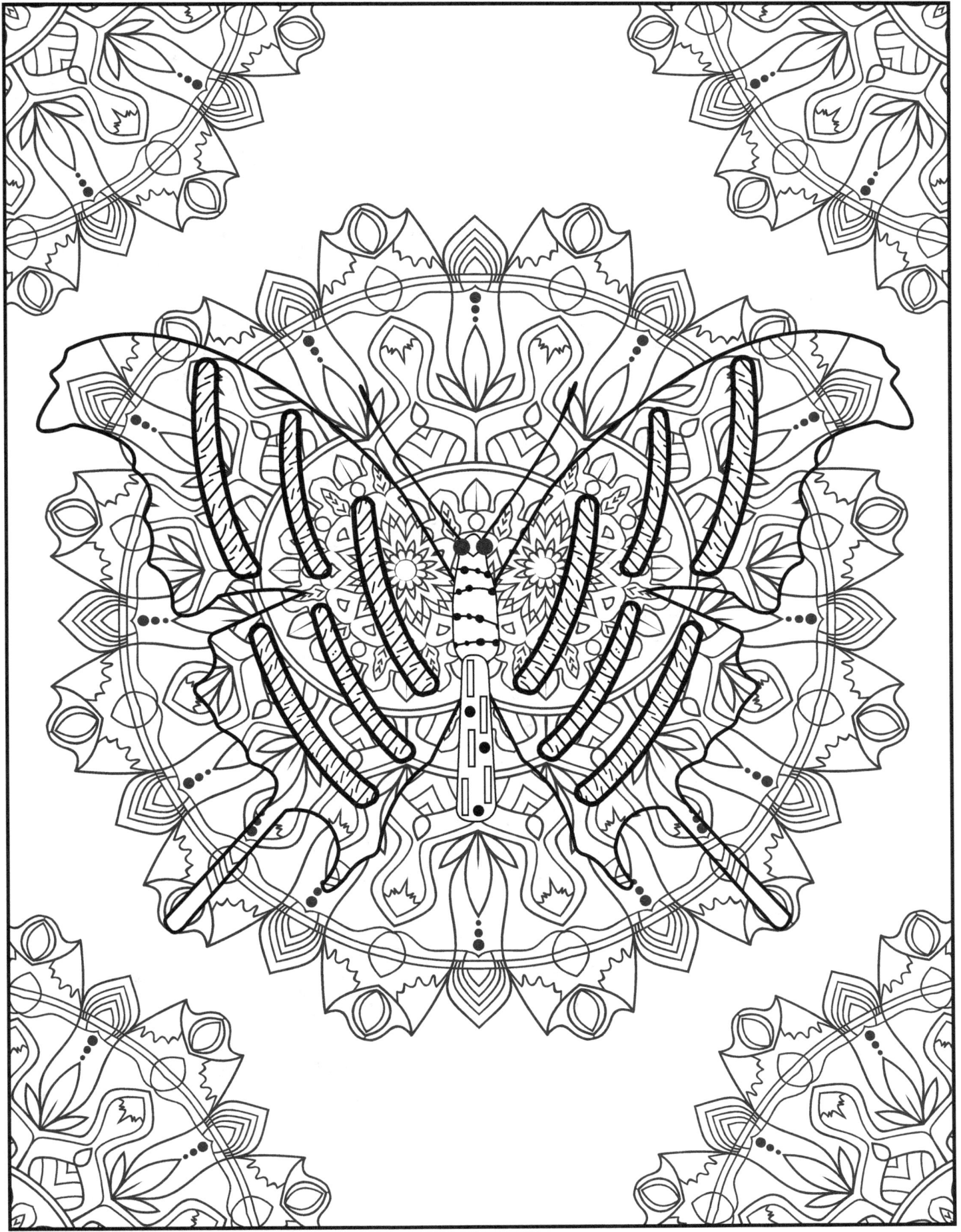

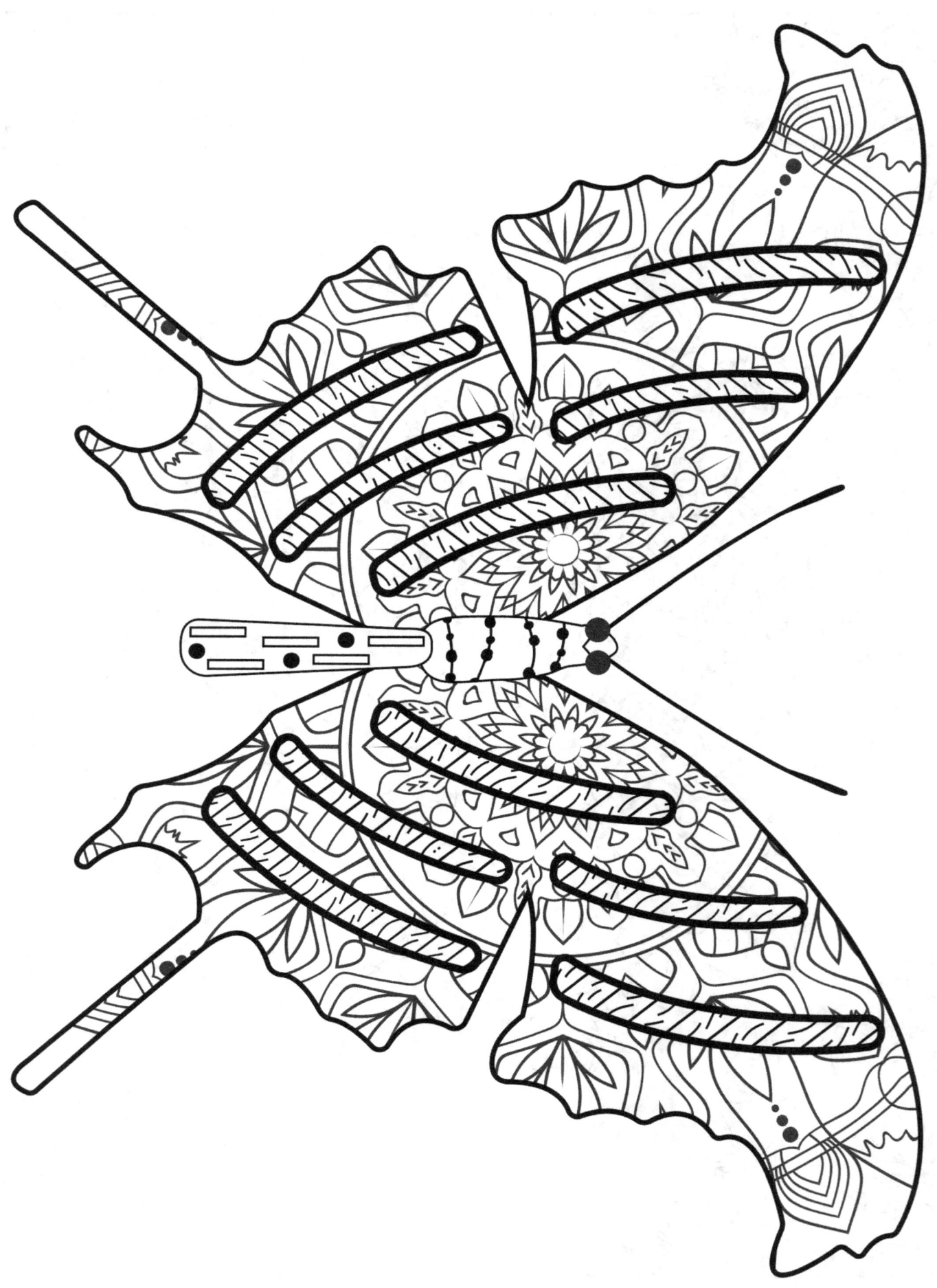

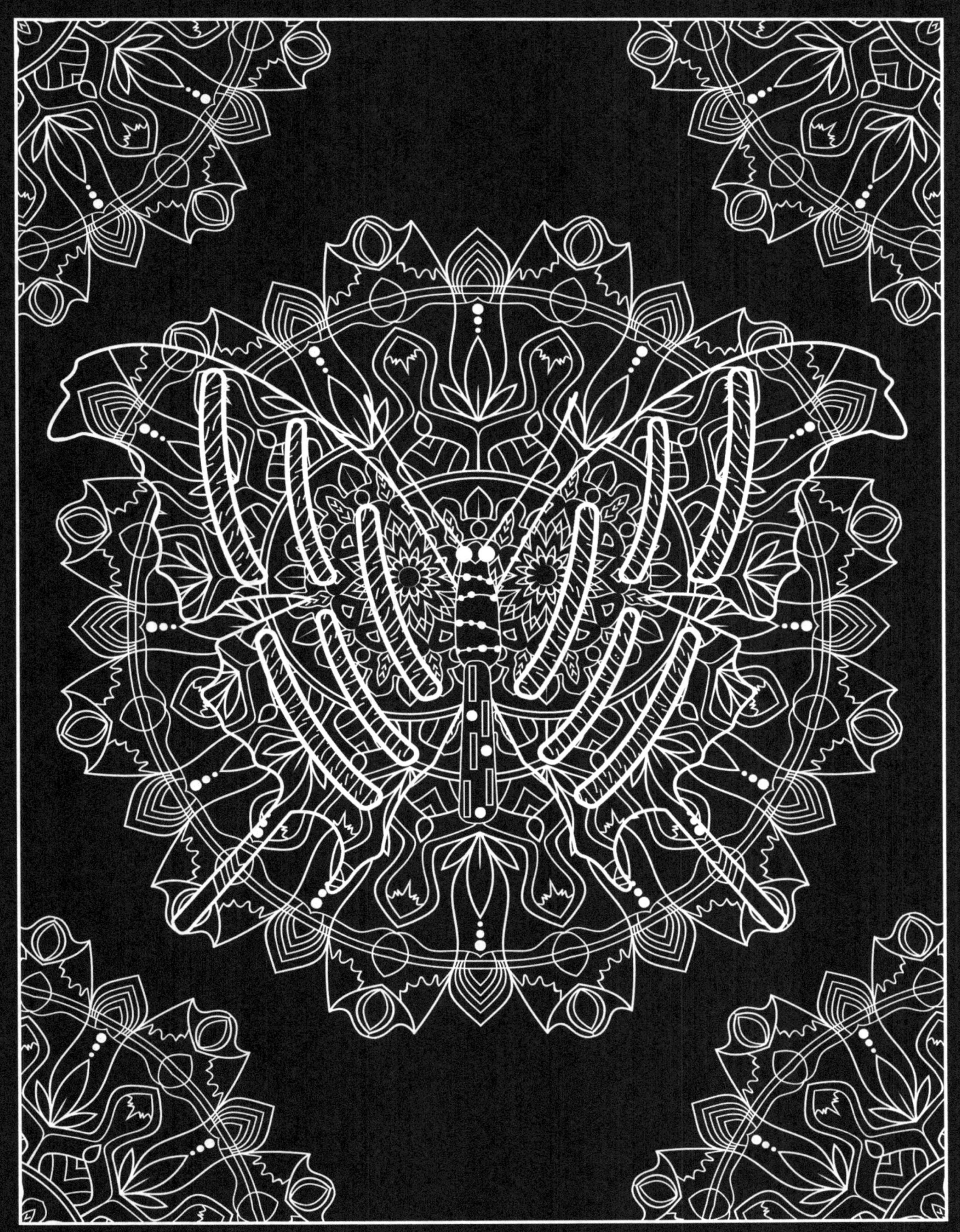

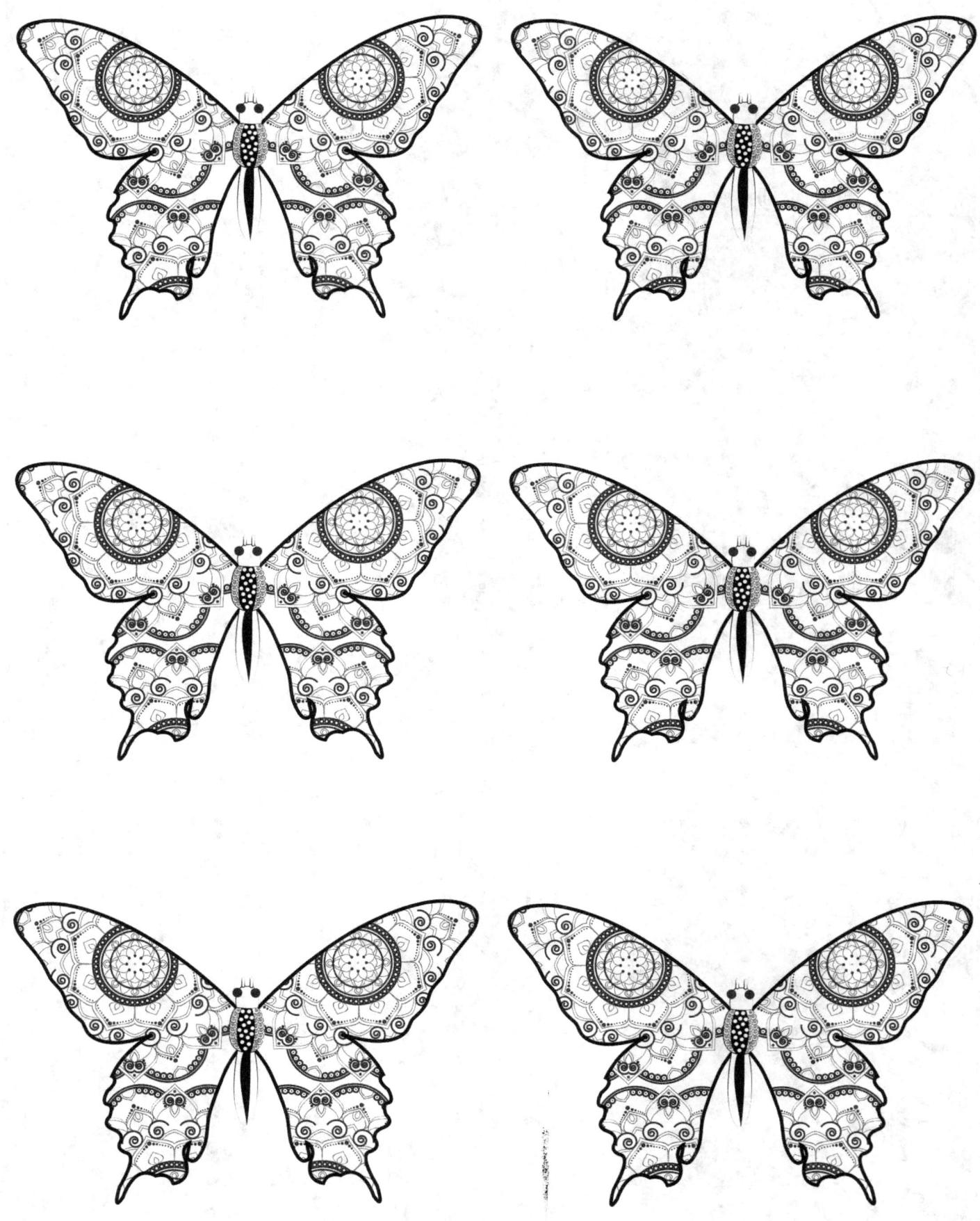

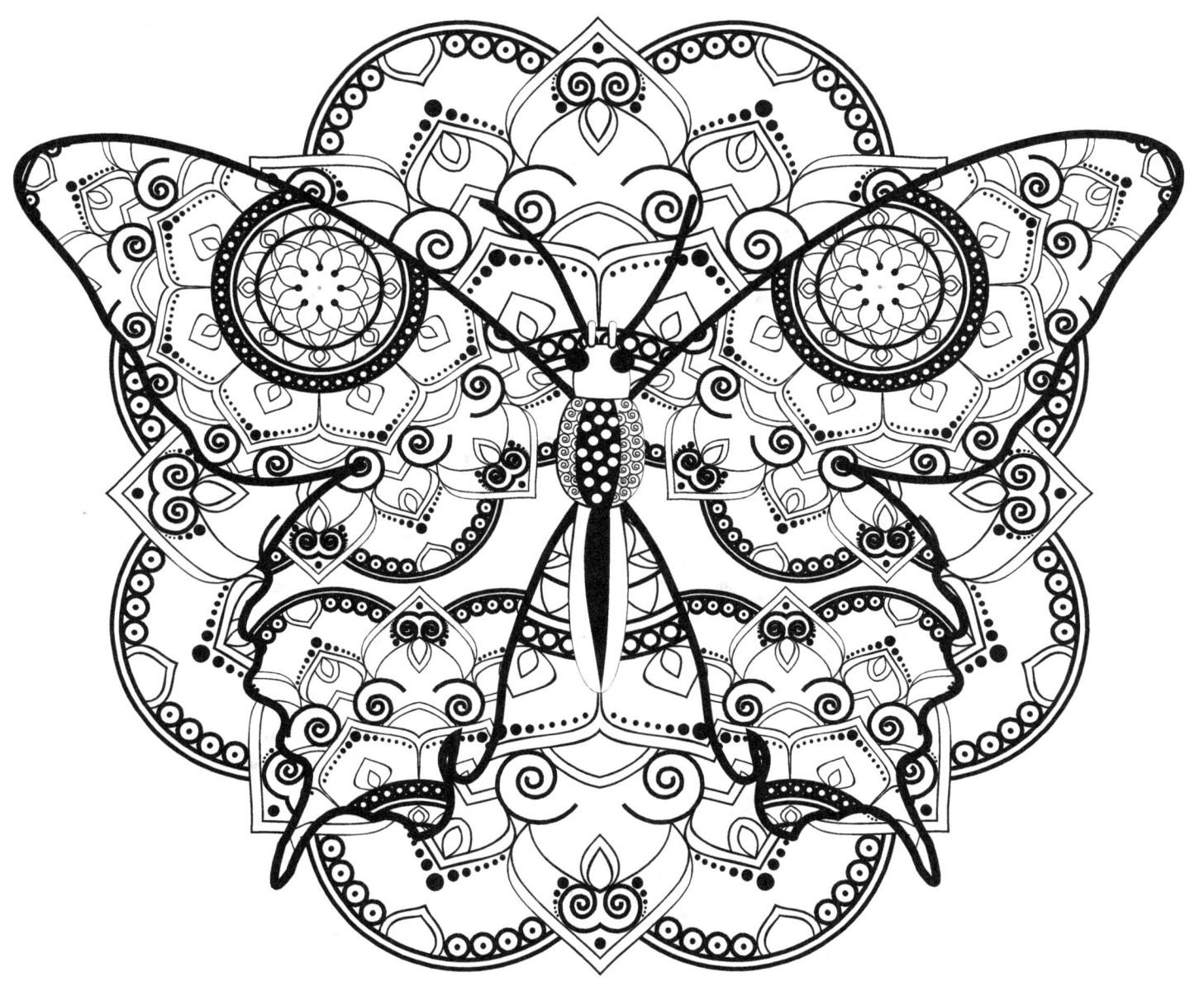

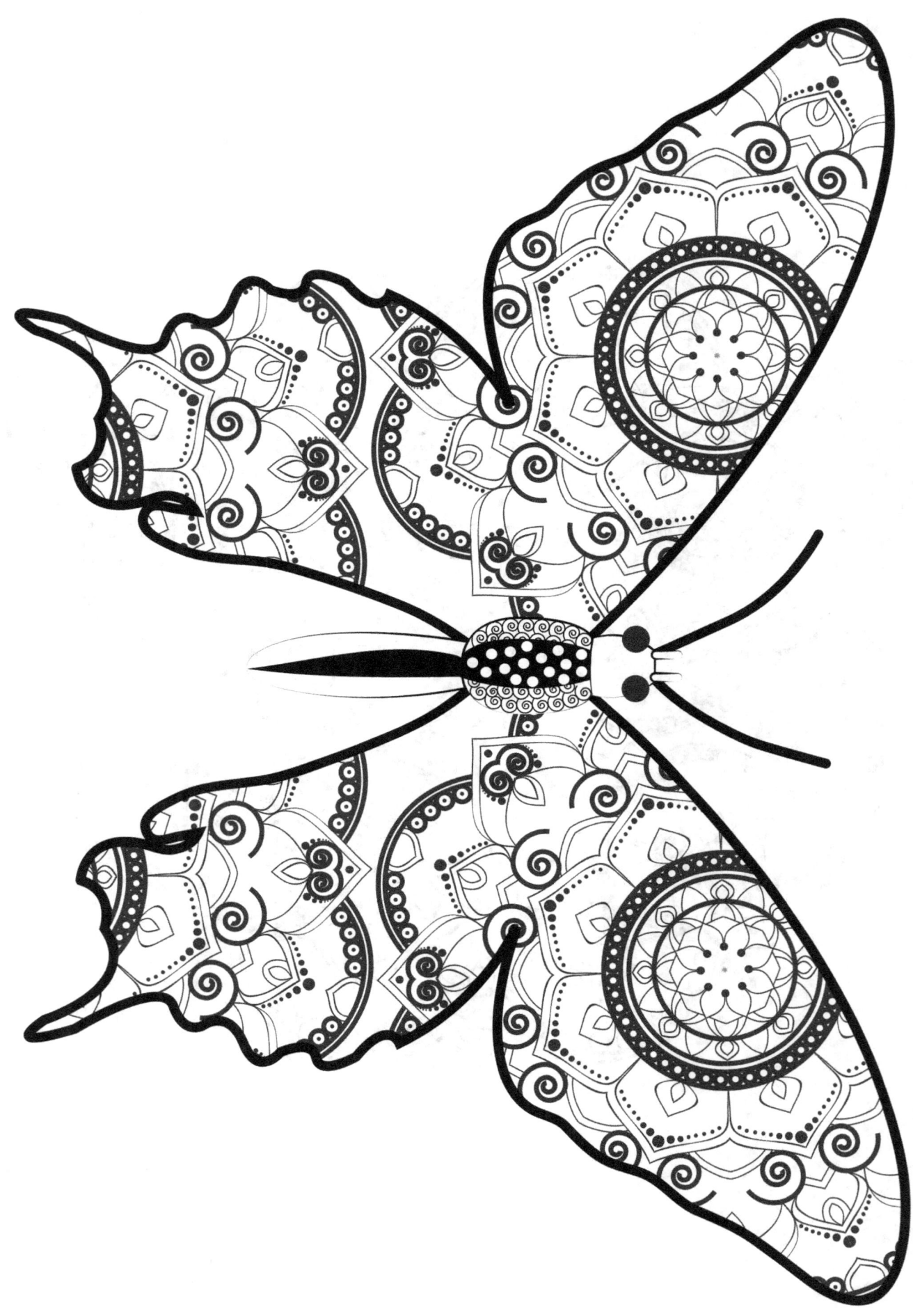

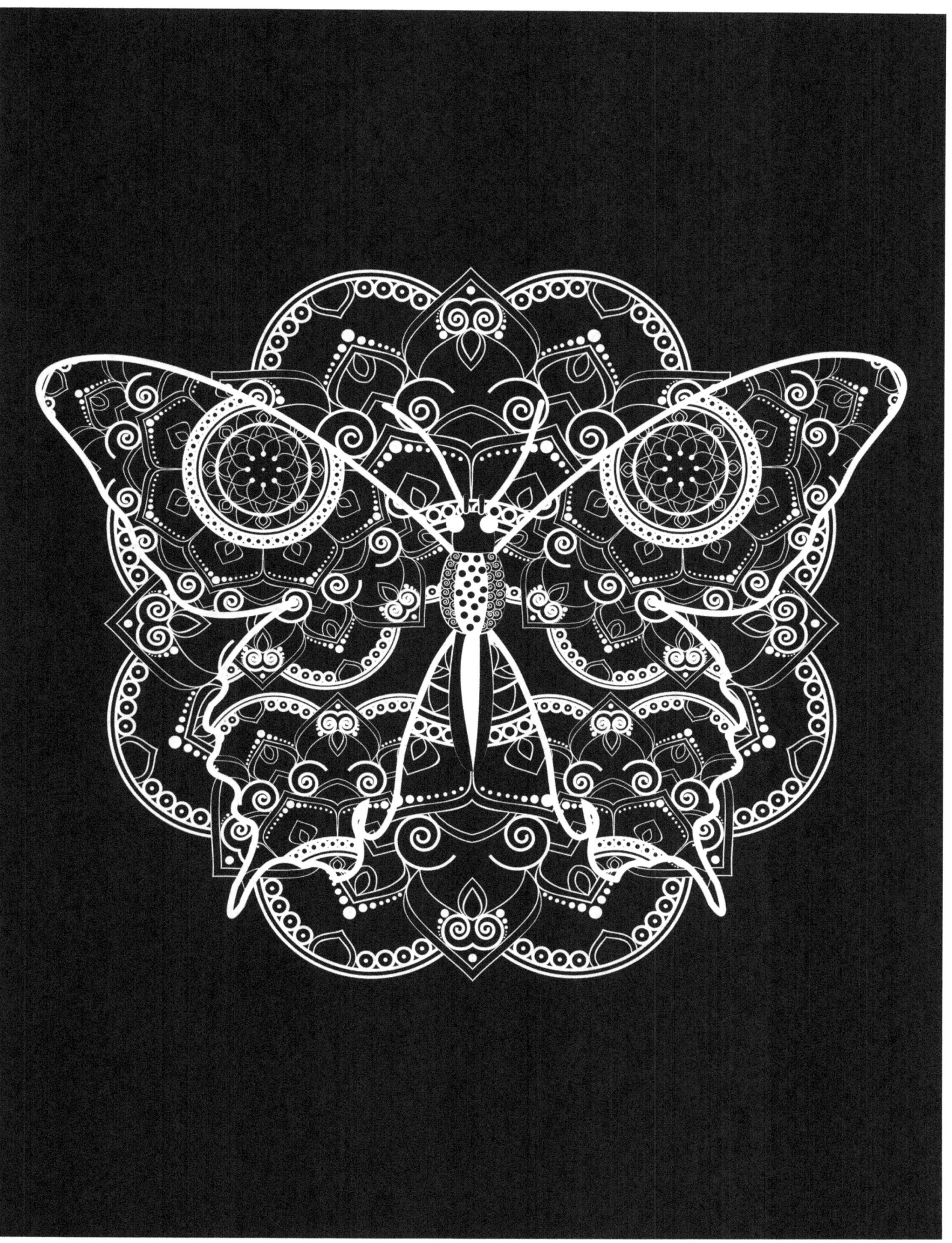

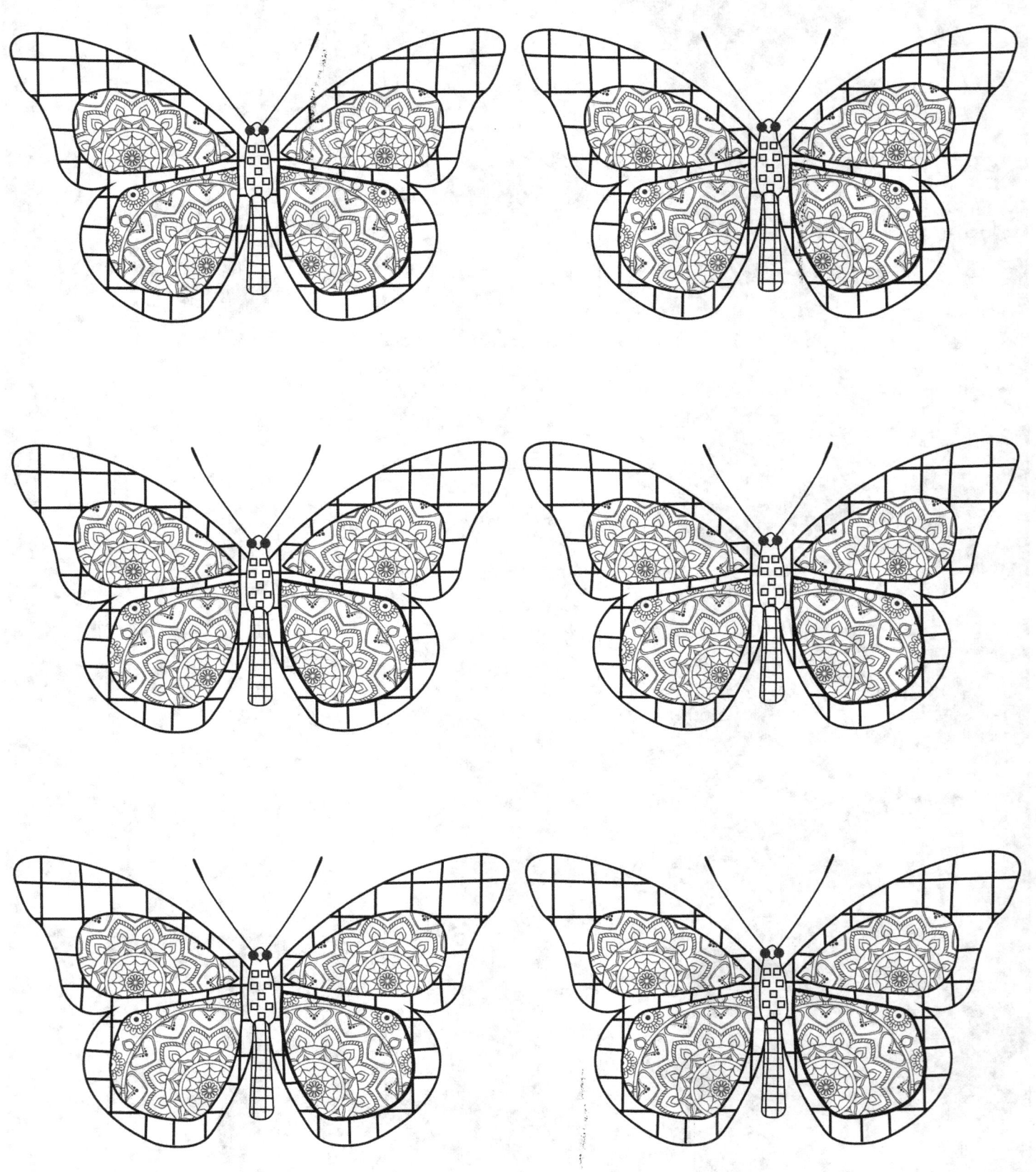

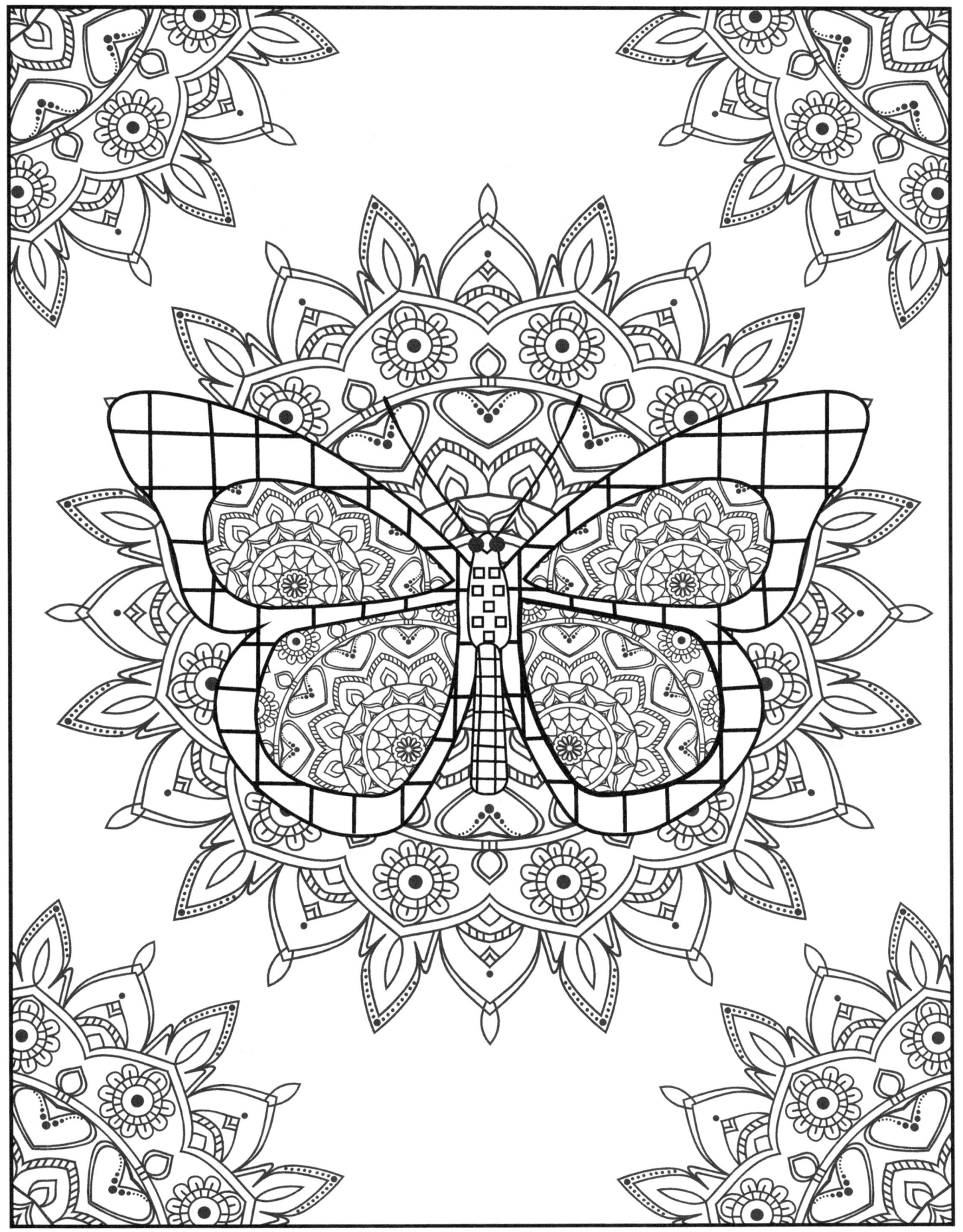

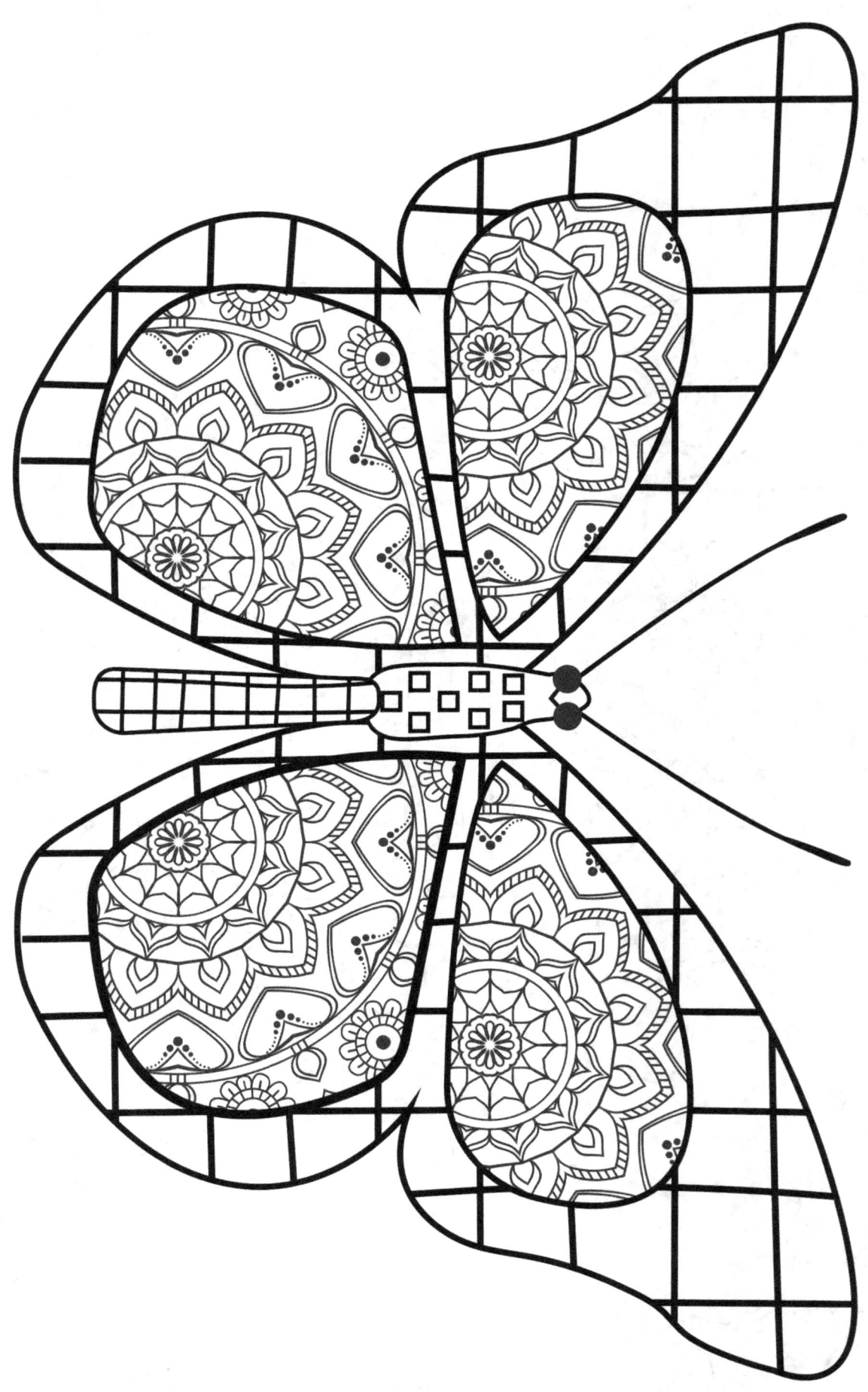

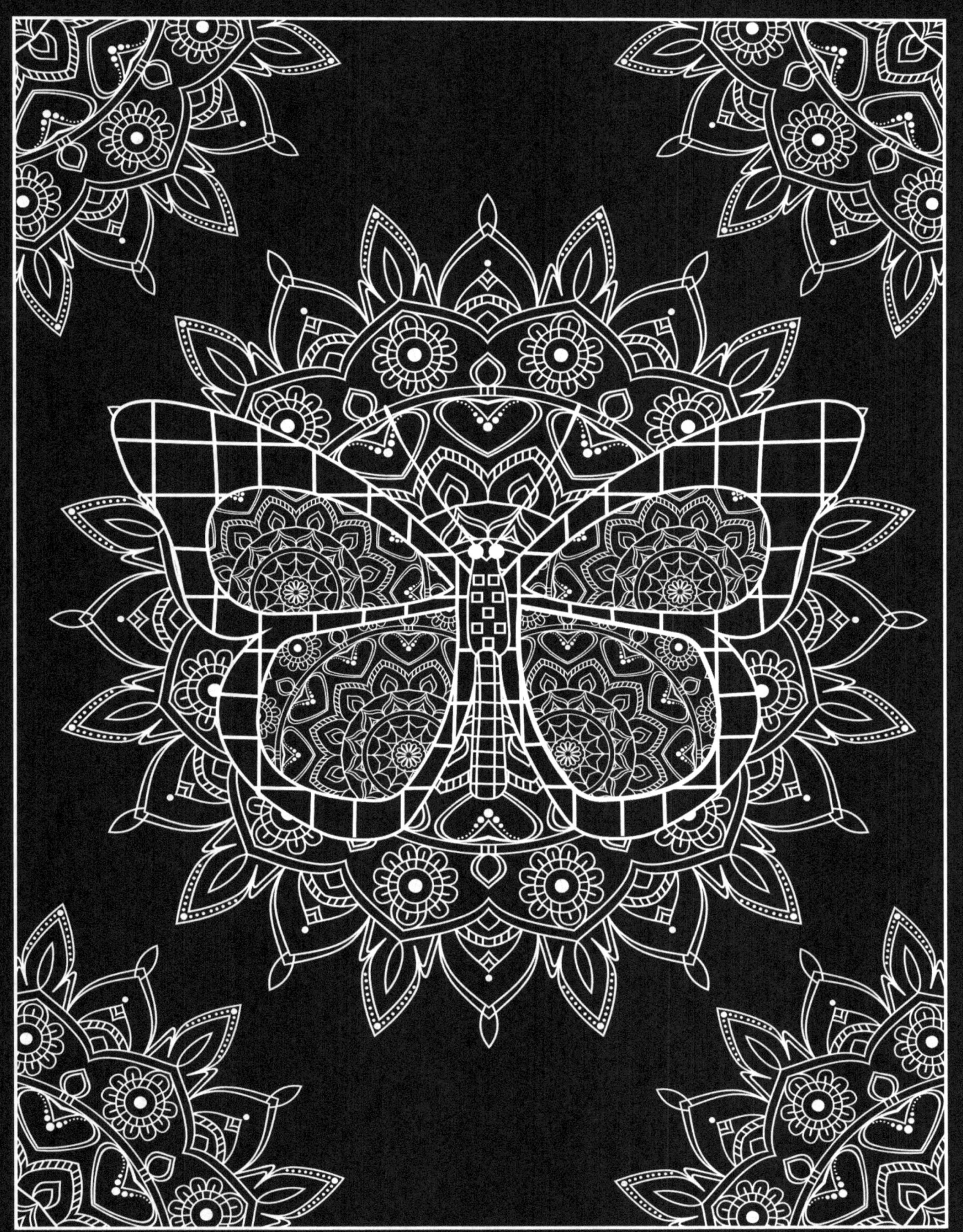

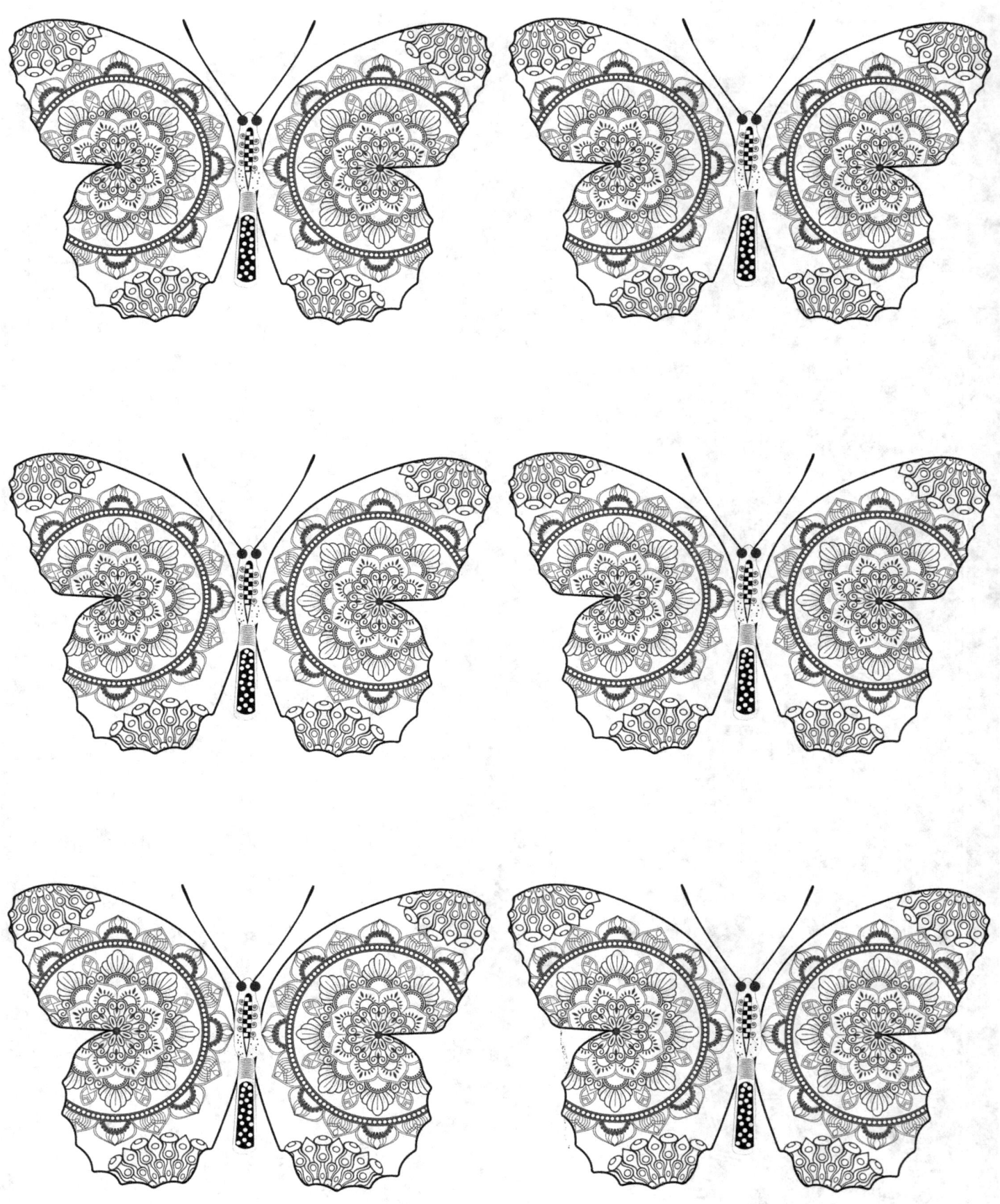

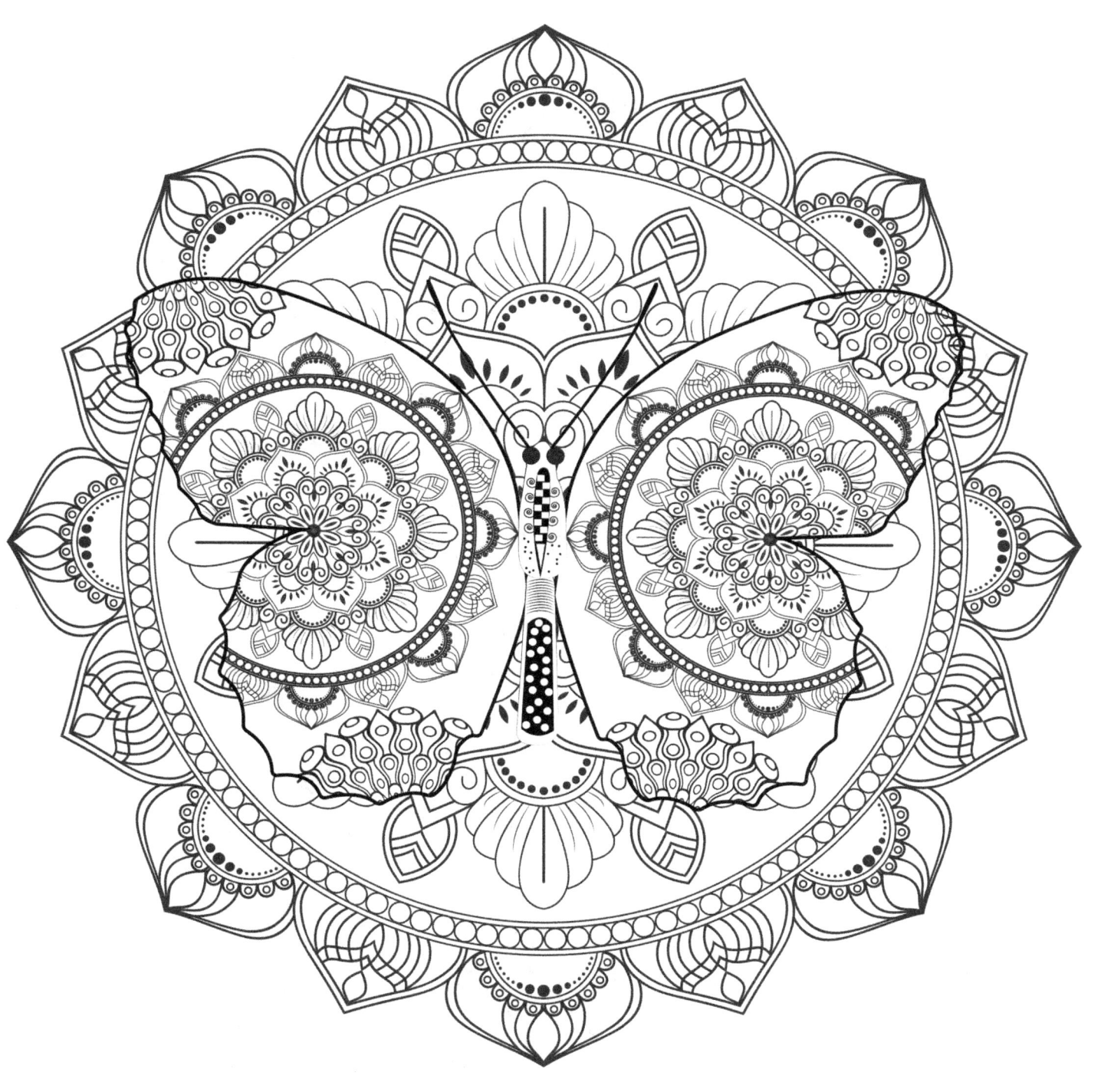

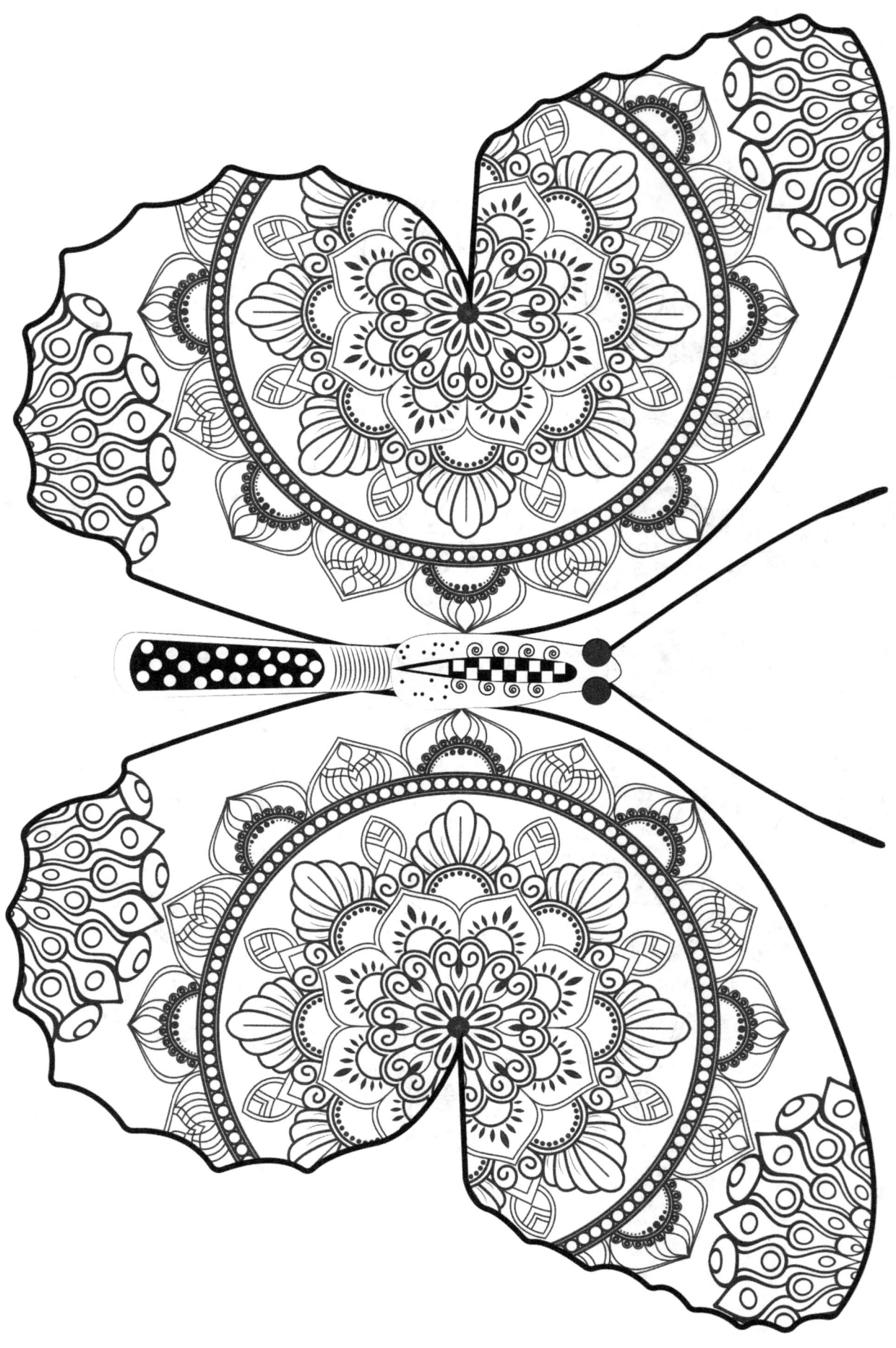

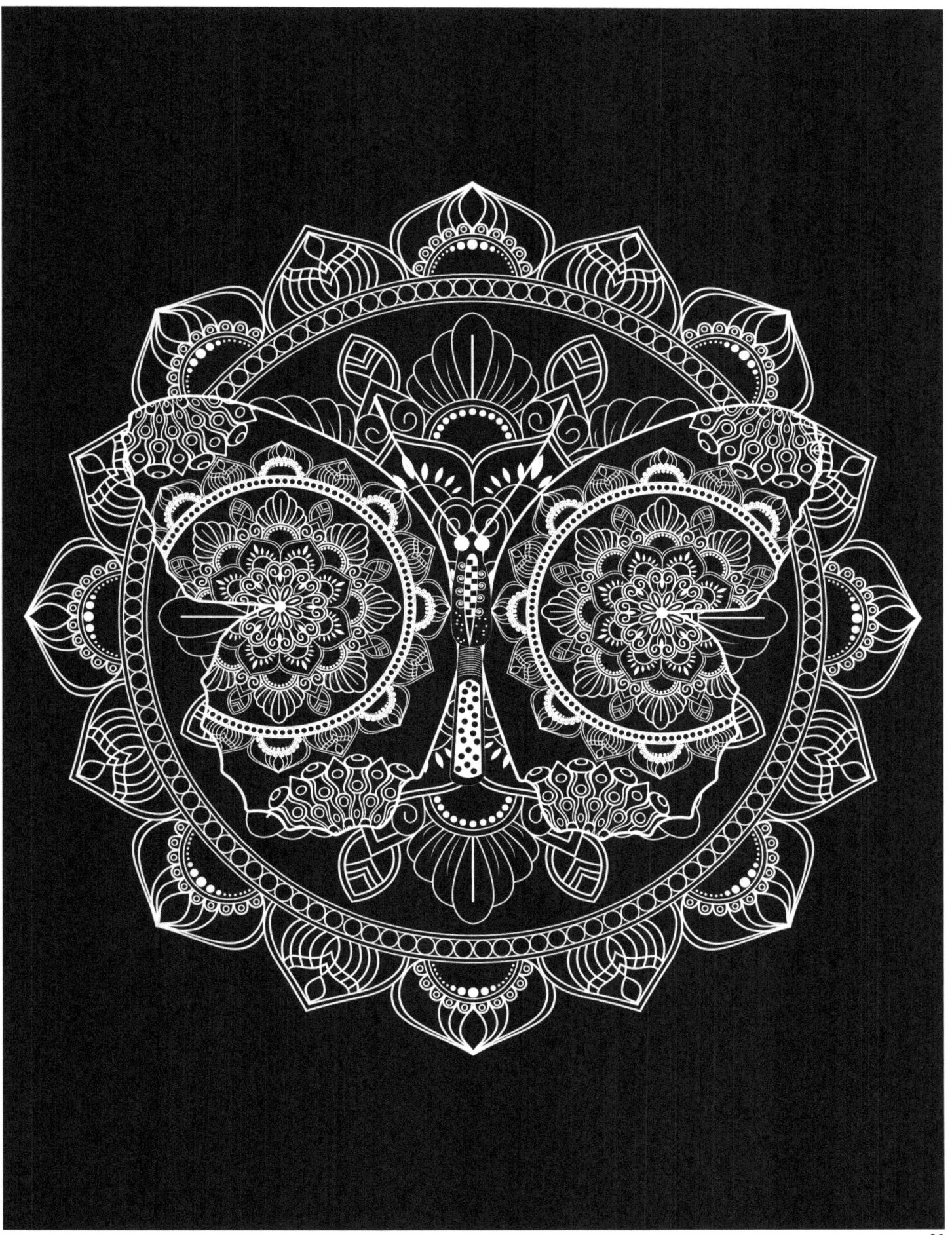

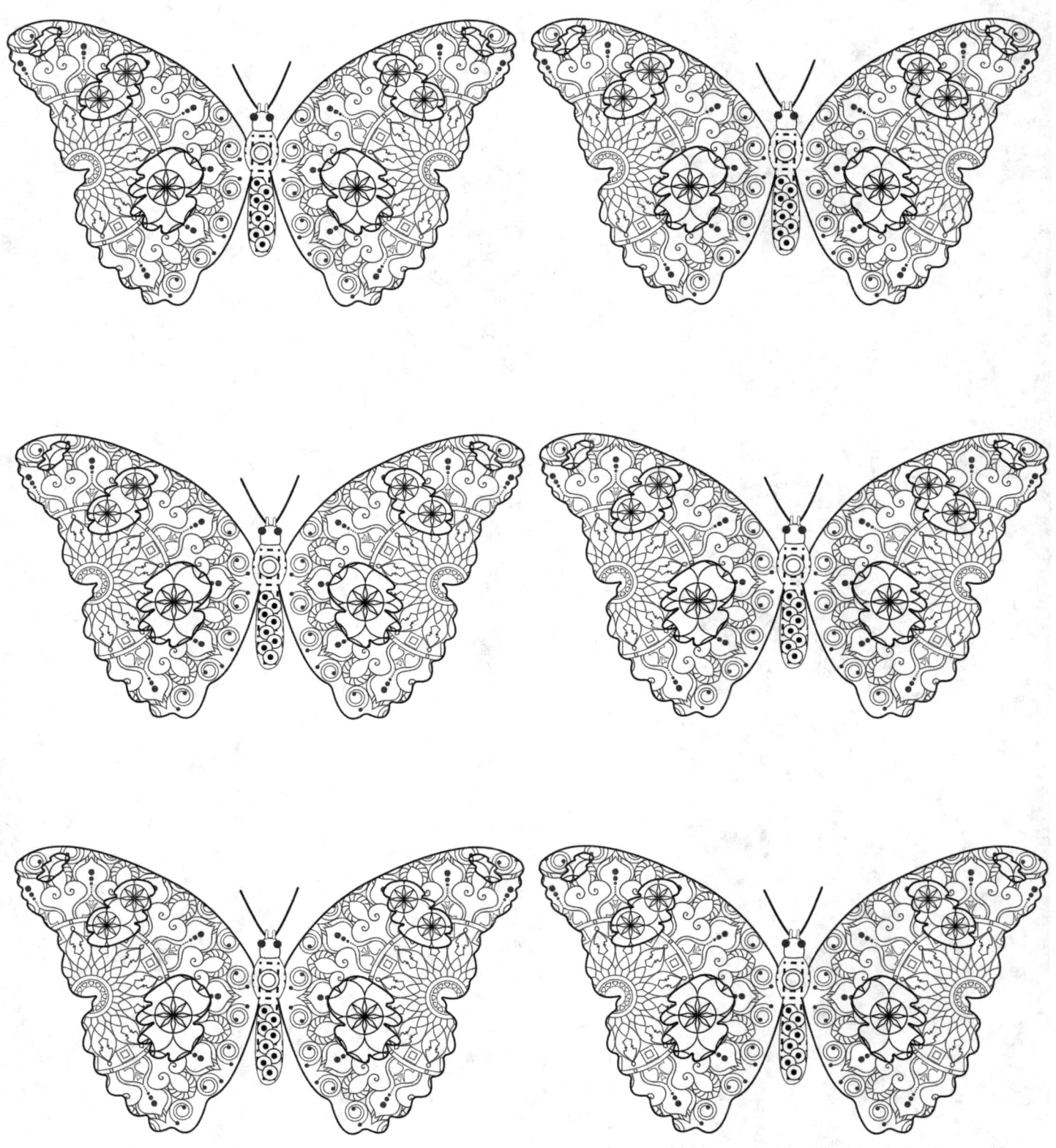

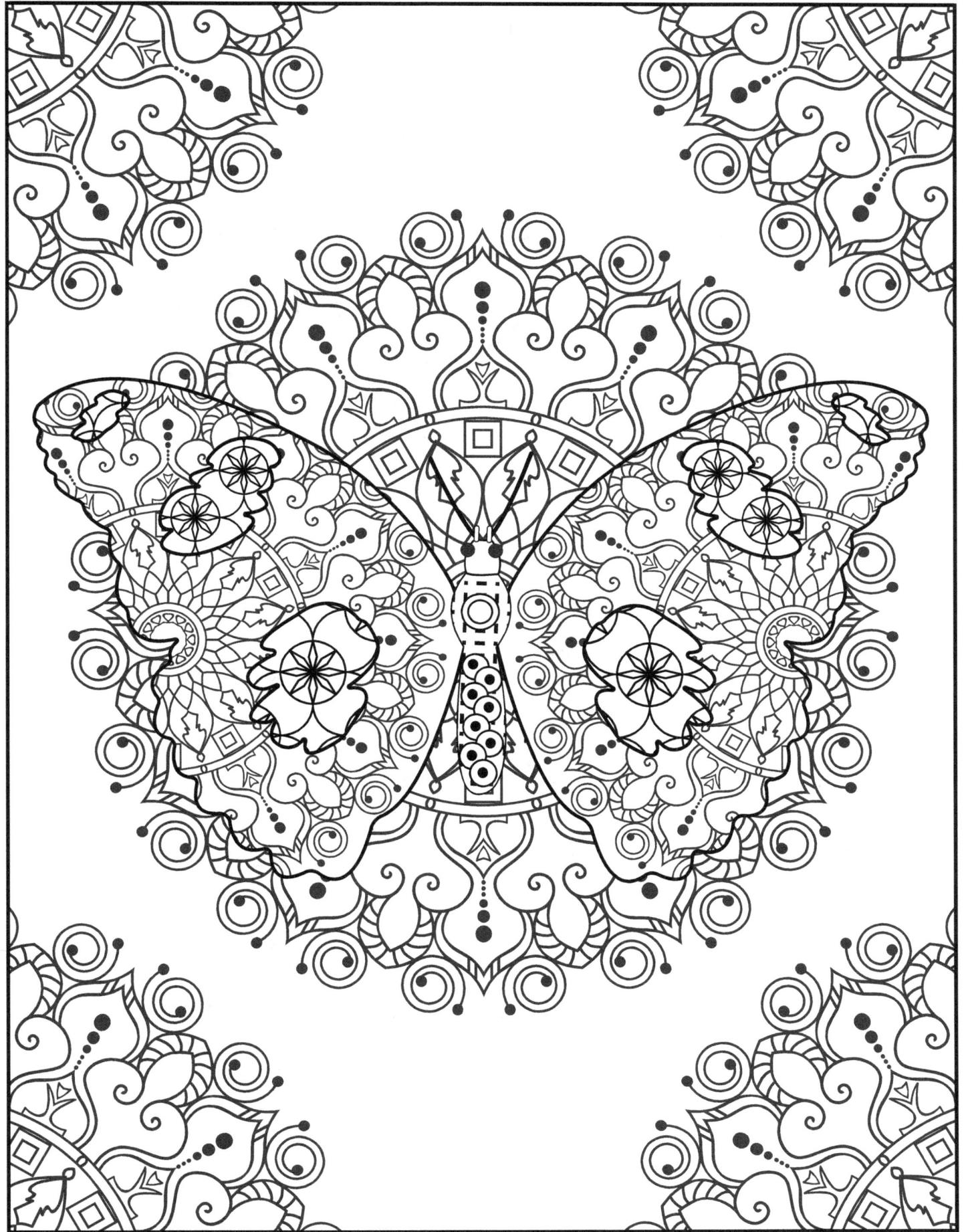

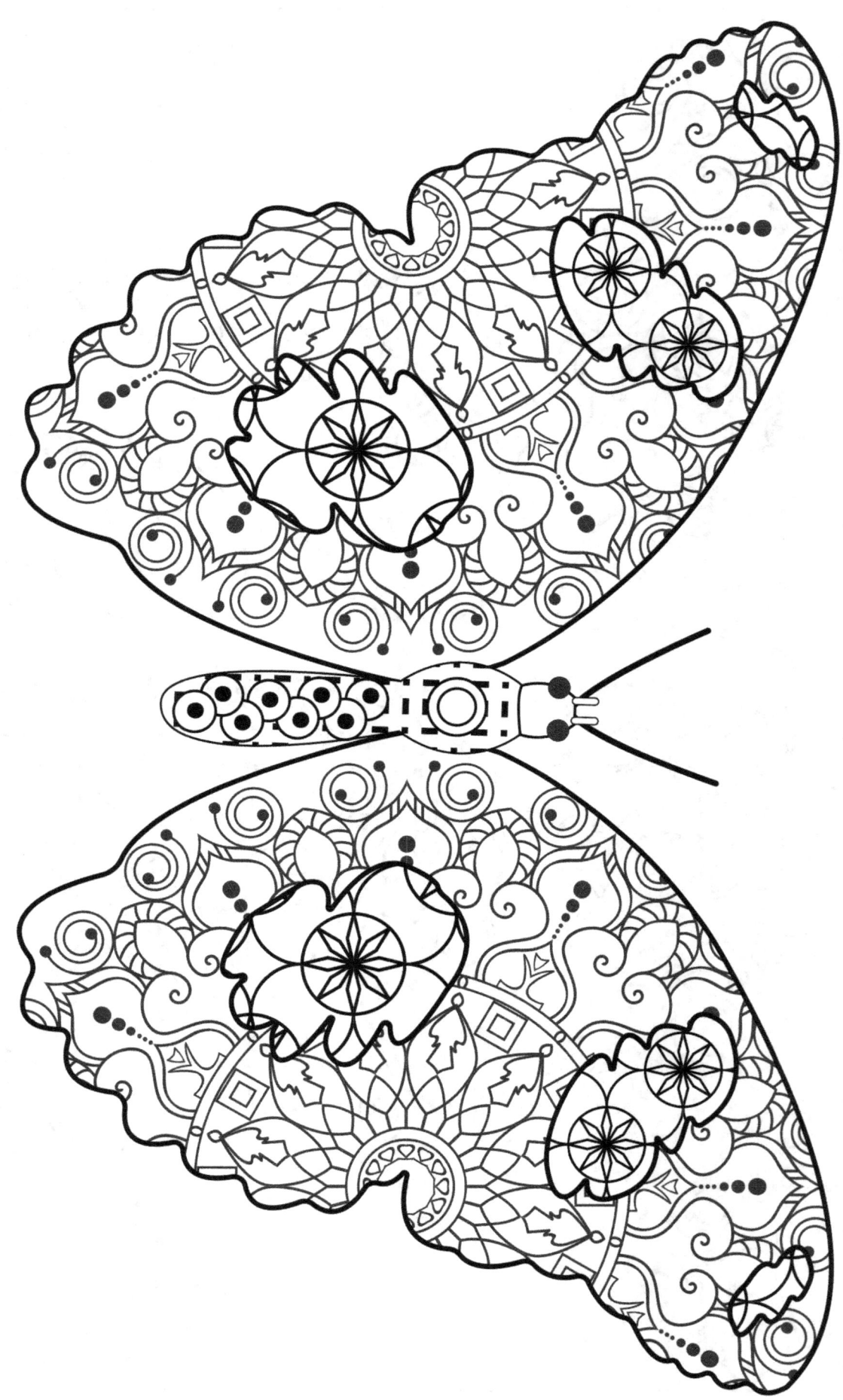

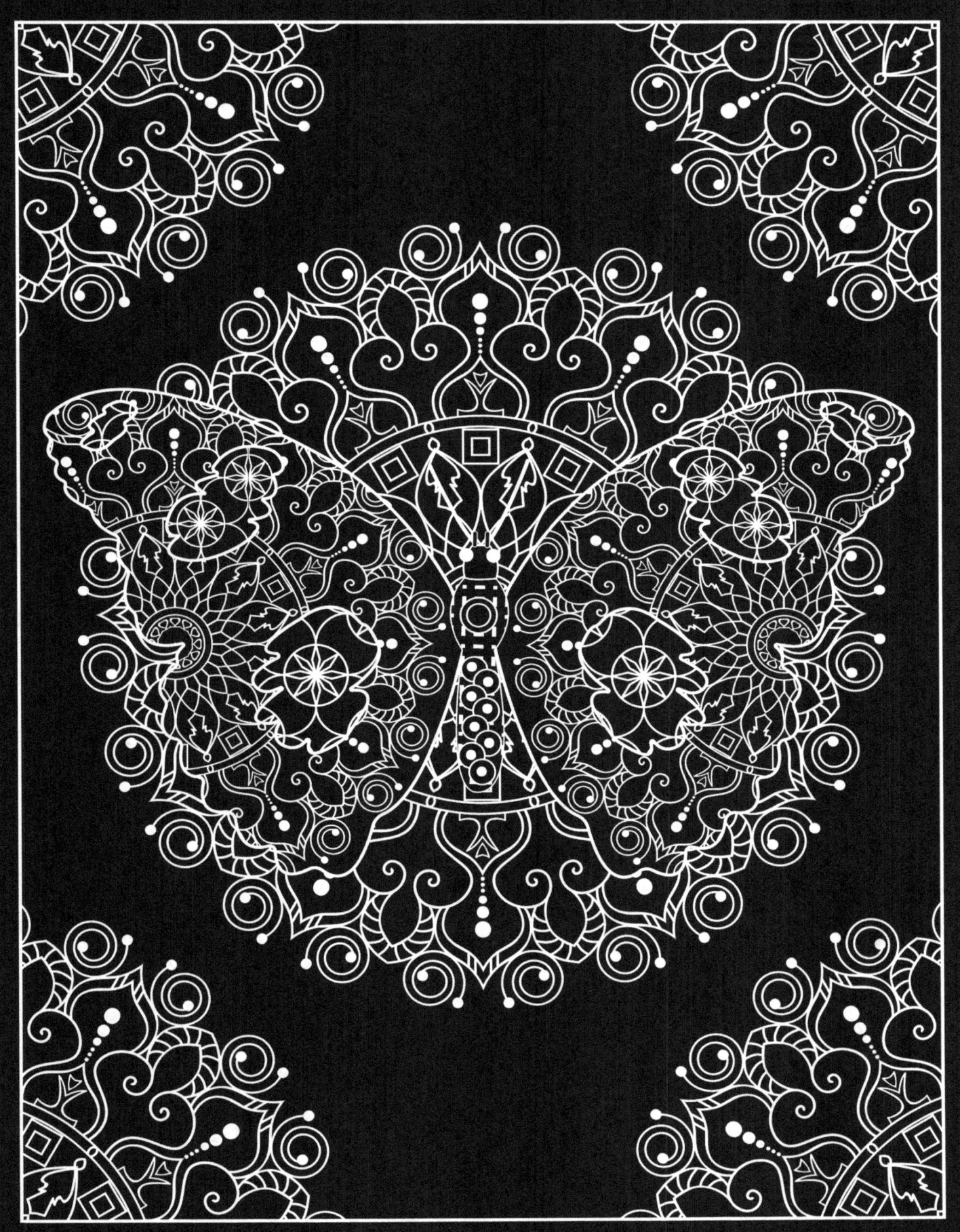

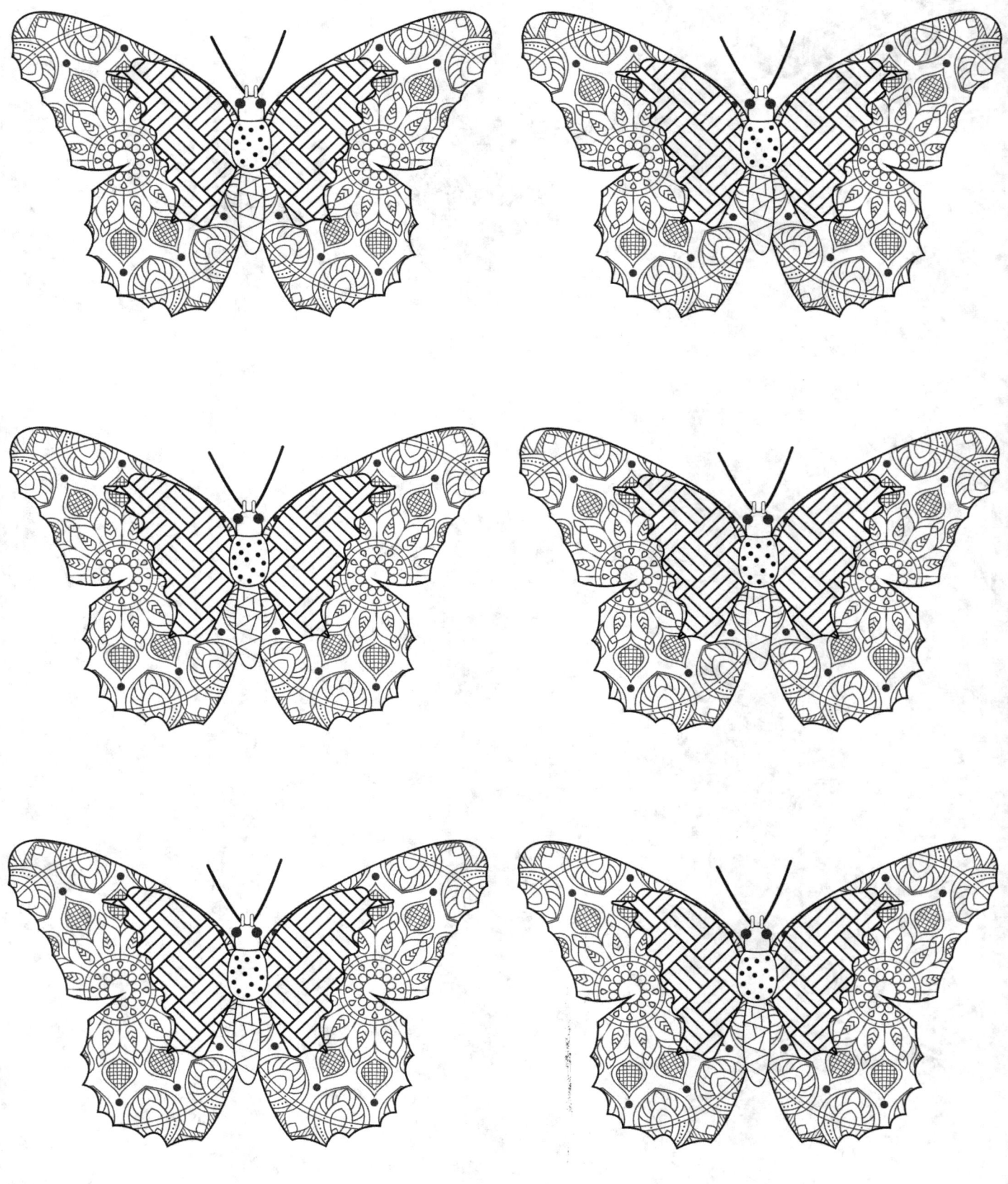

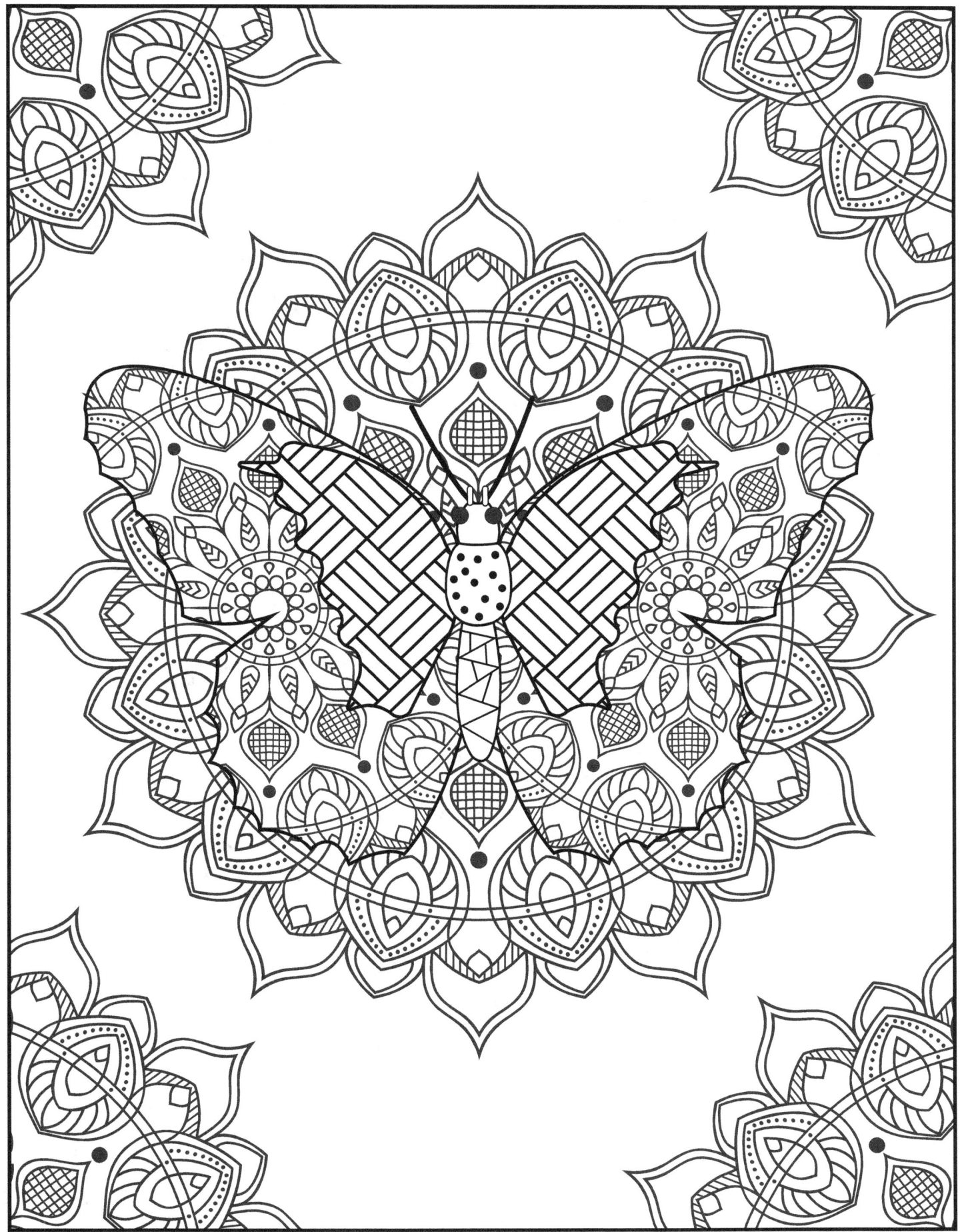

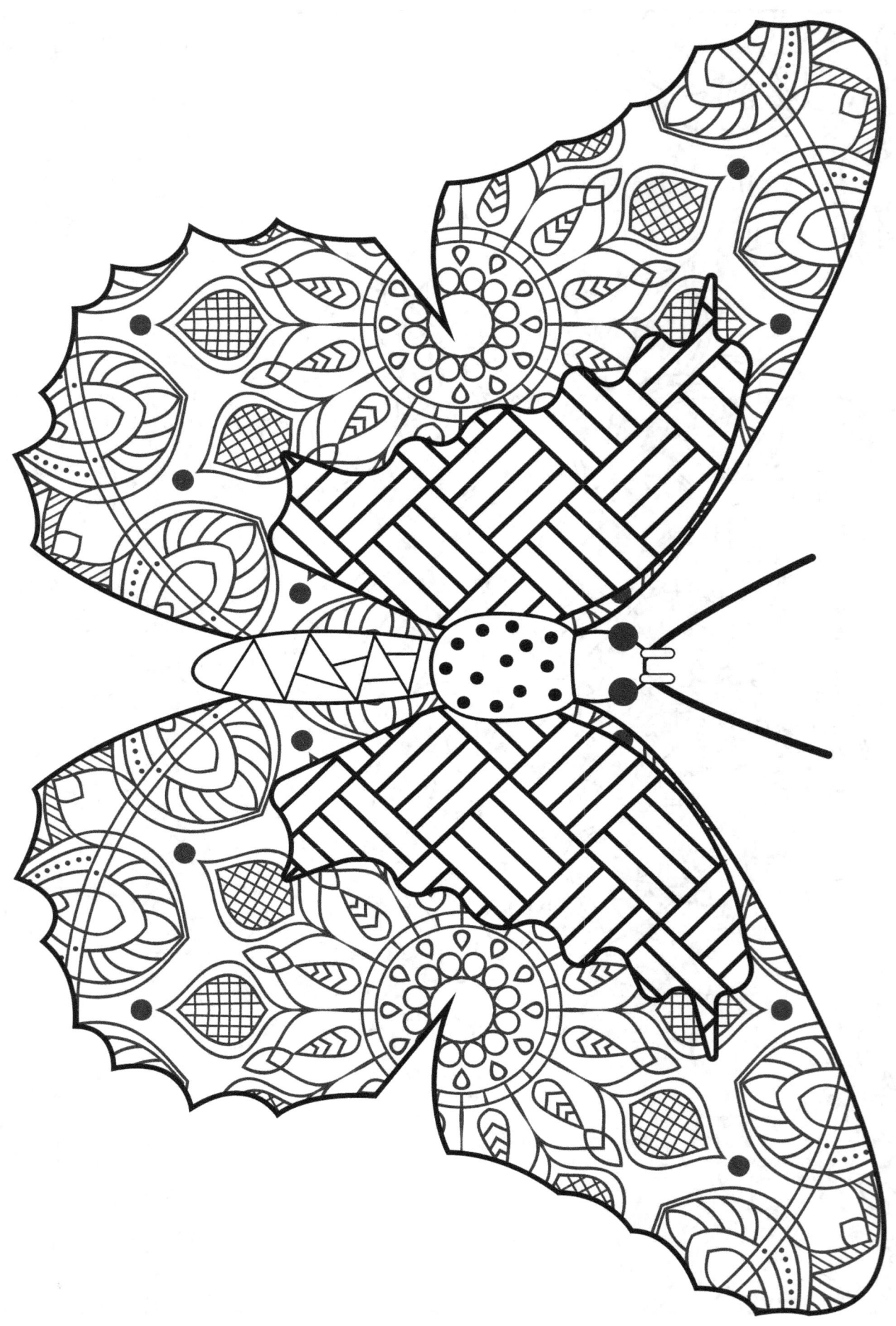

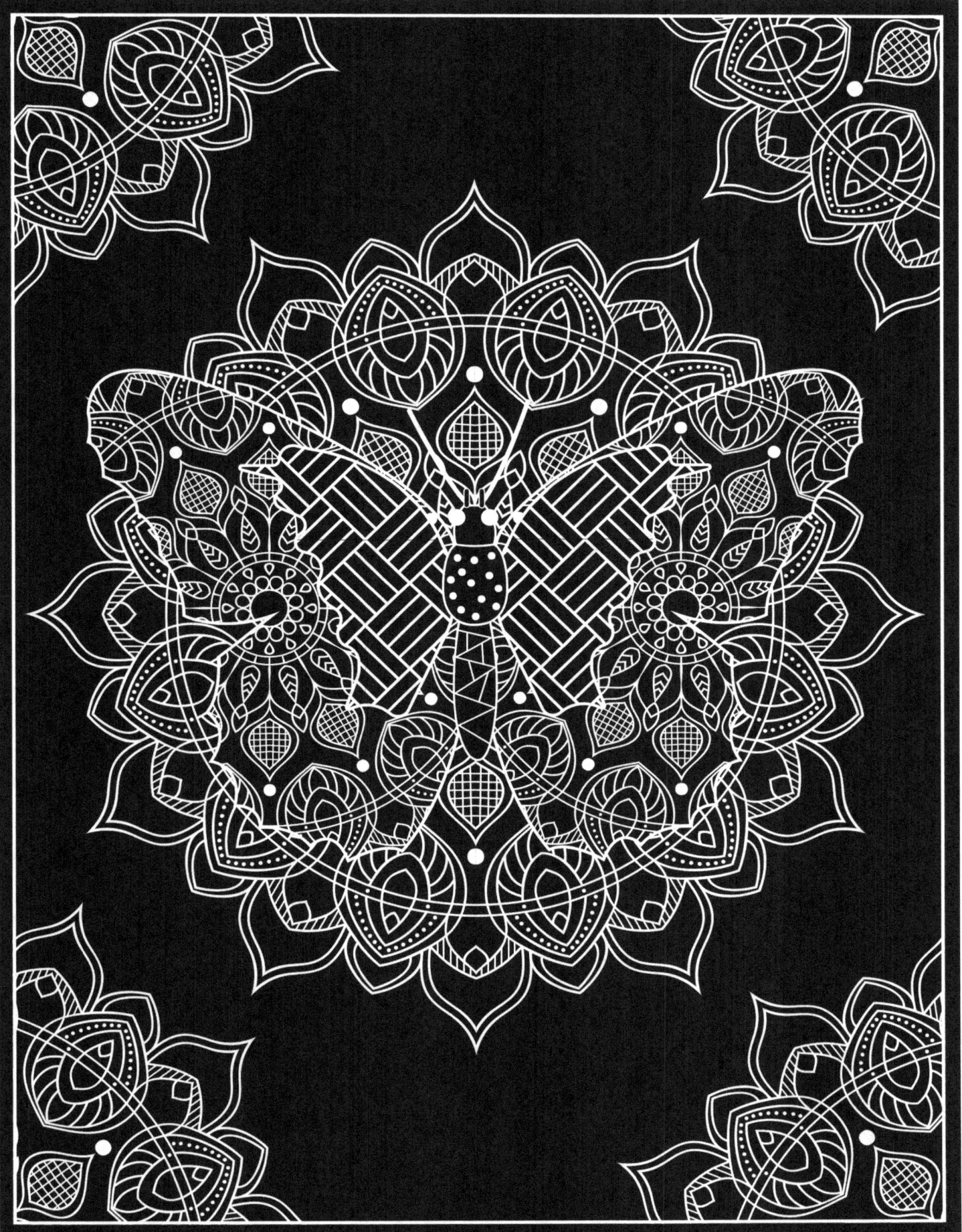

31

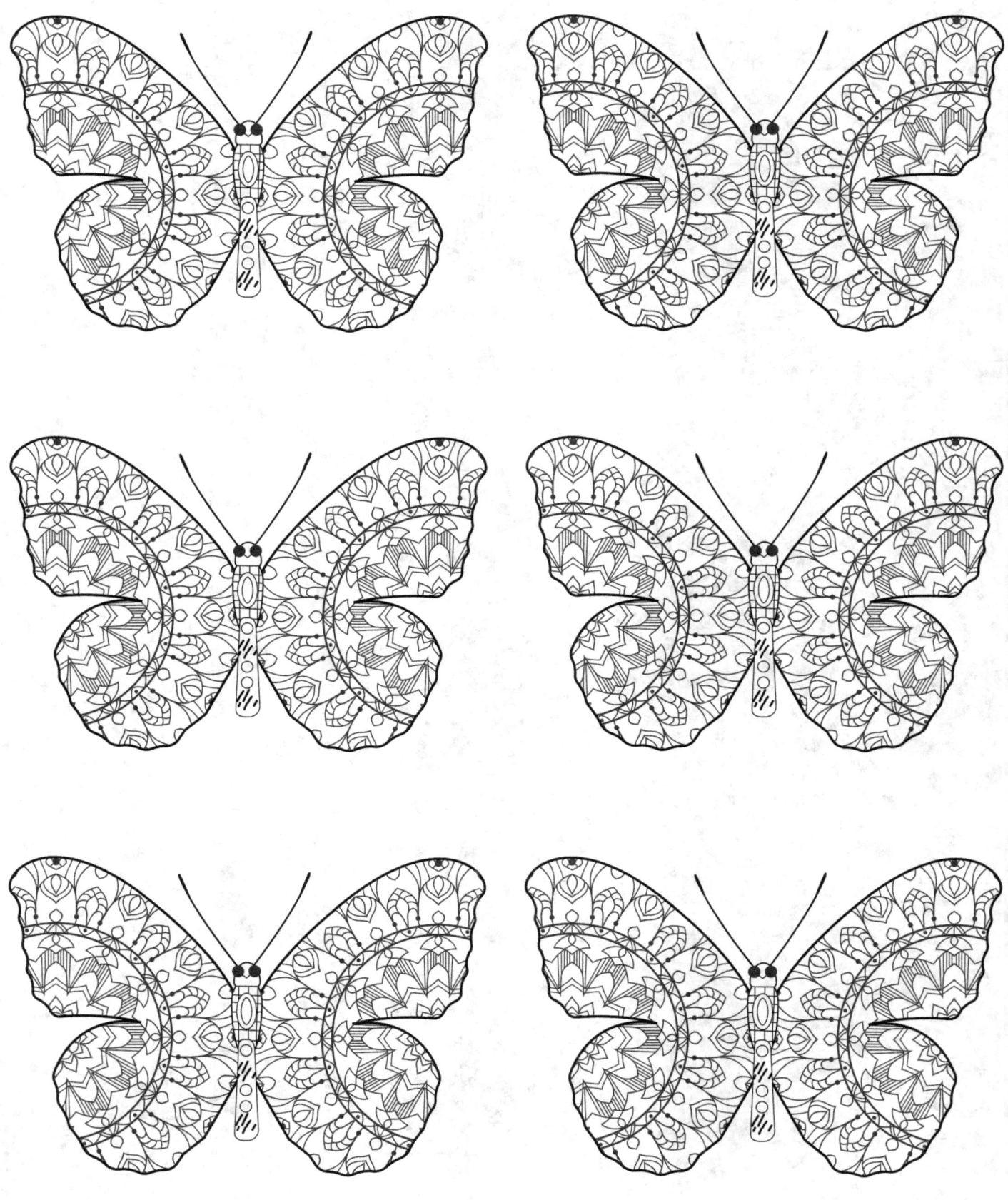

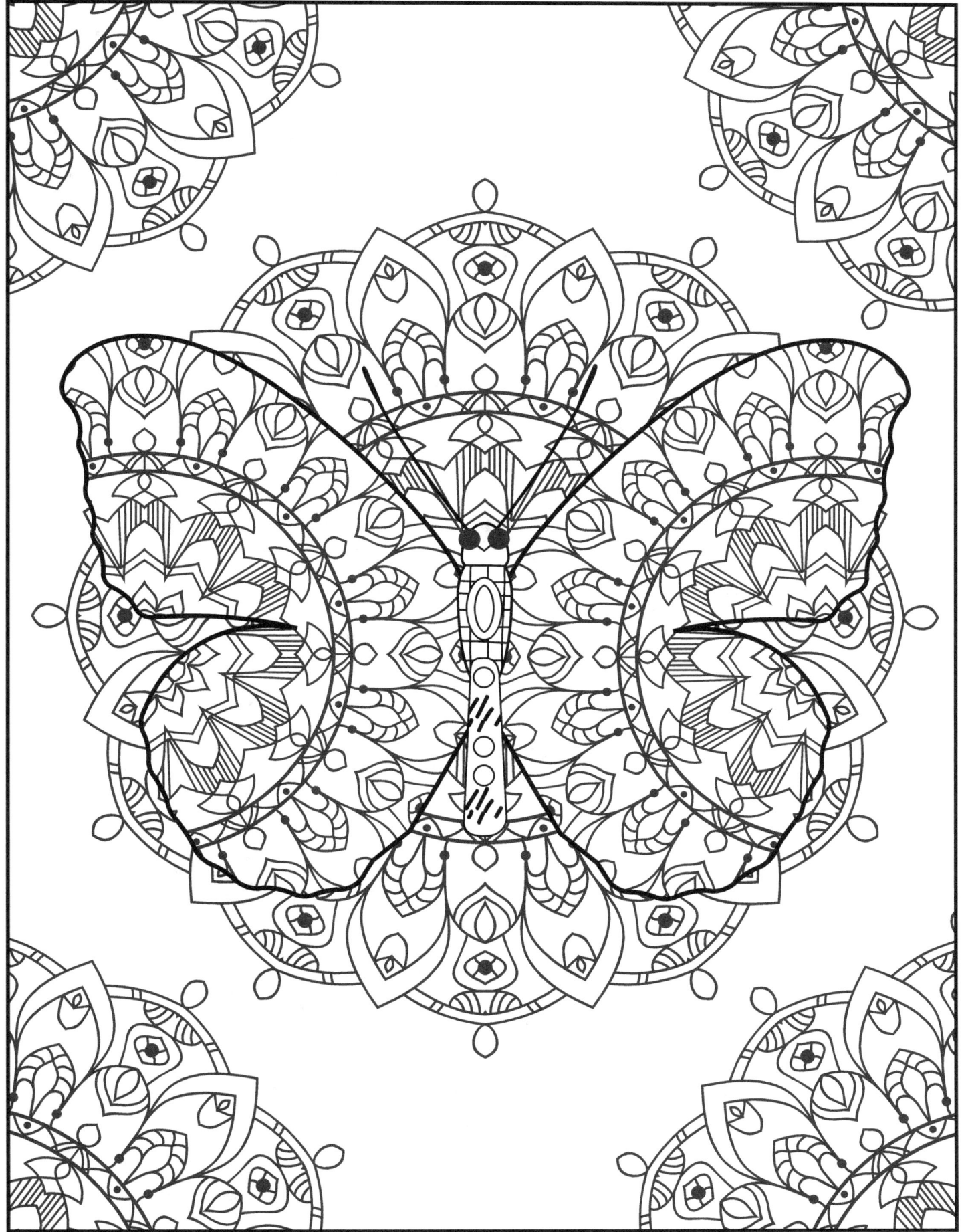

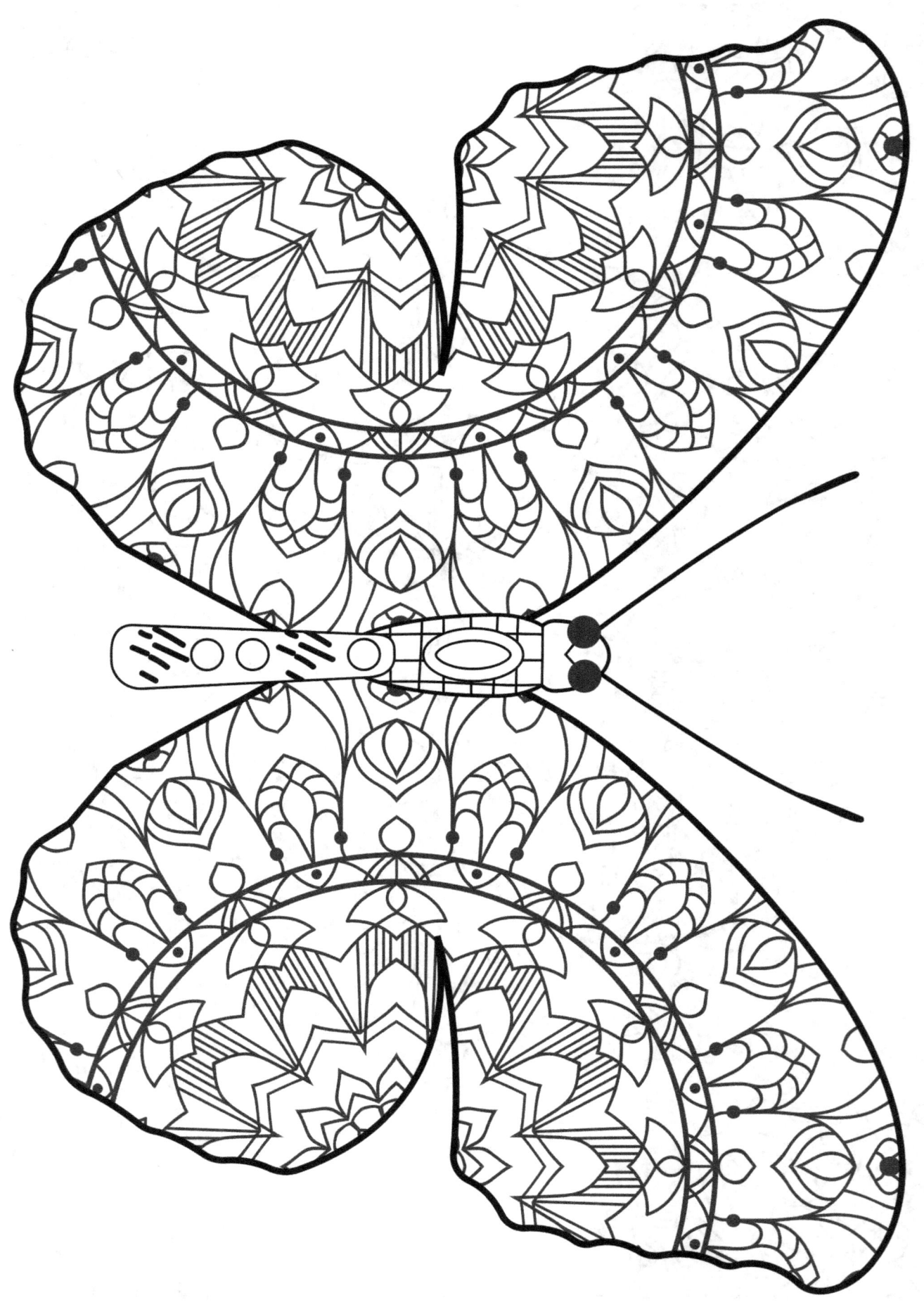

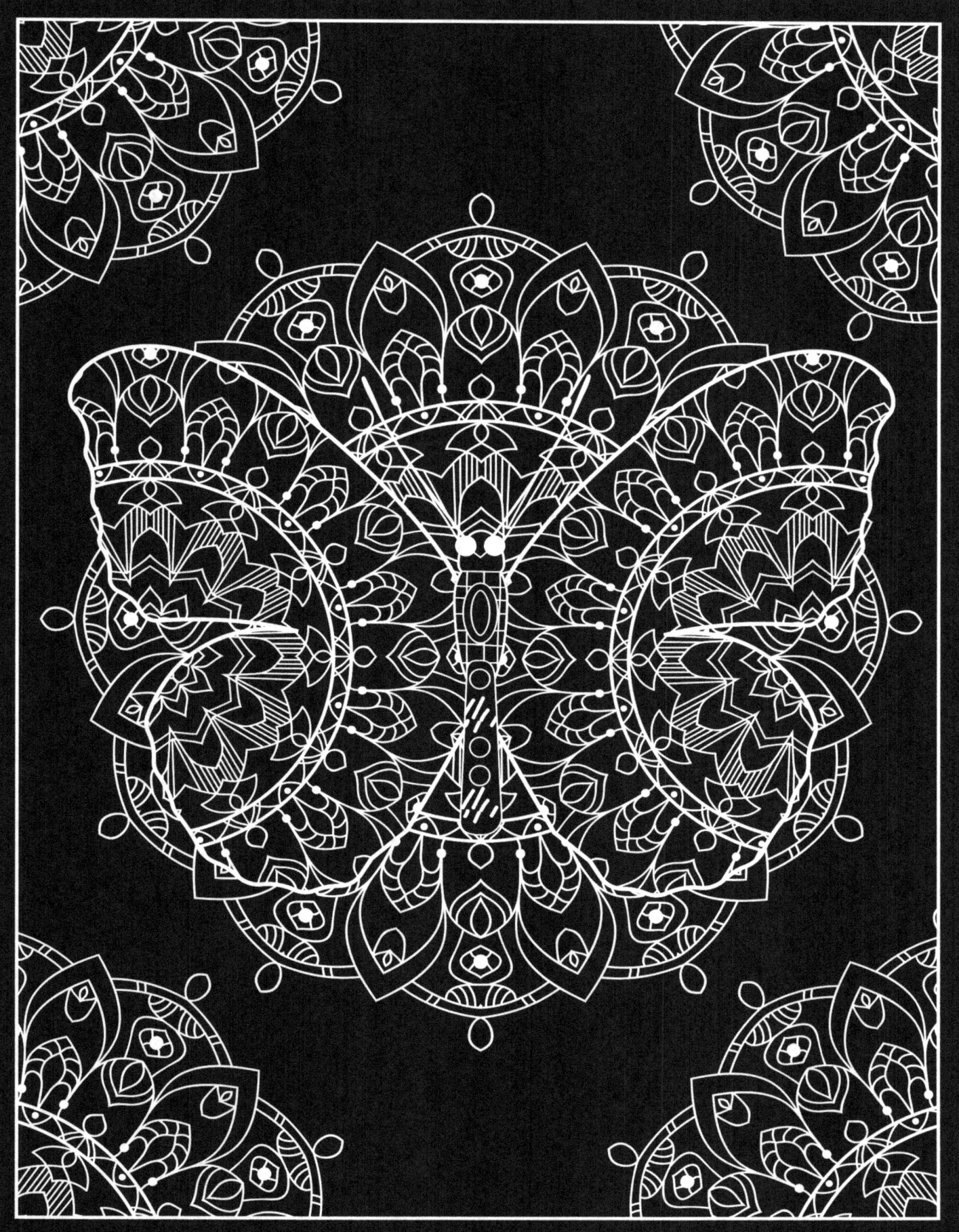

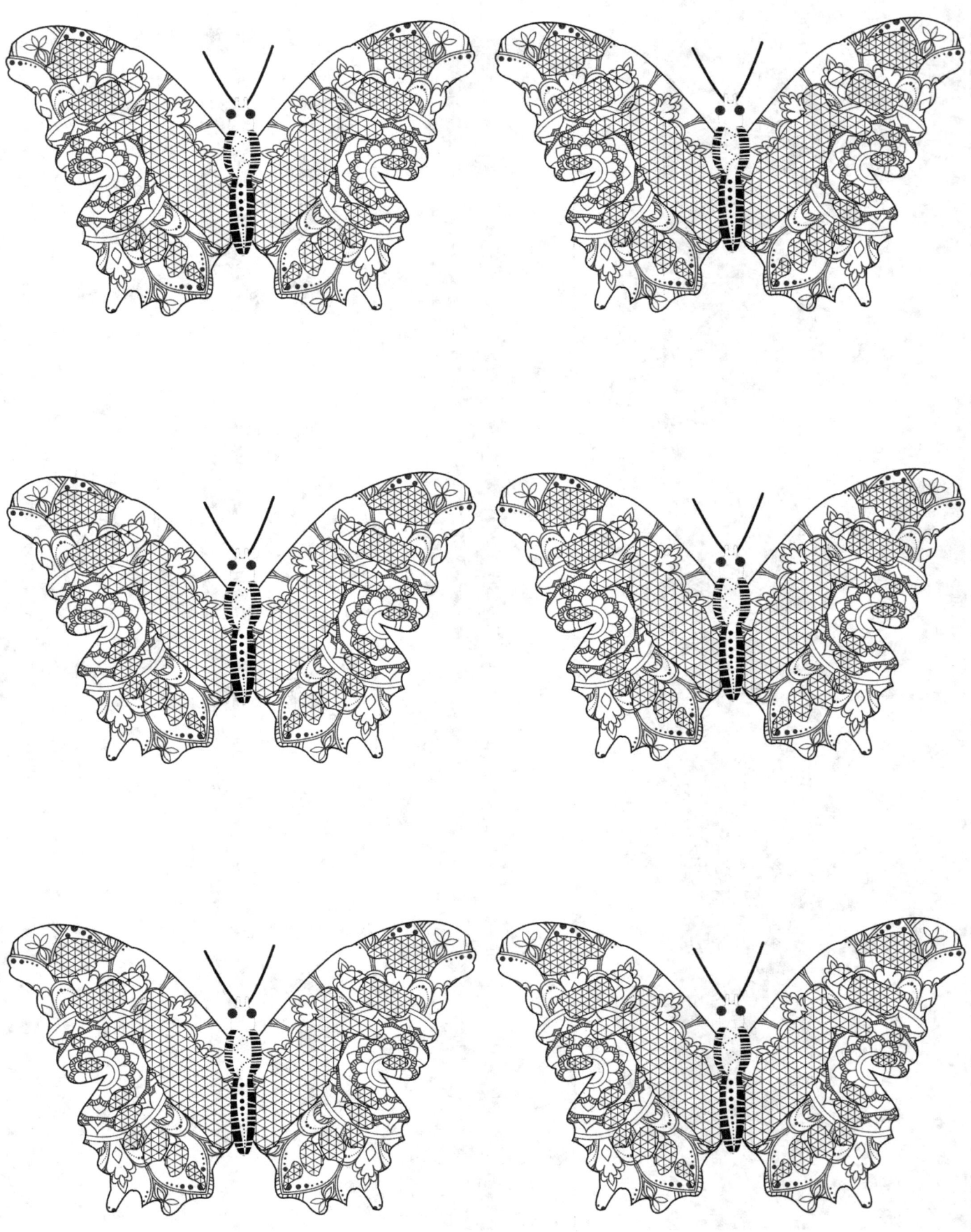

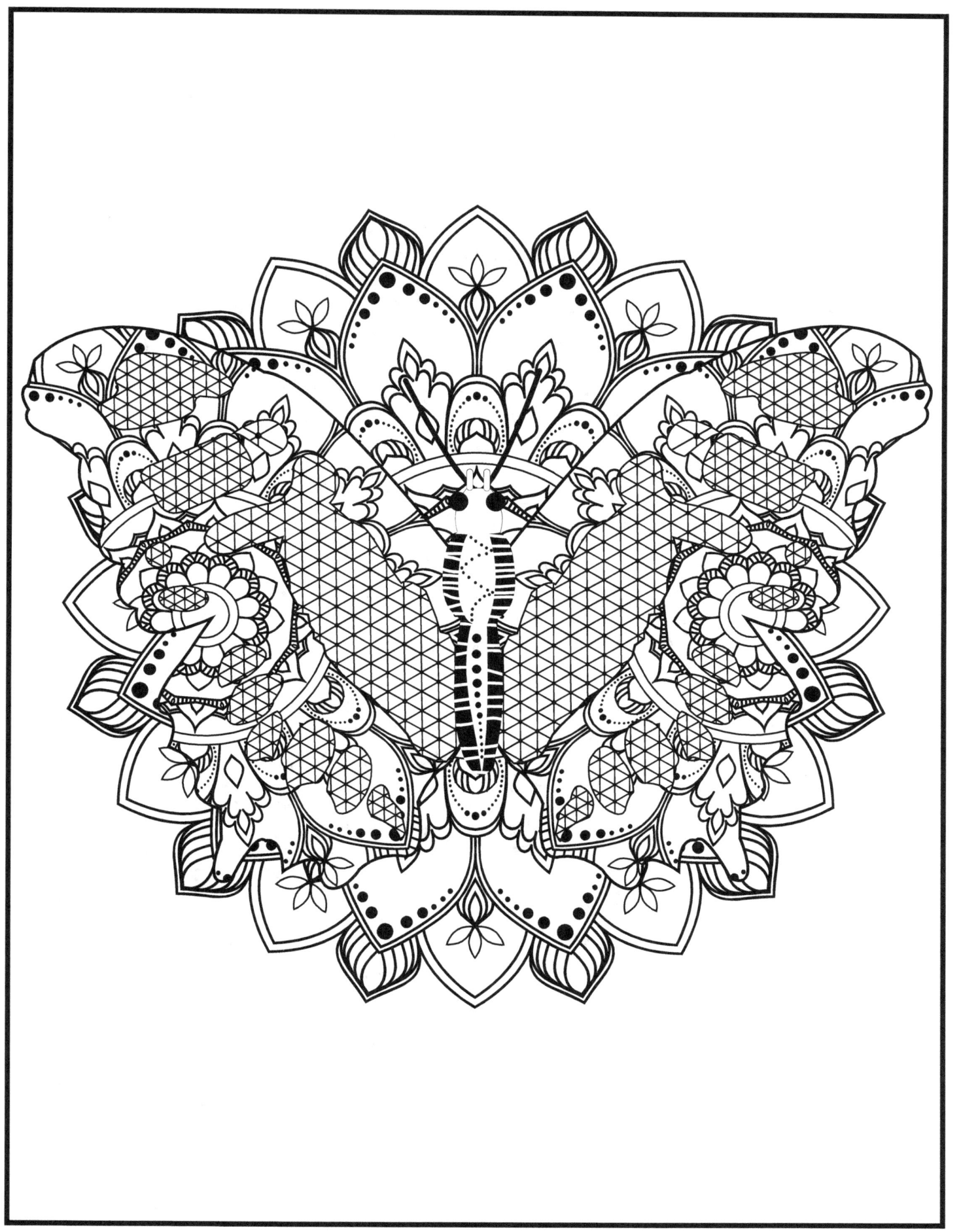

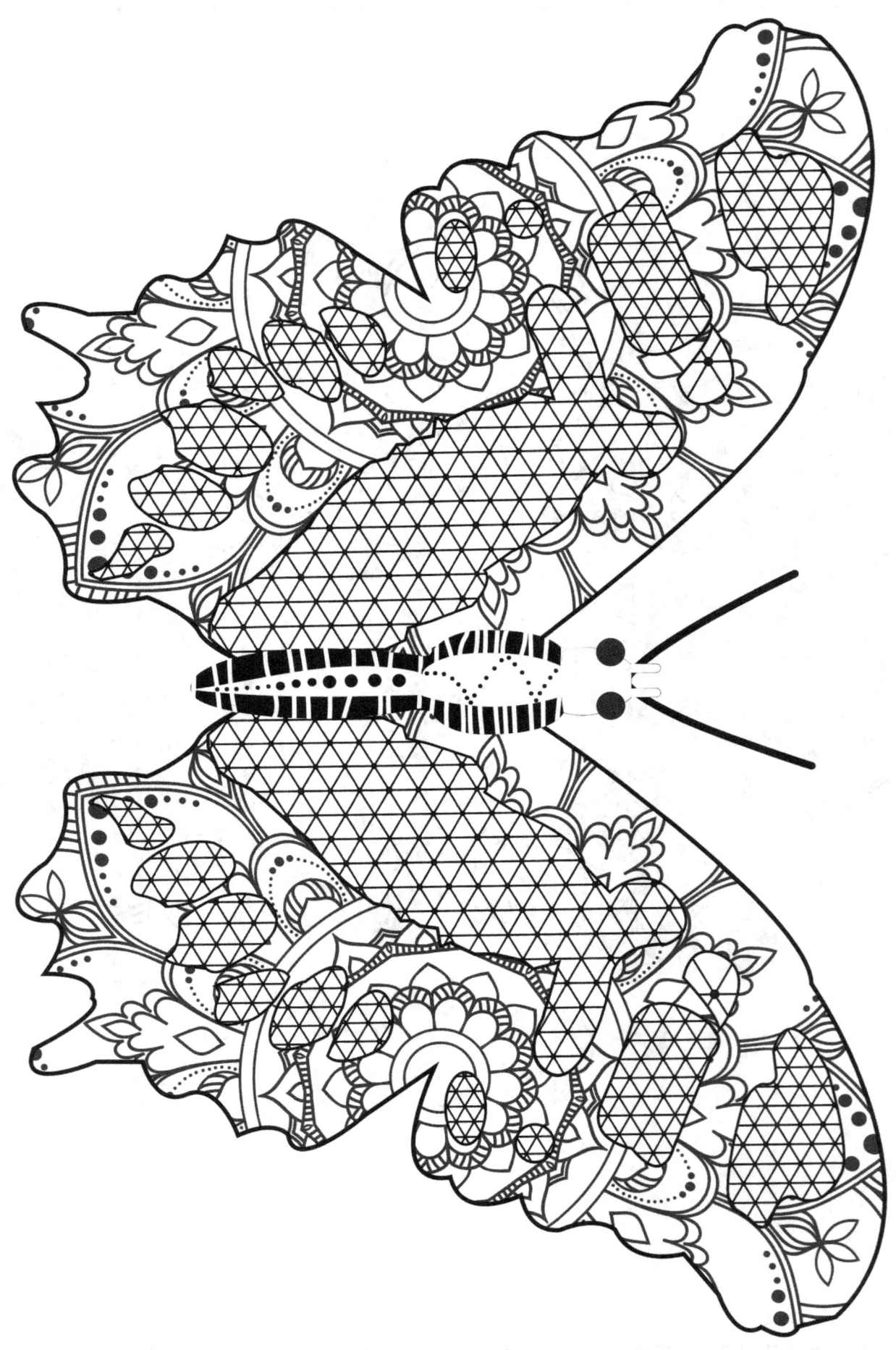

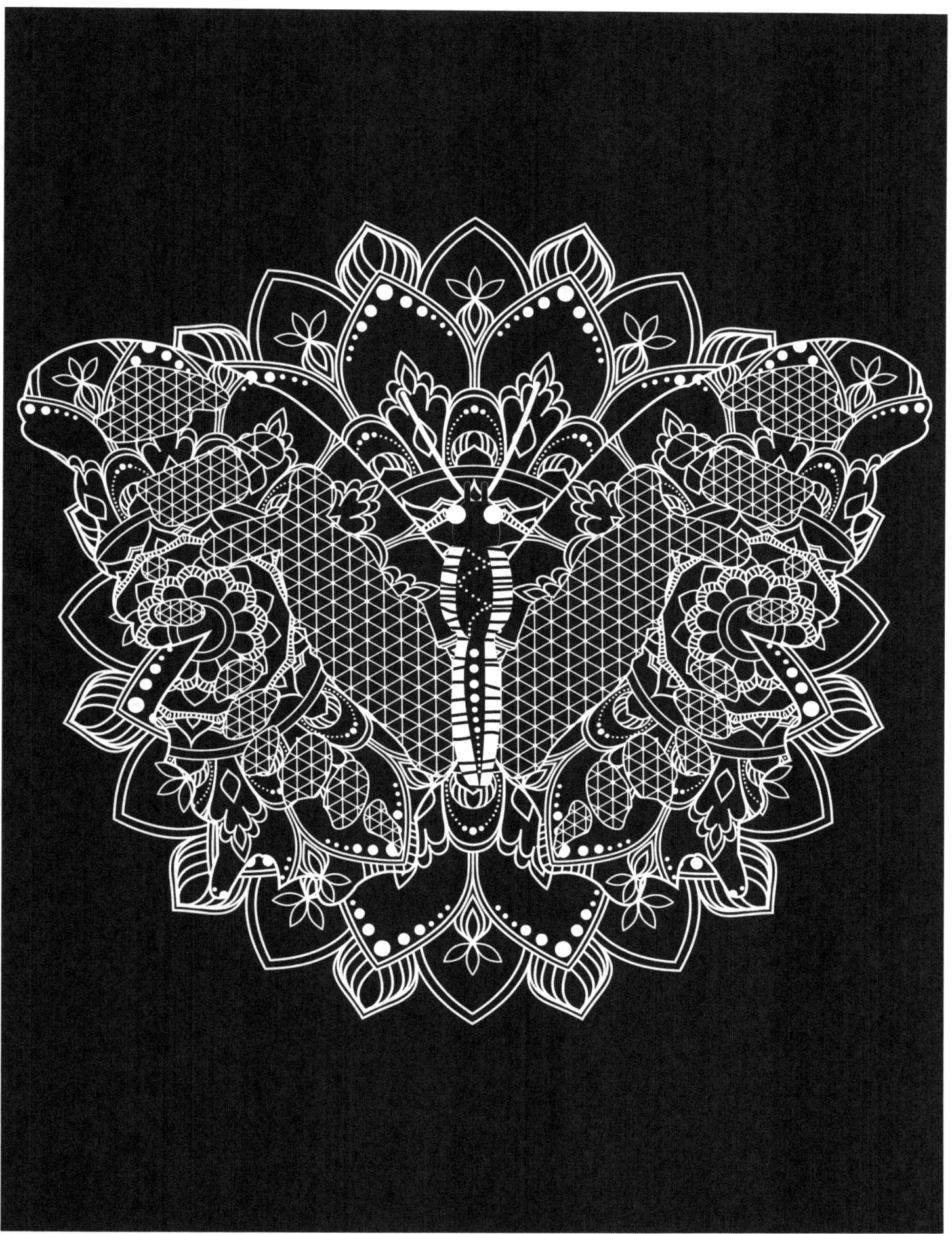

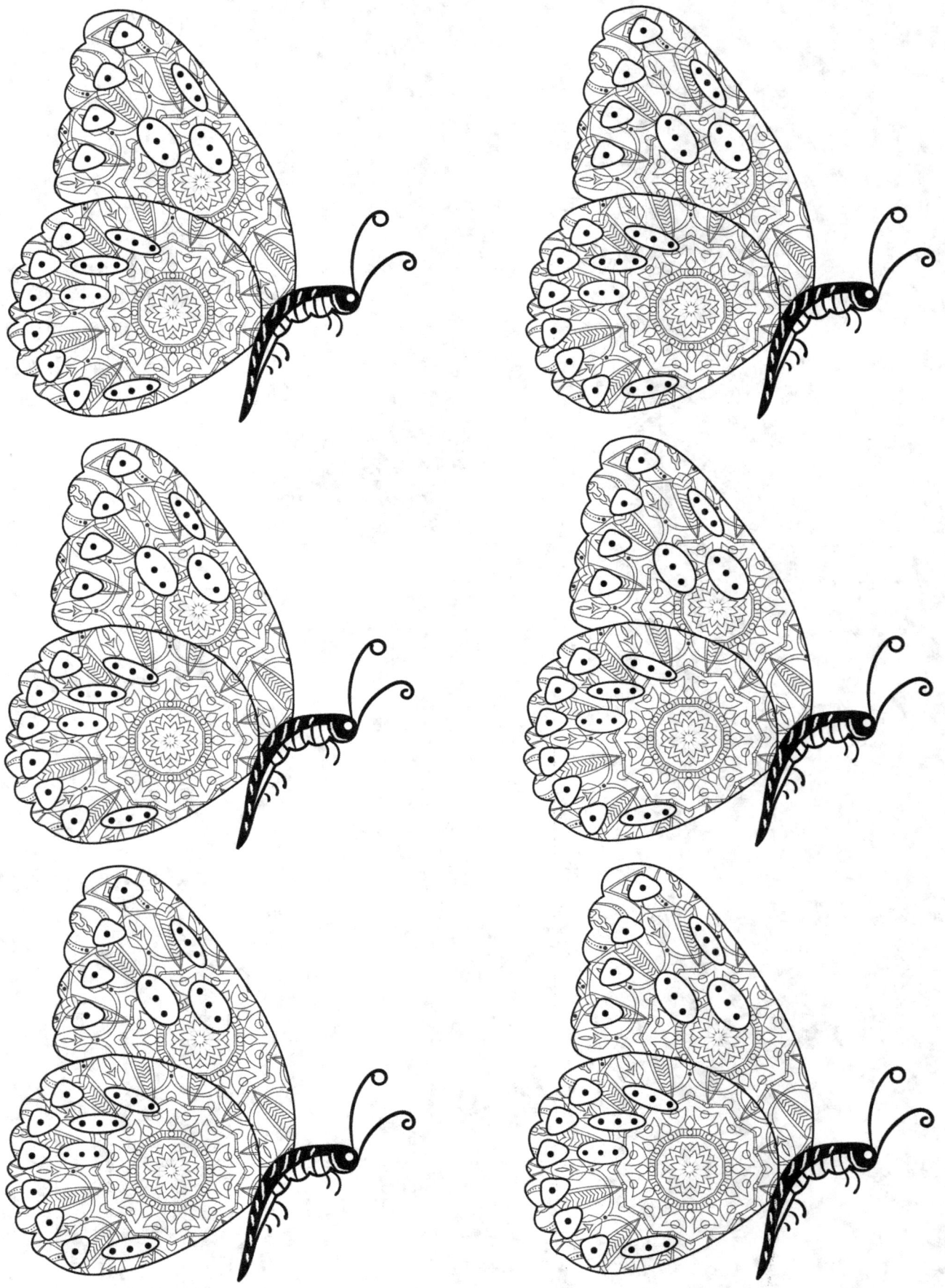

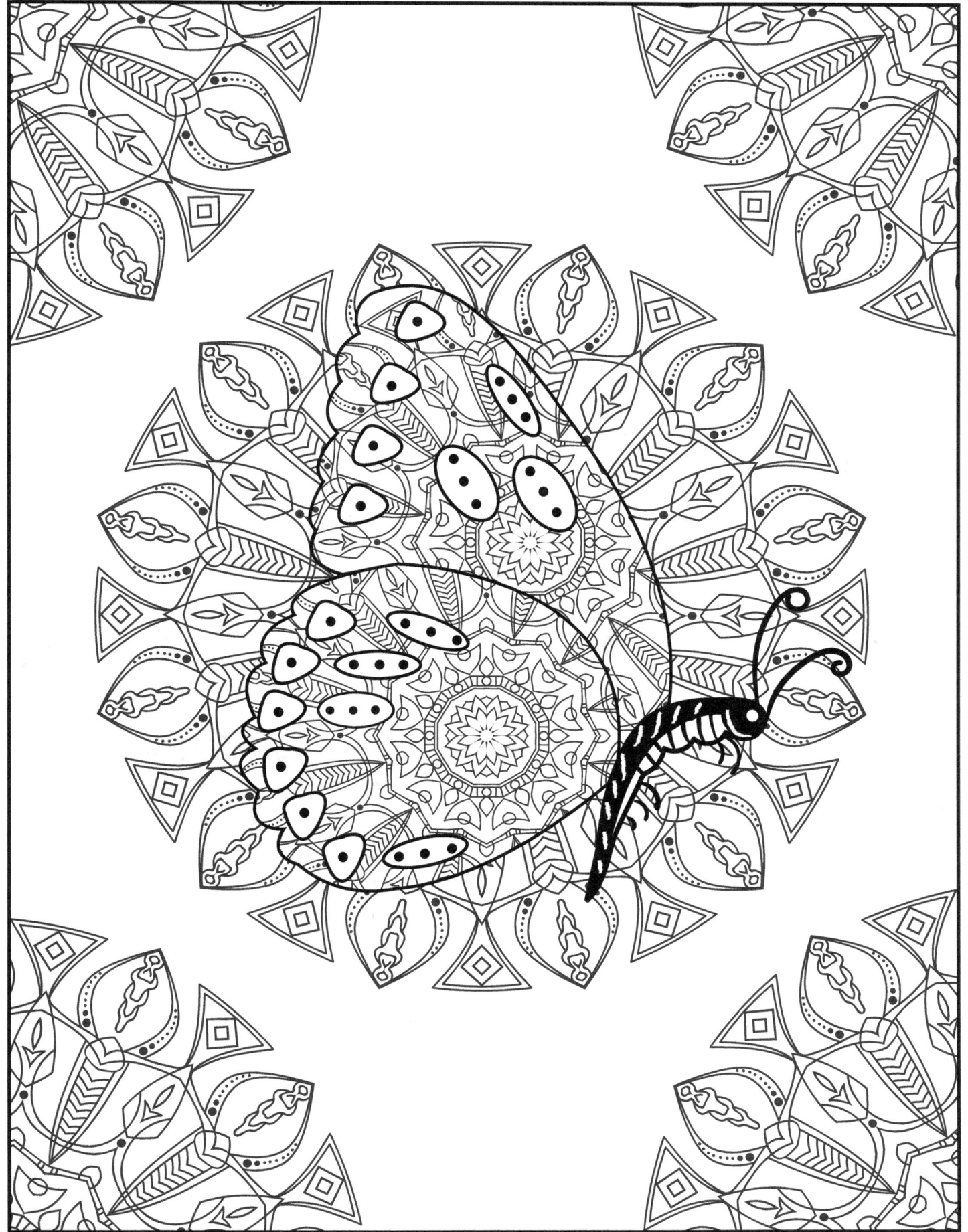

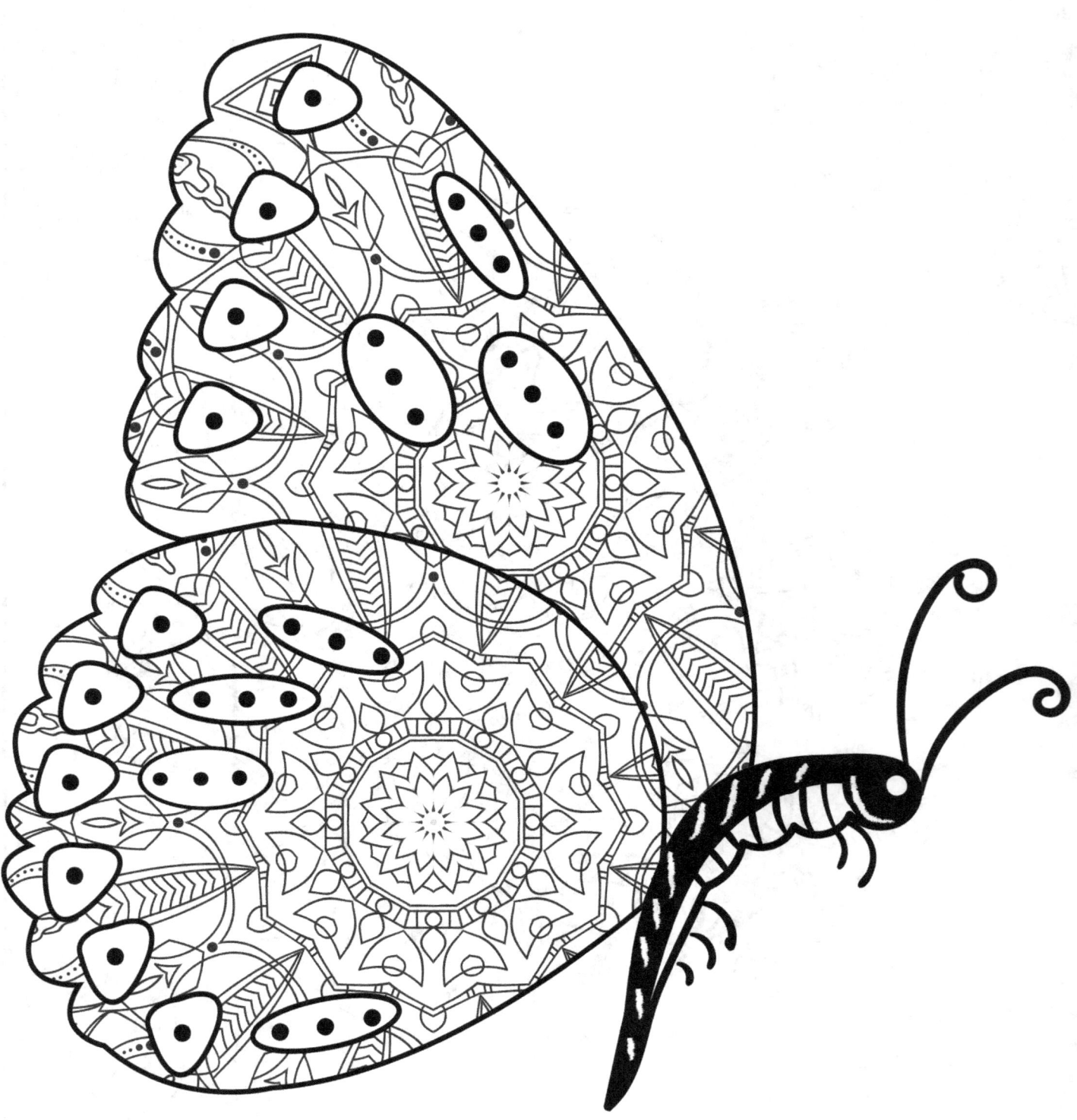

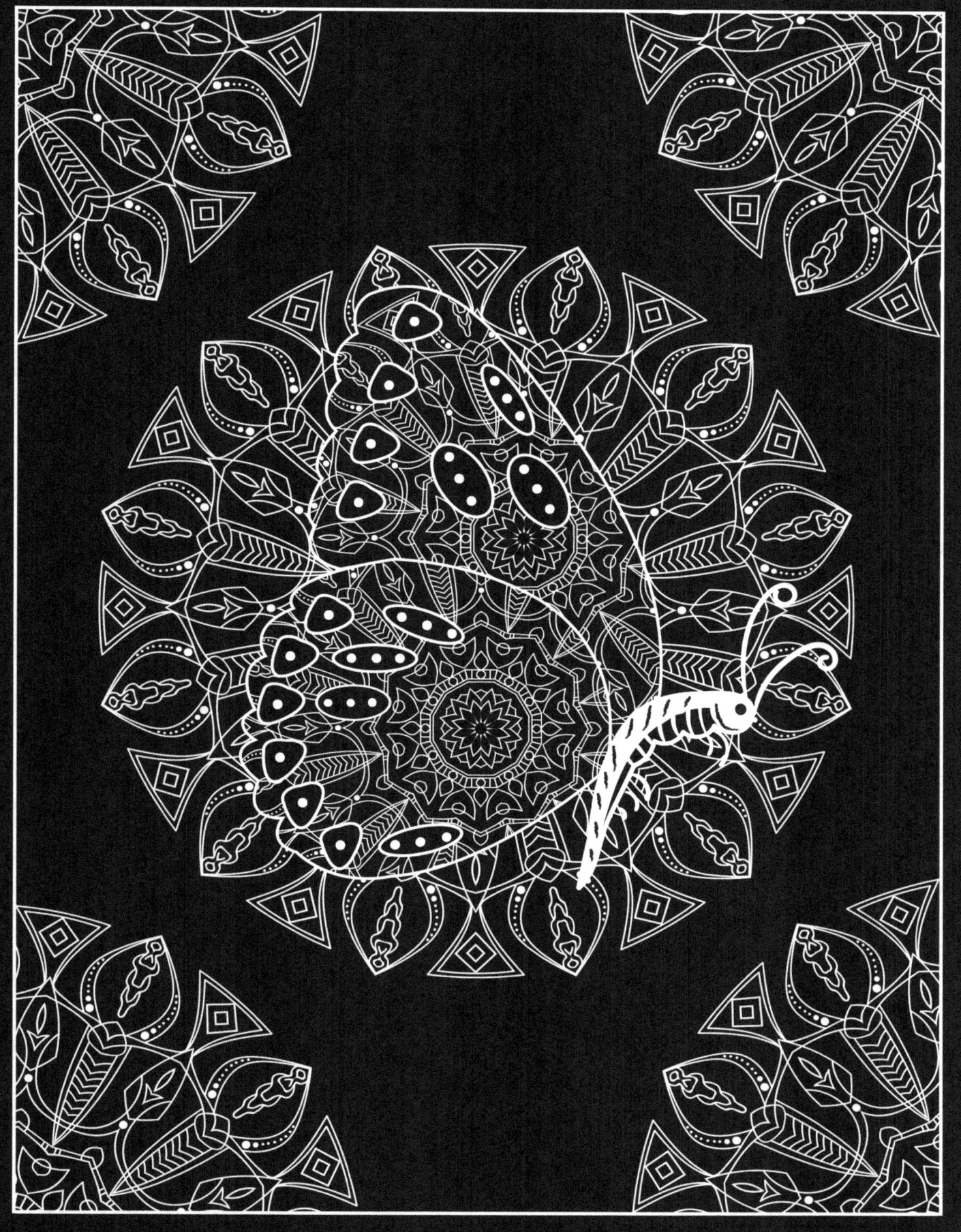

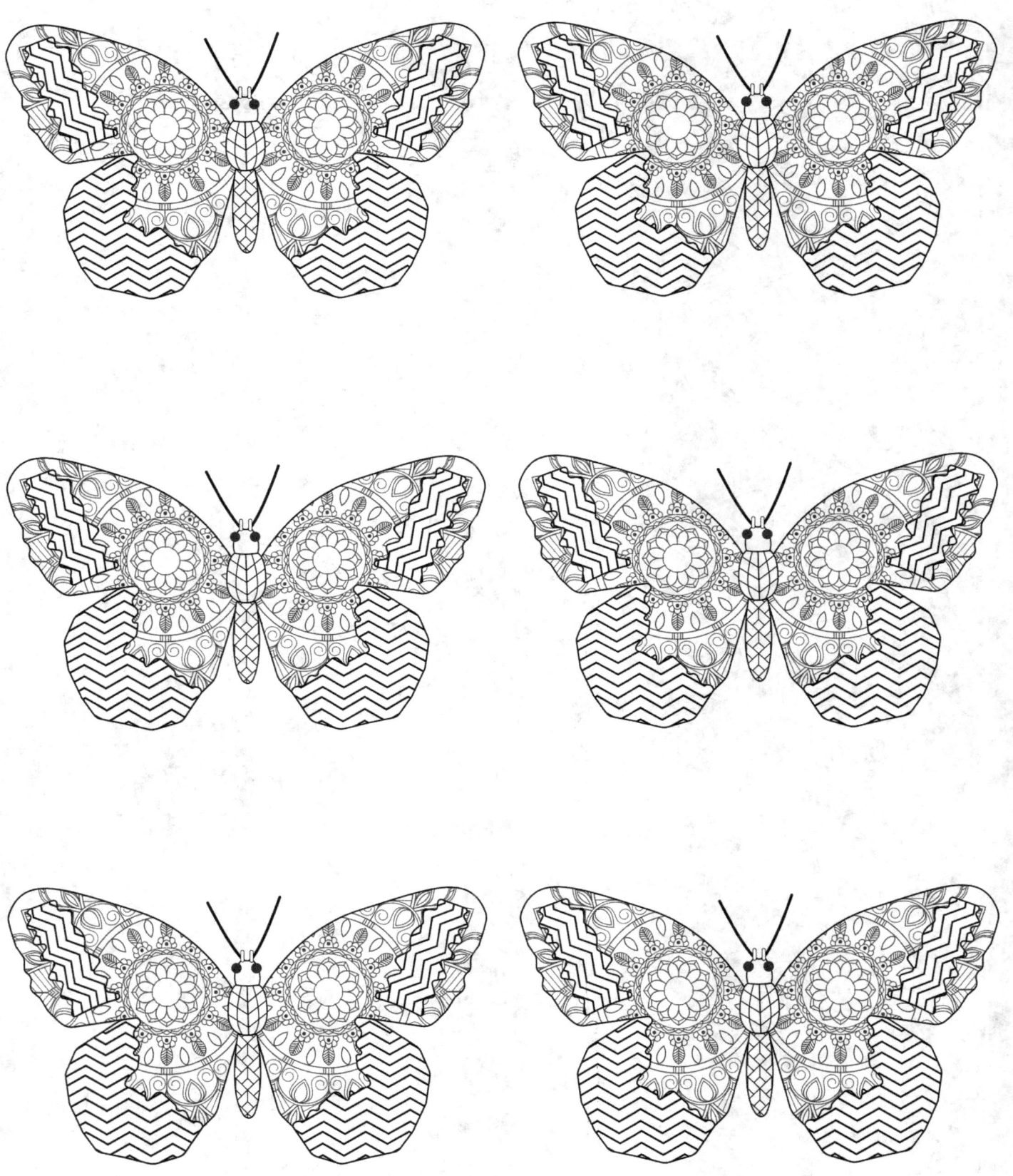

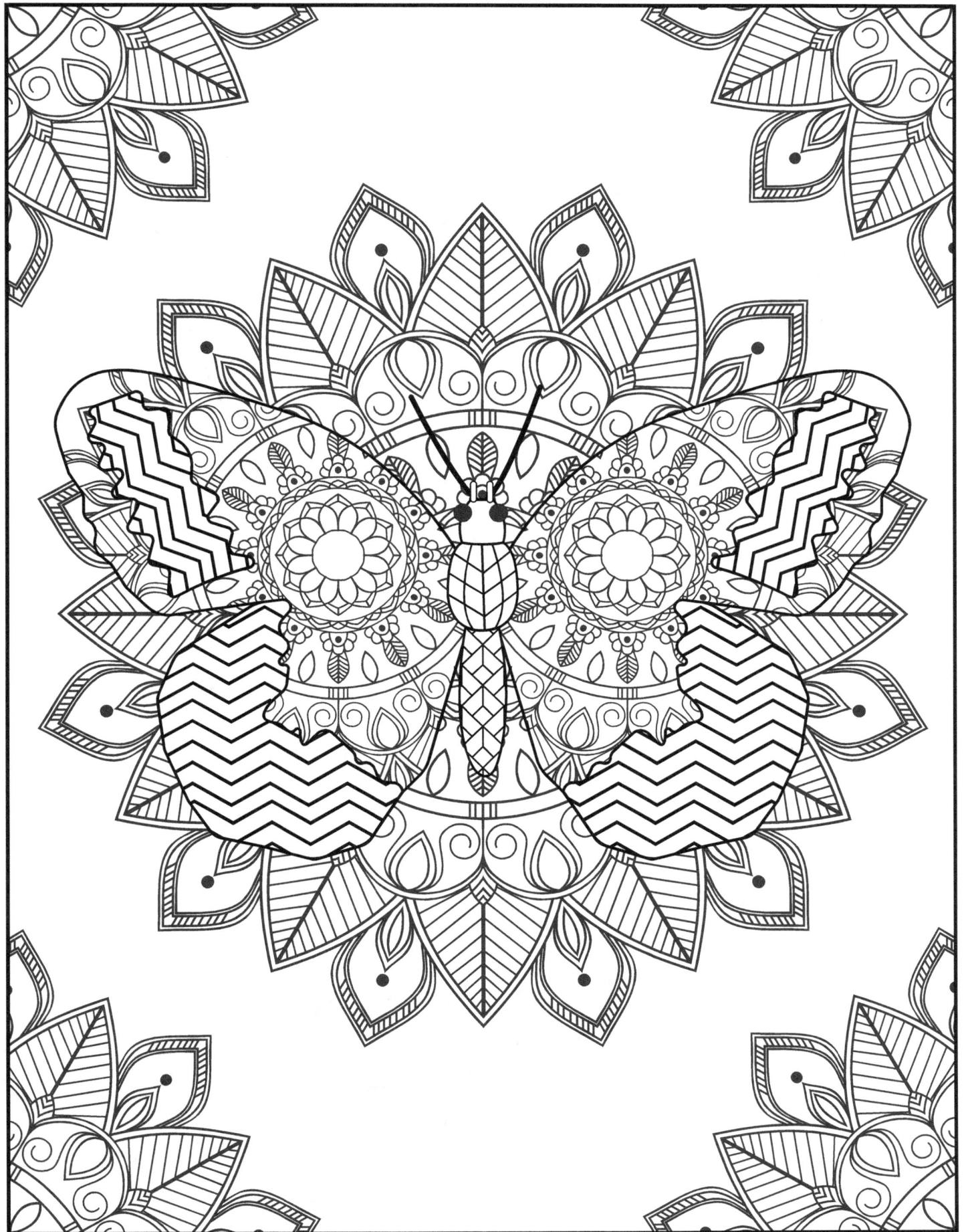

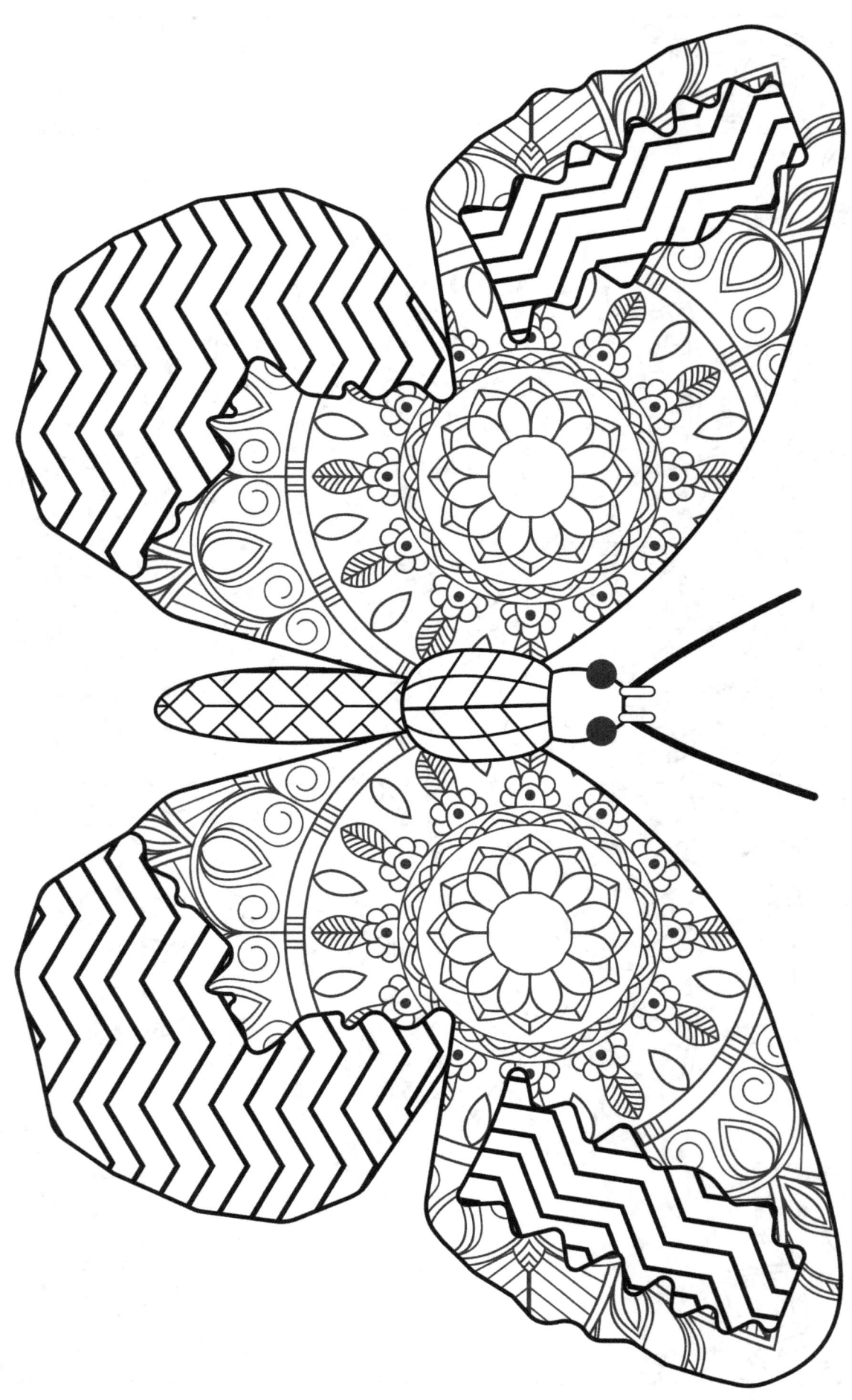

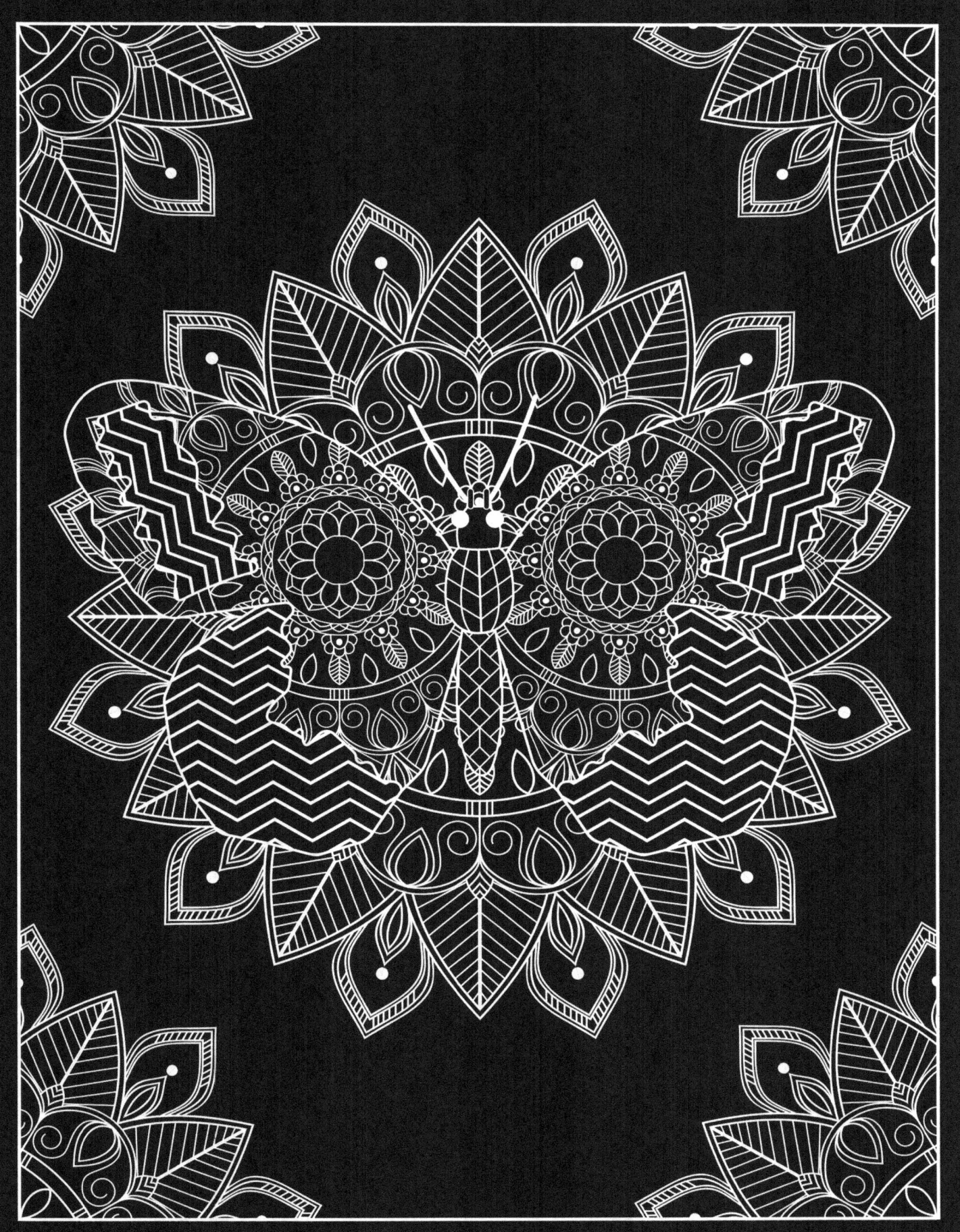

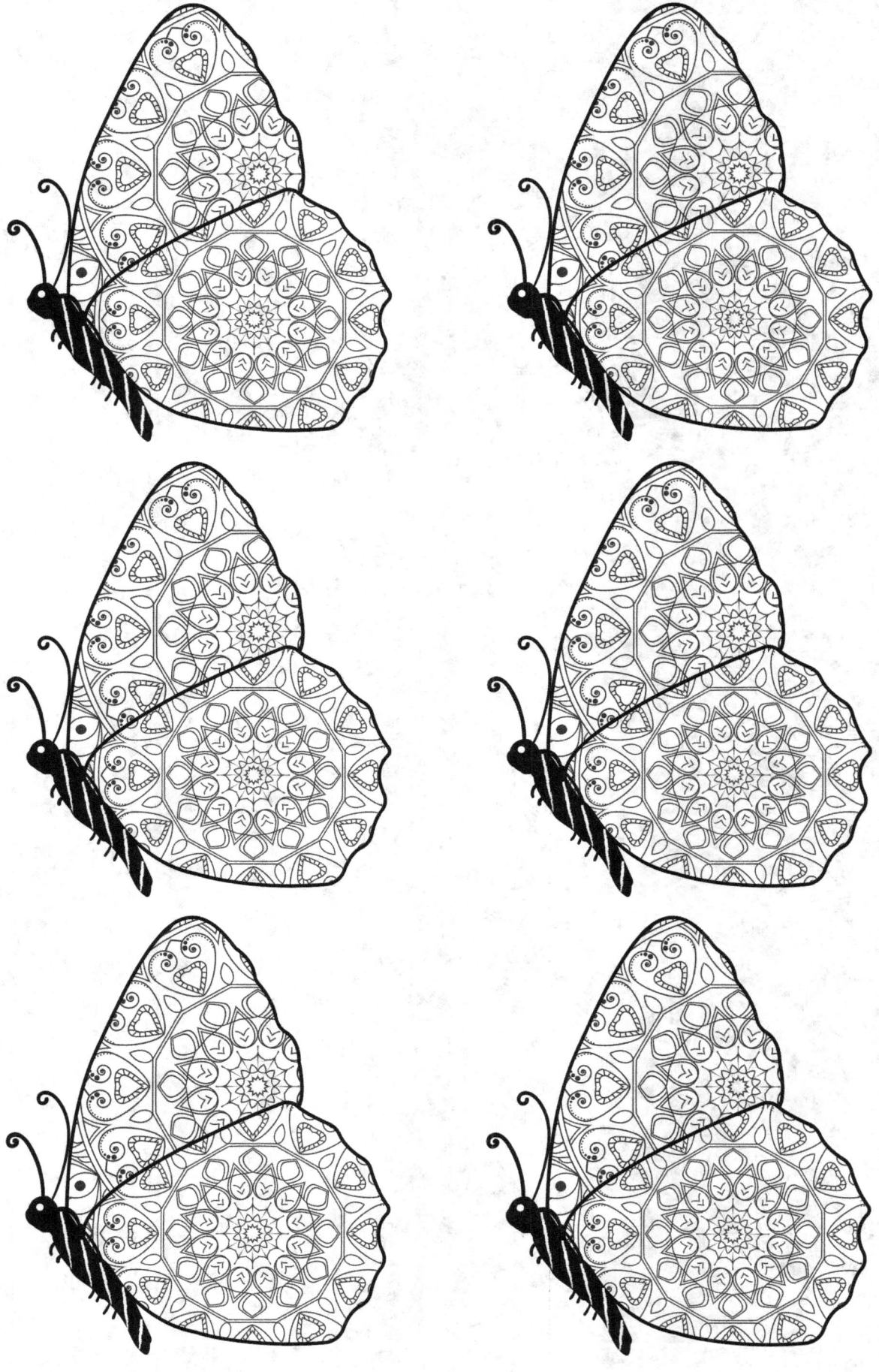

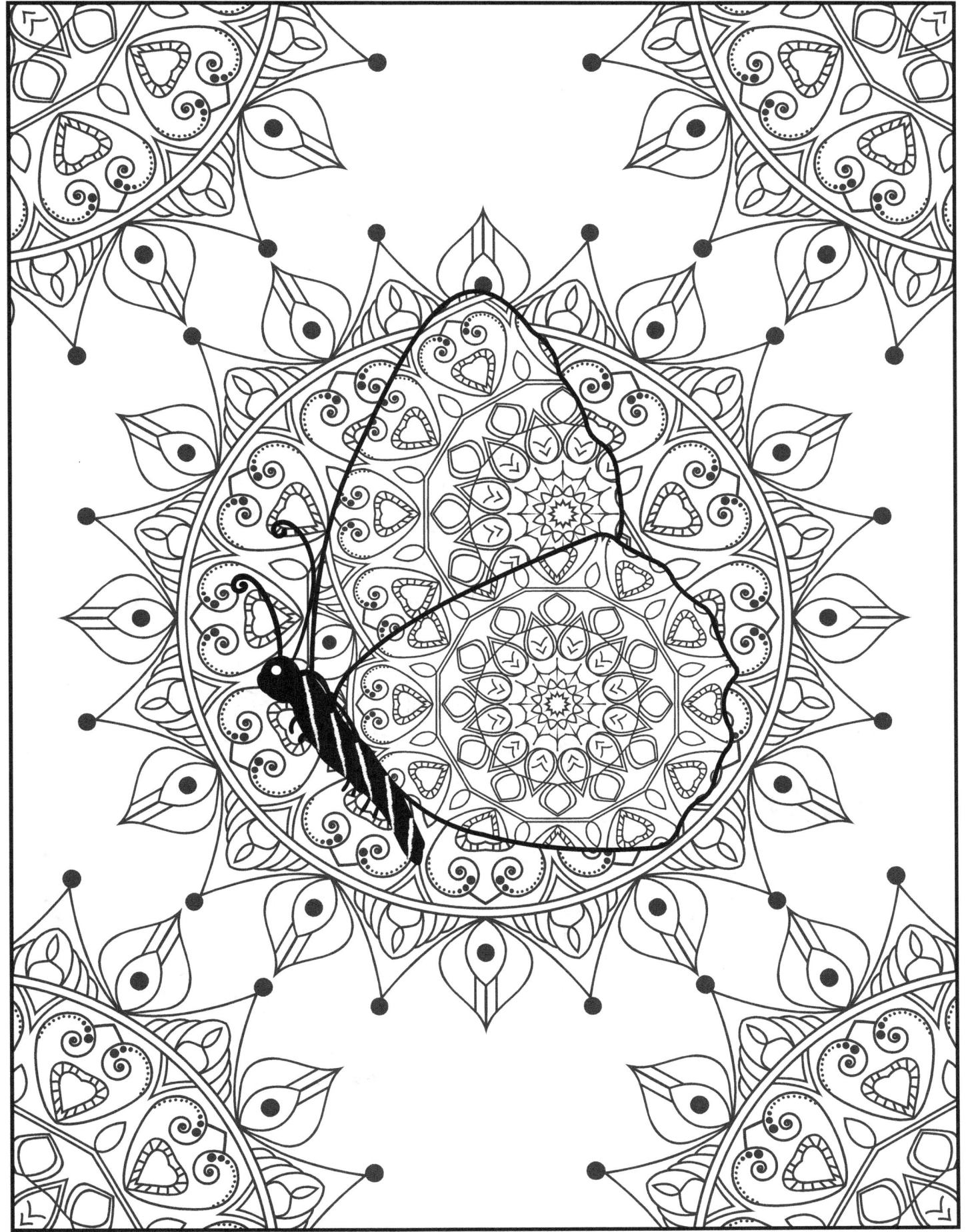

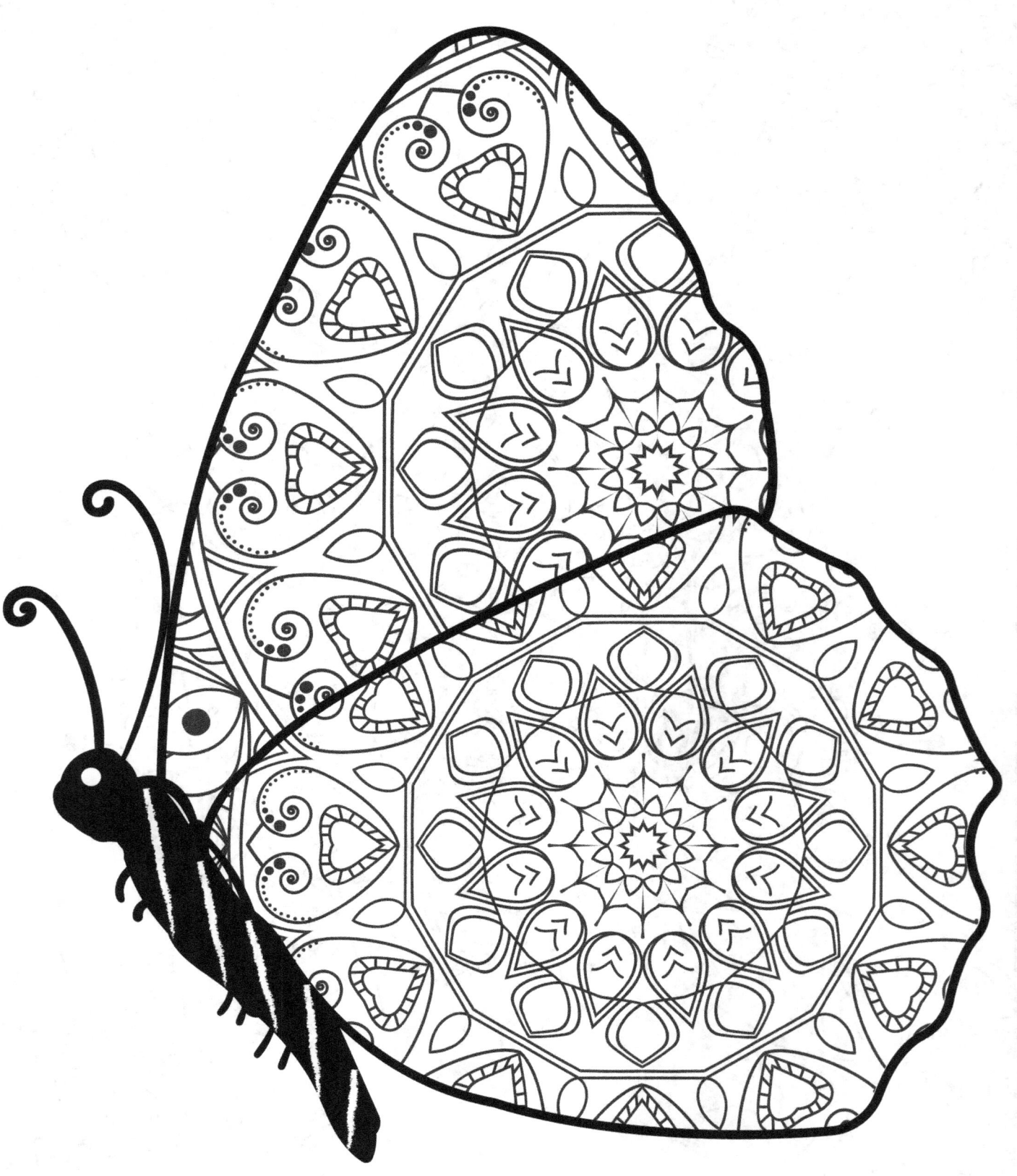

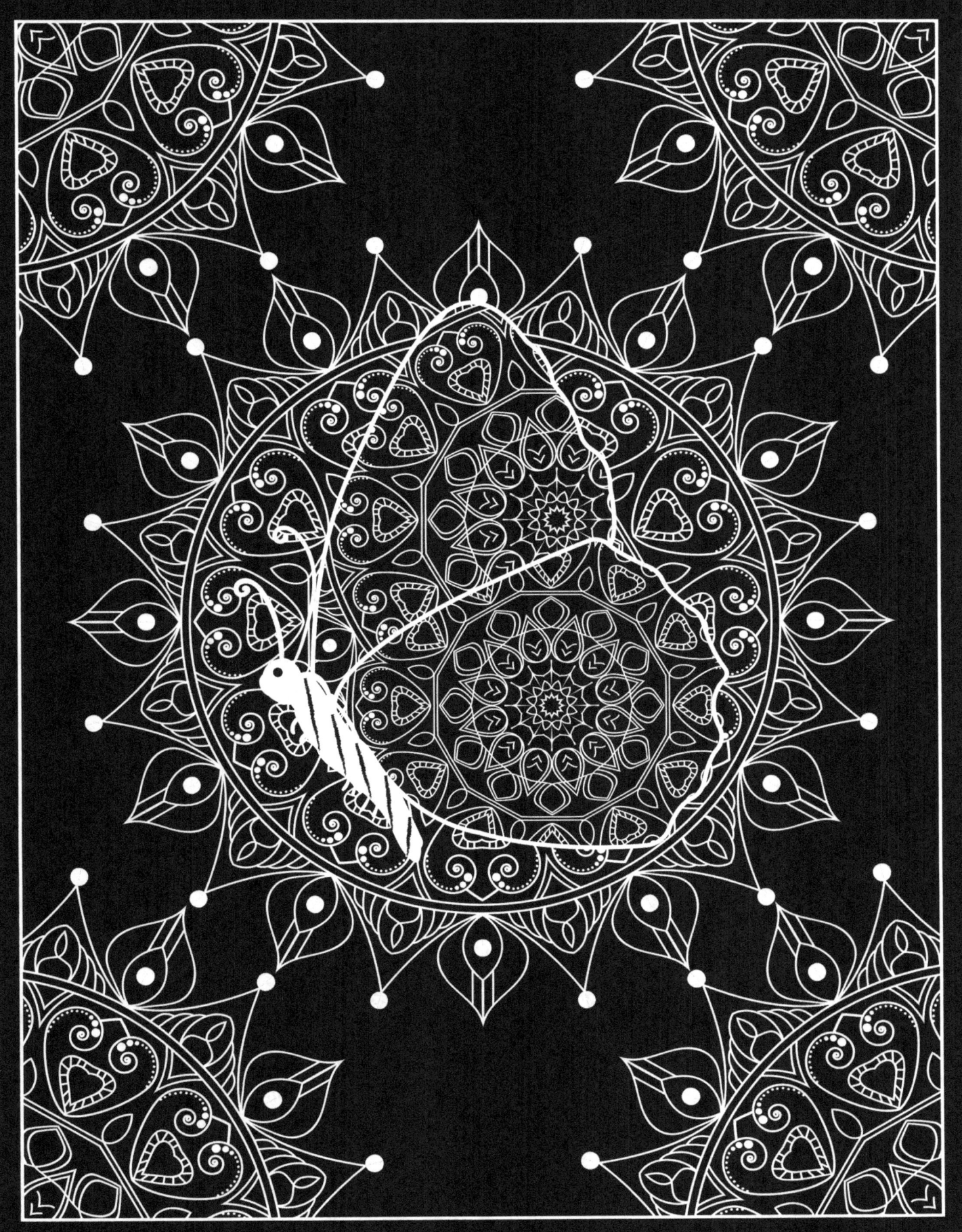

51

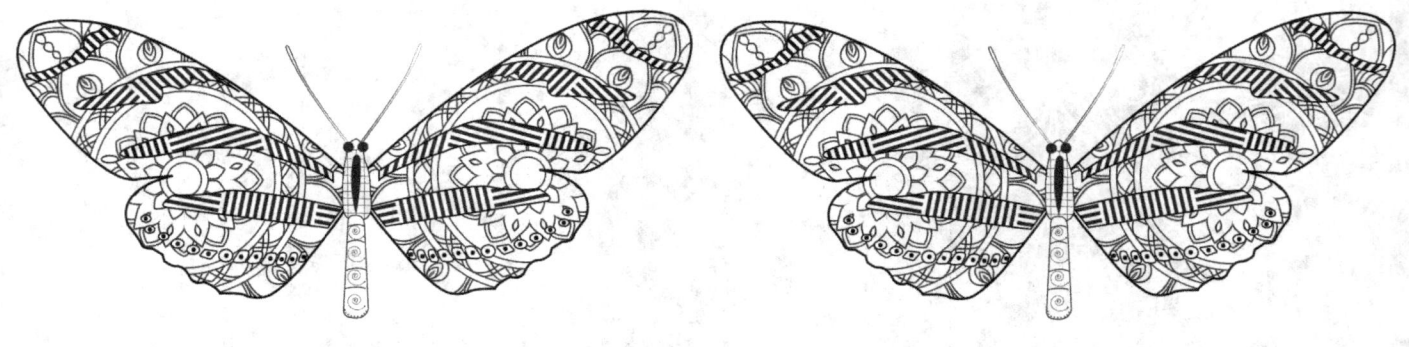

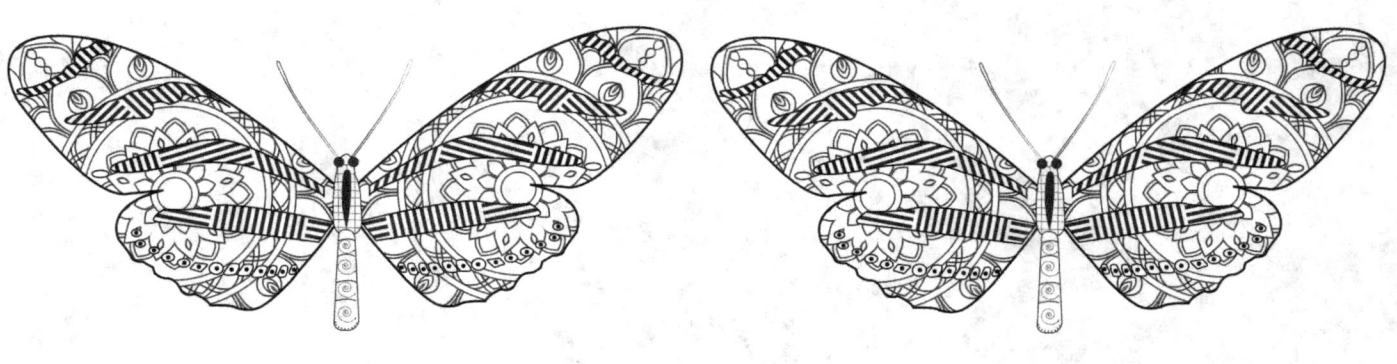

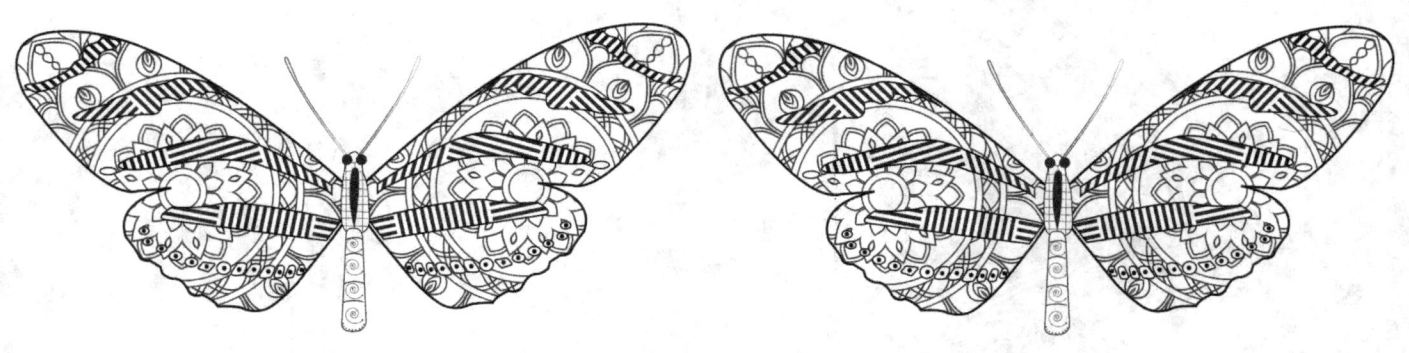

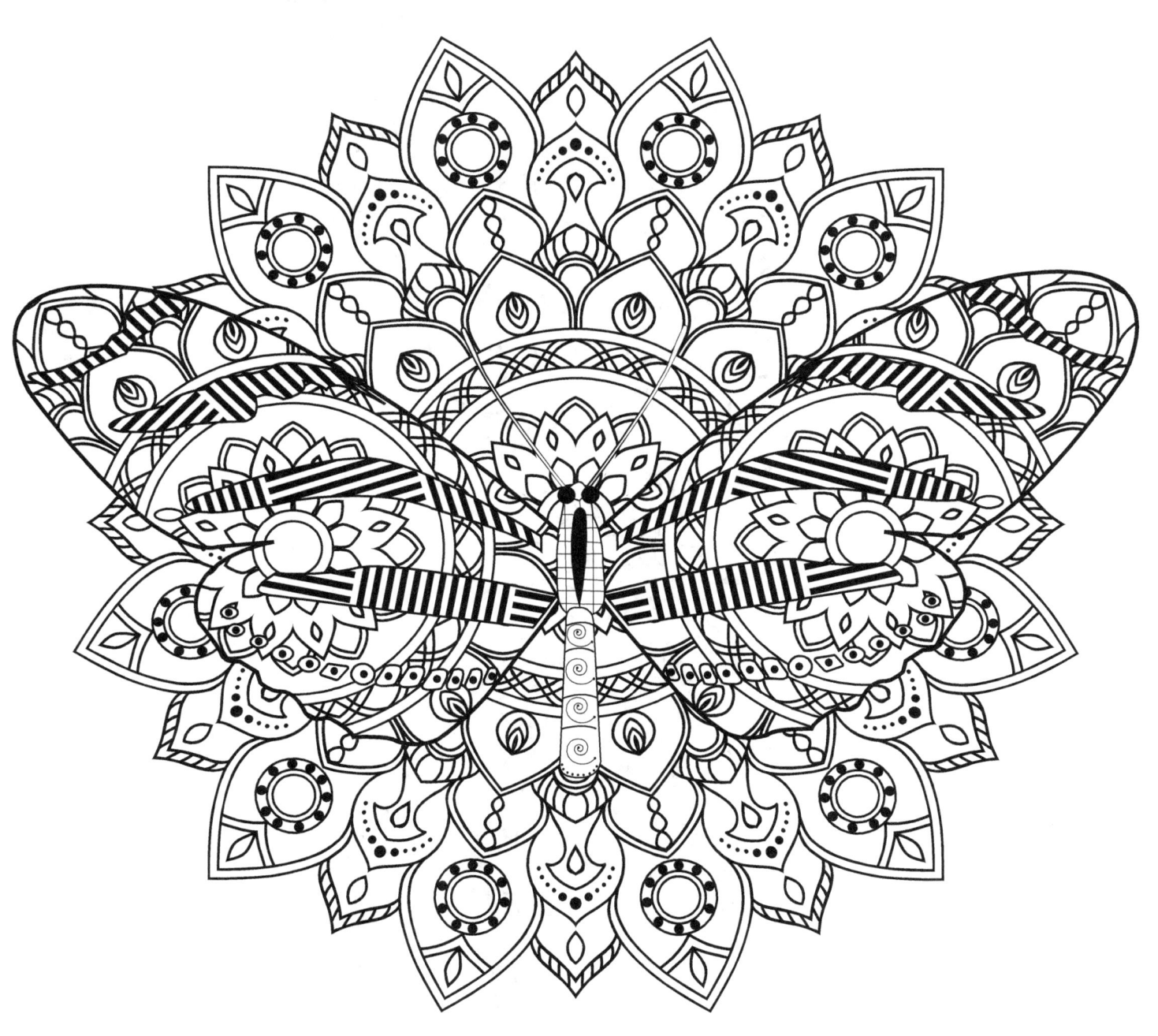

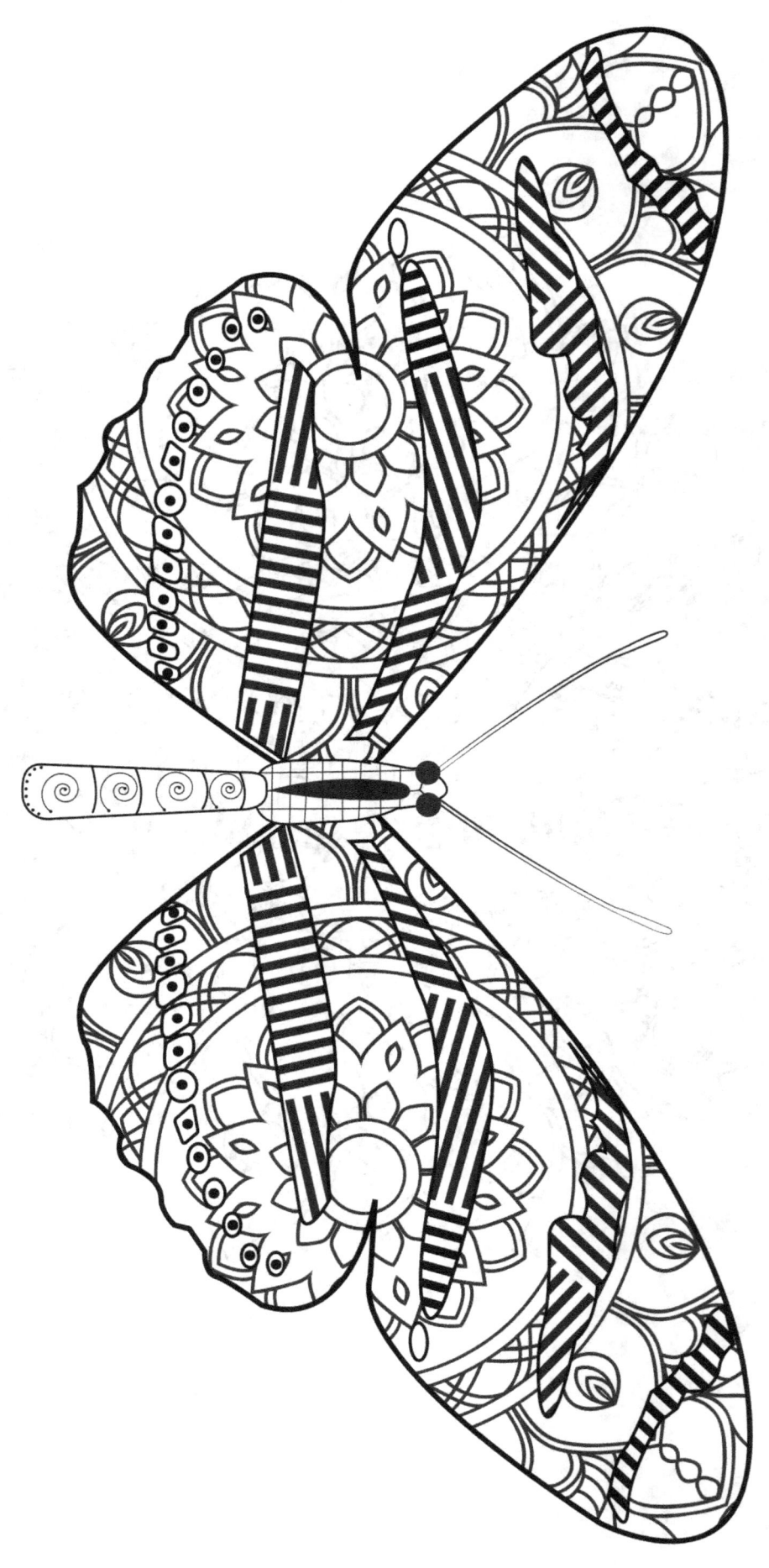

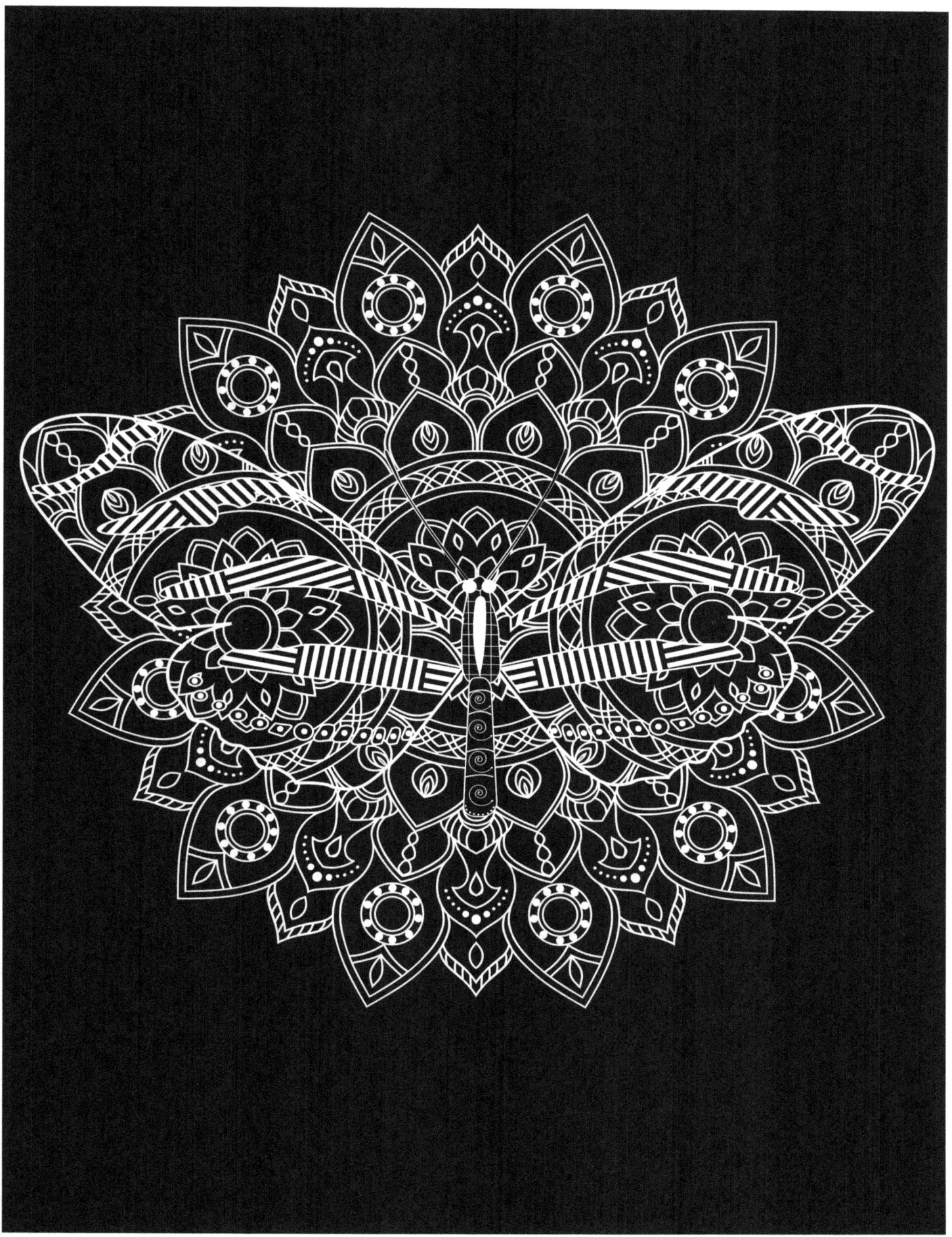

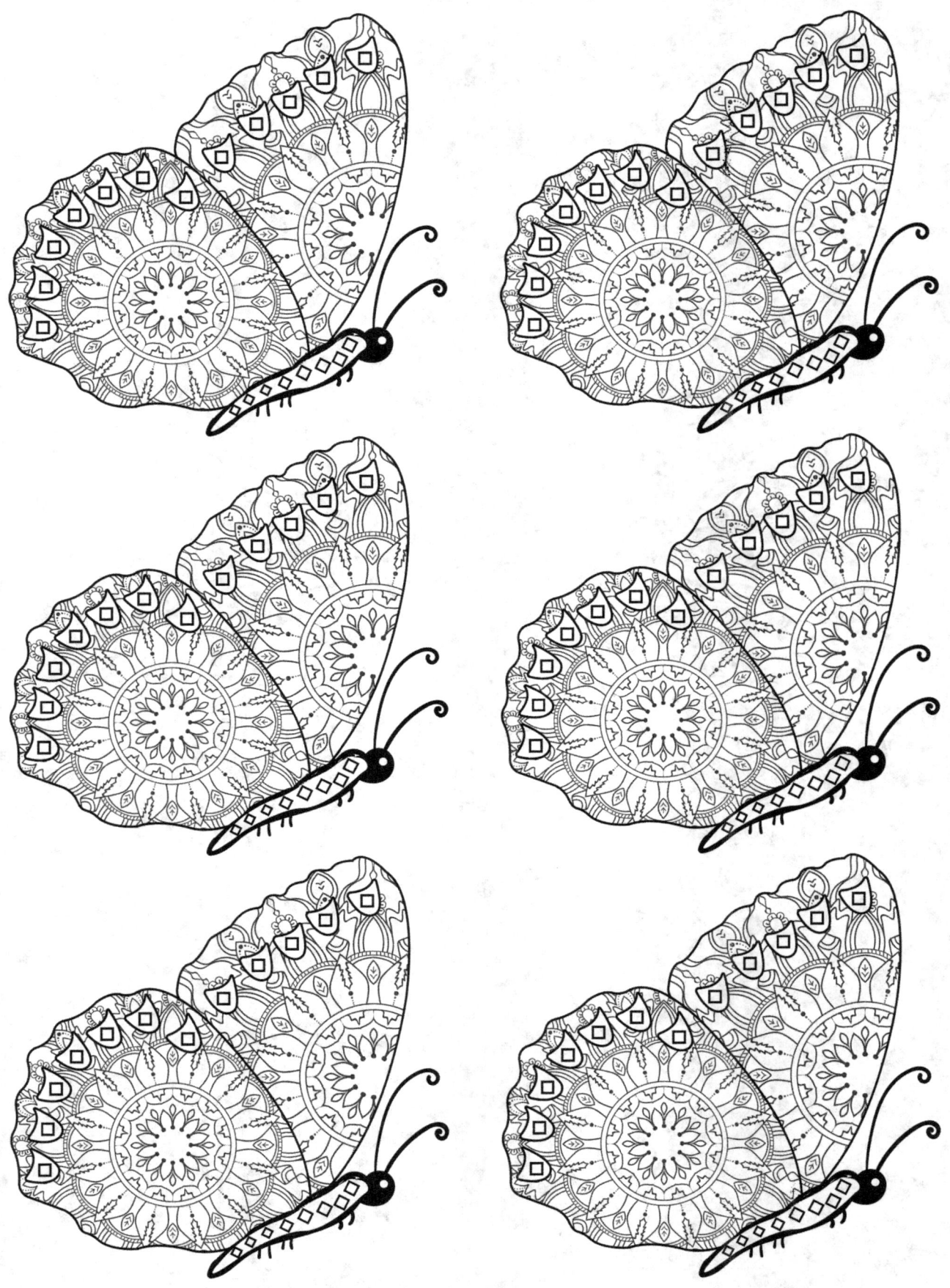

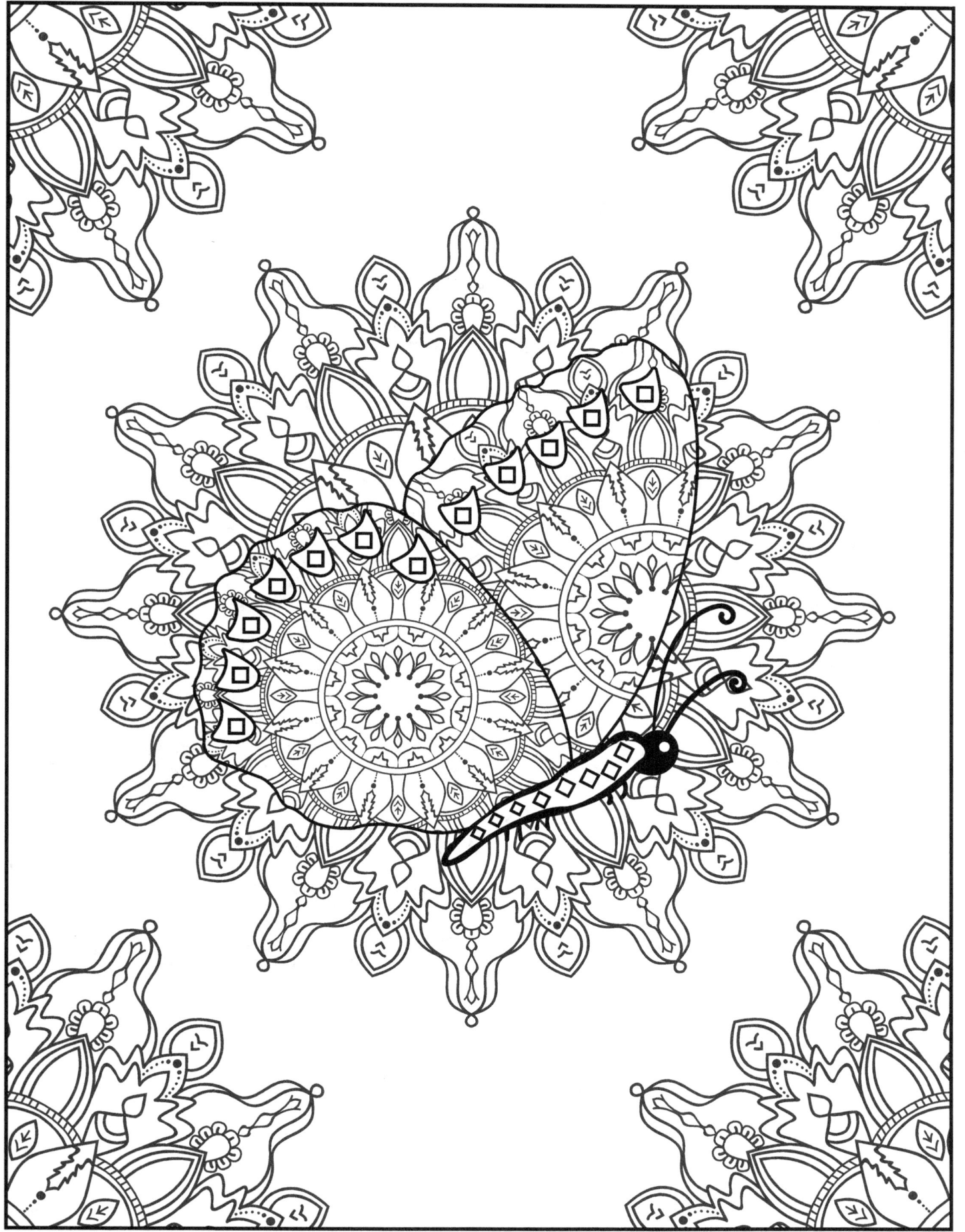

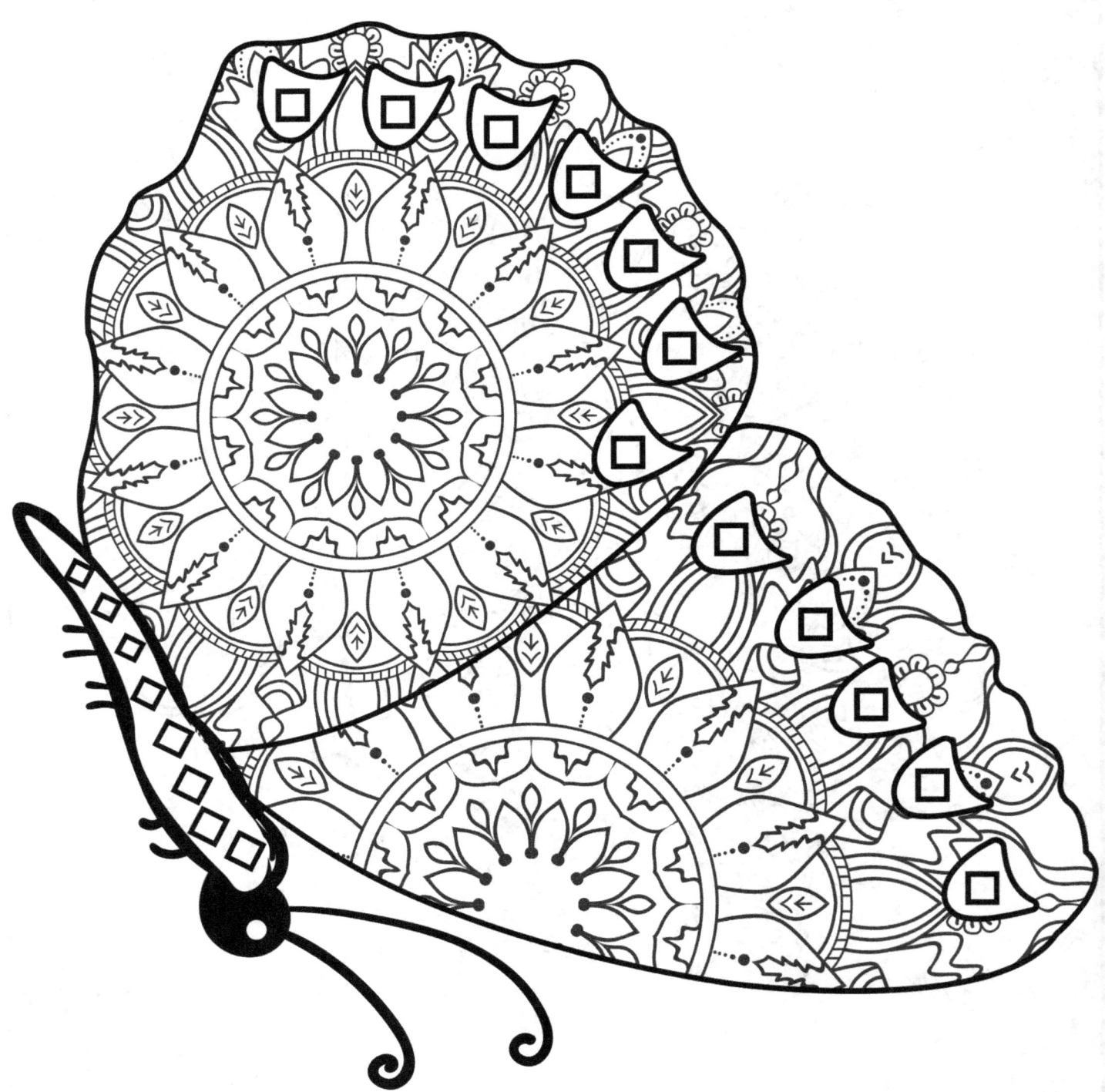

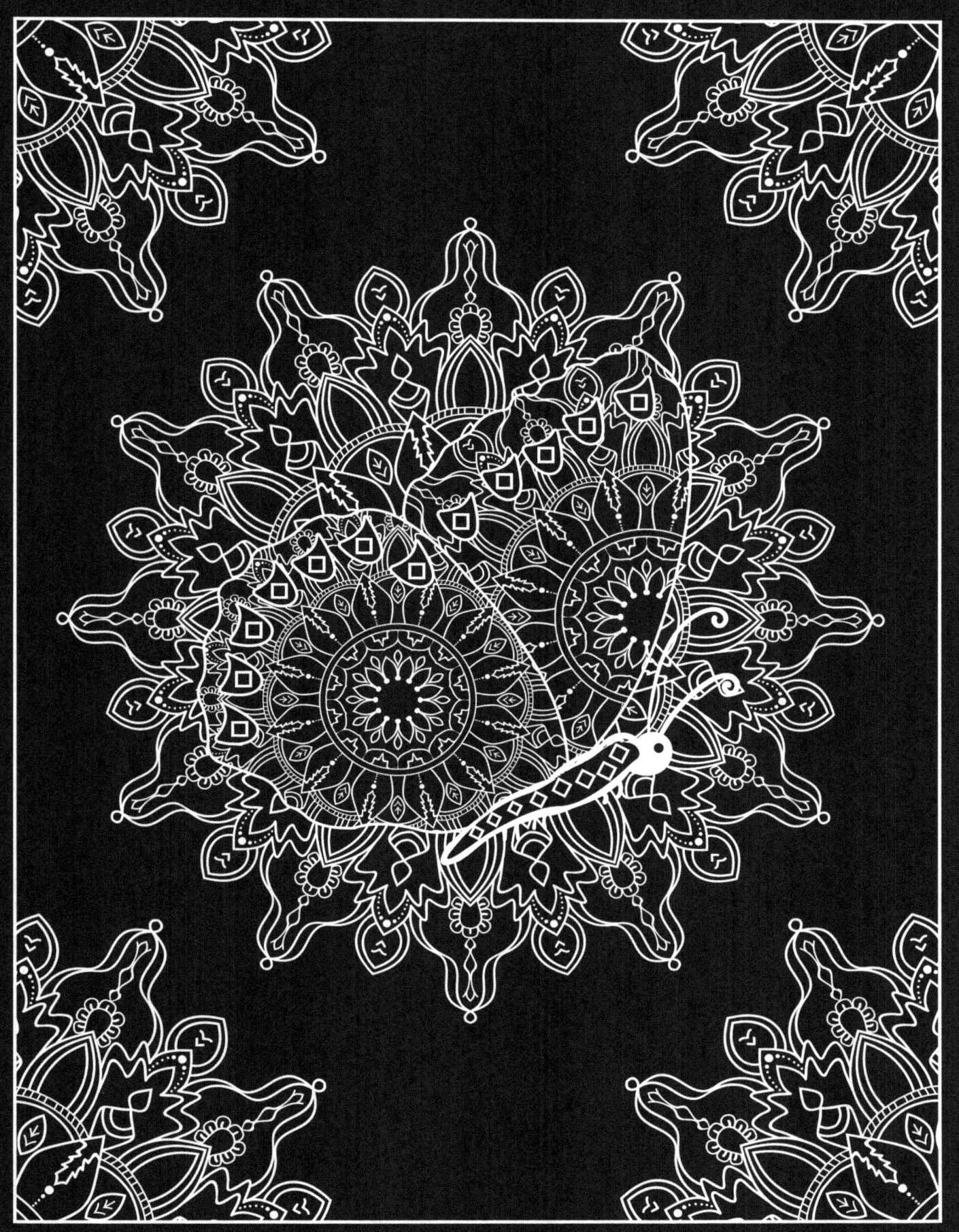

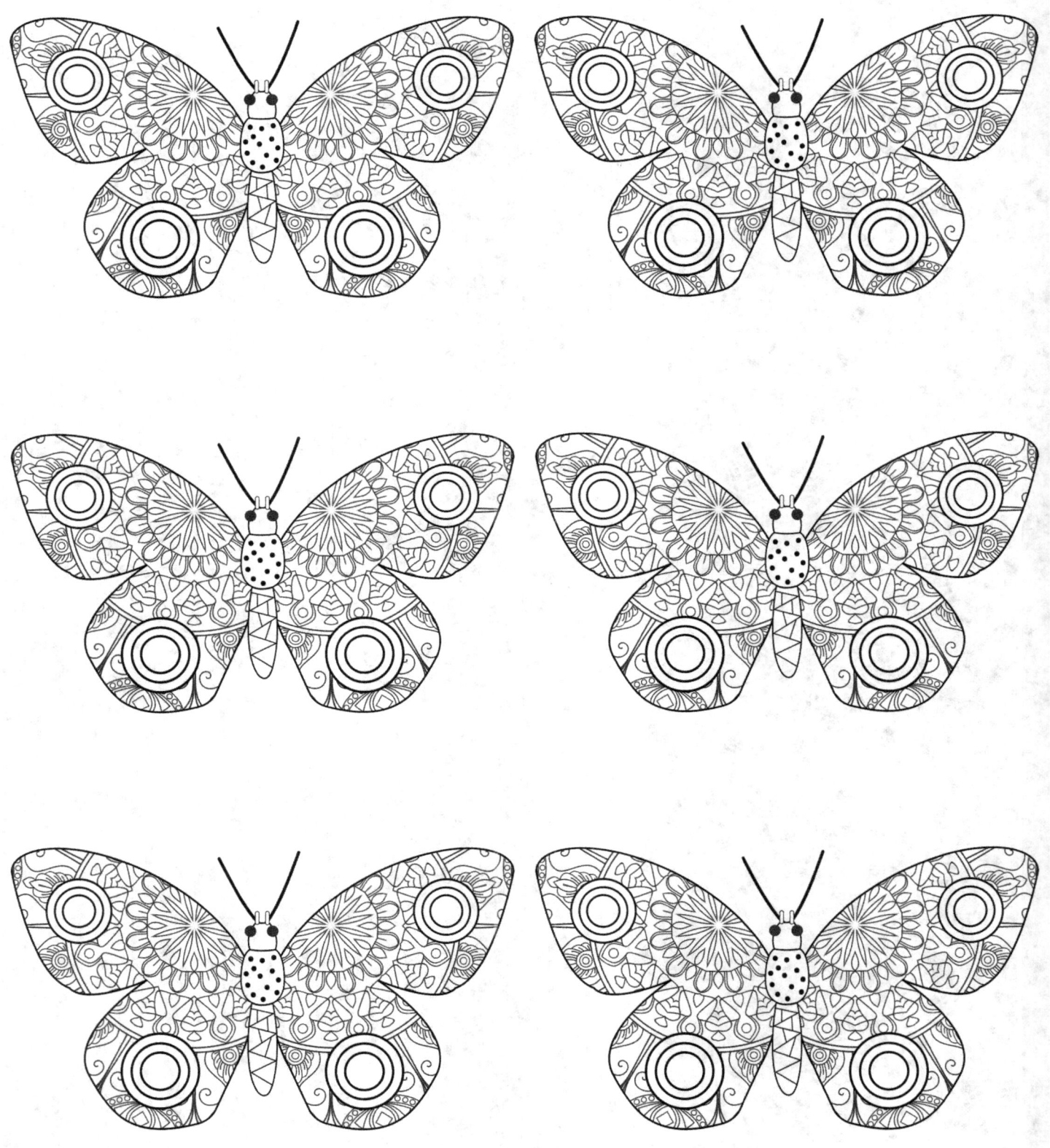

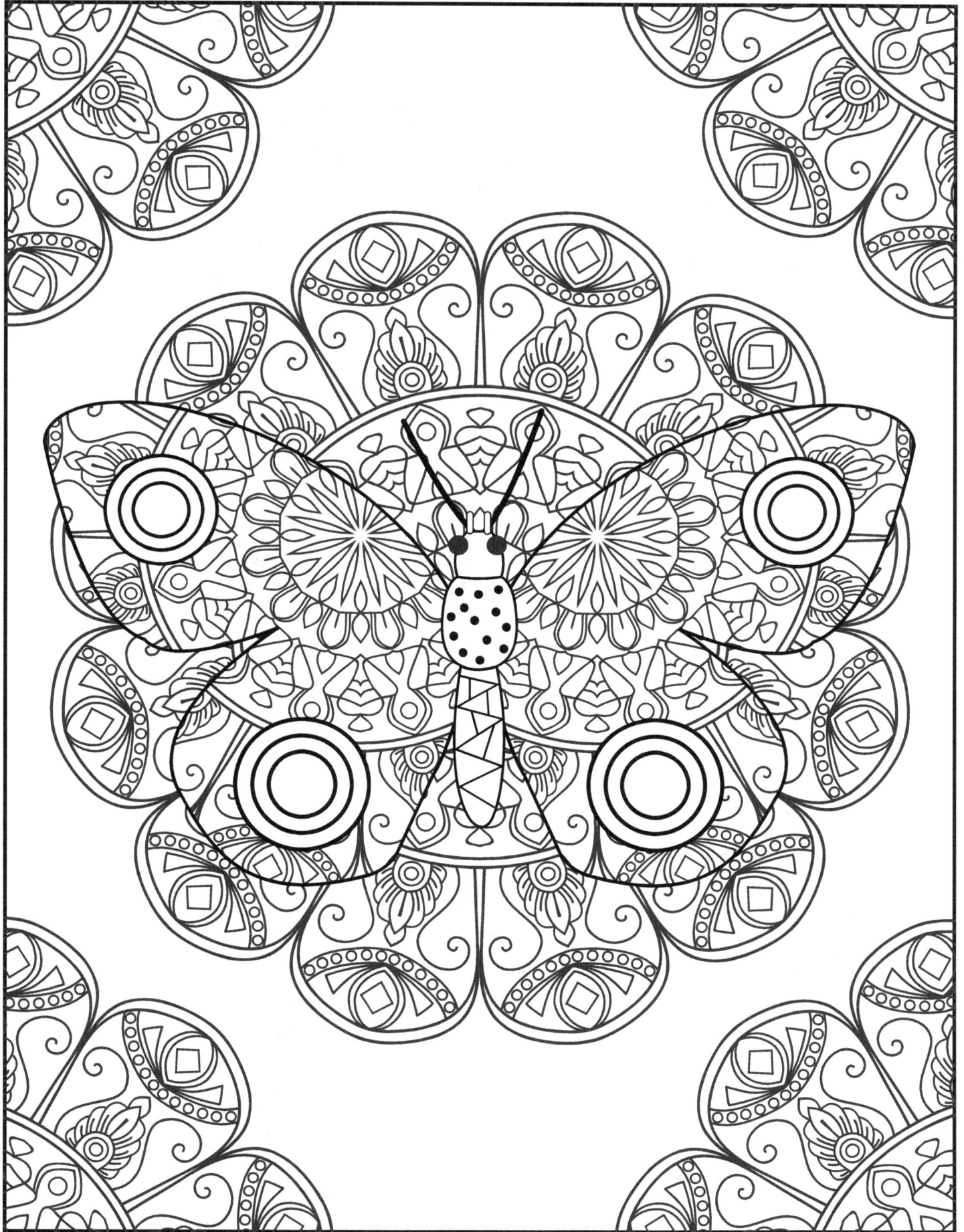

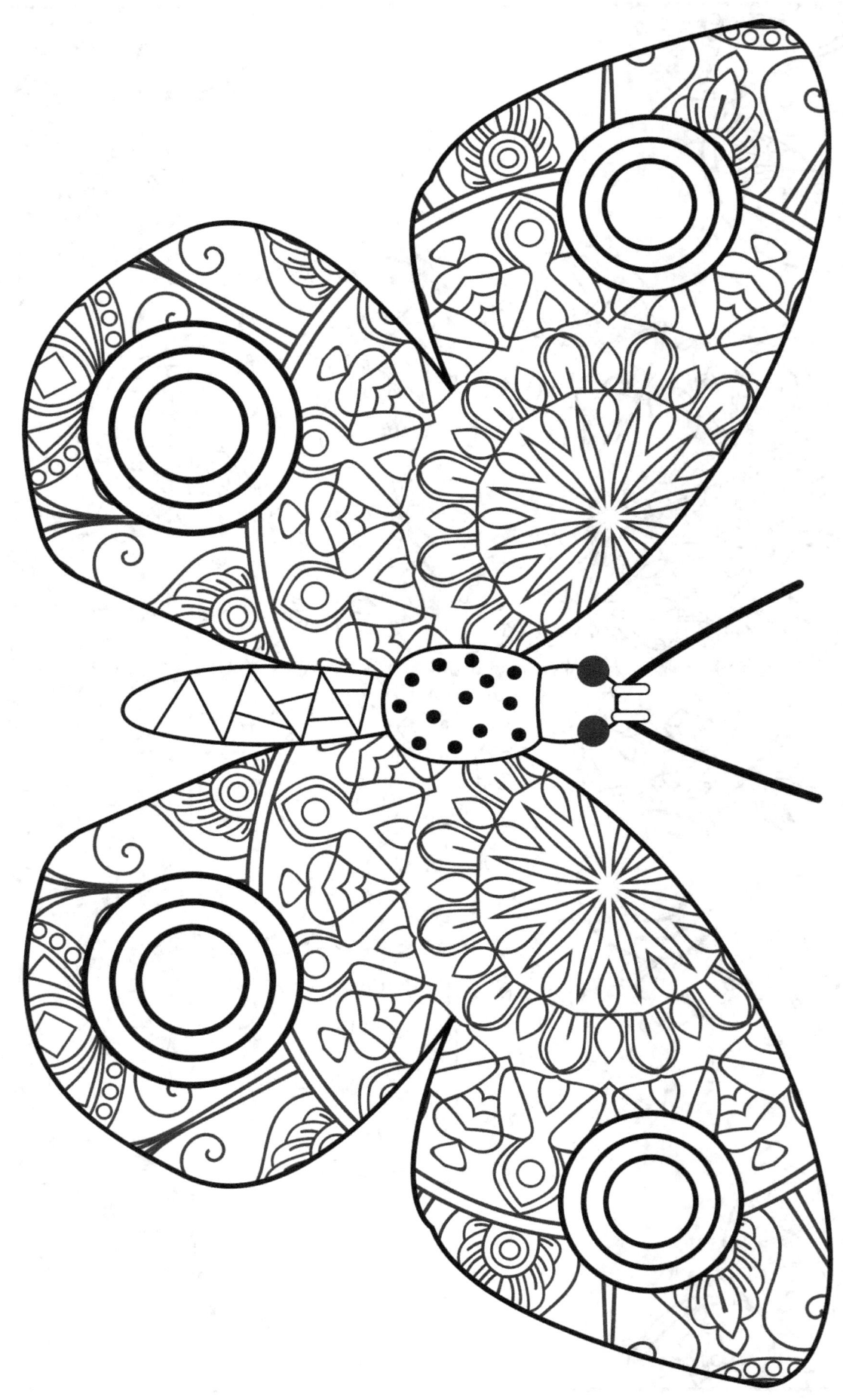

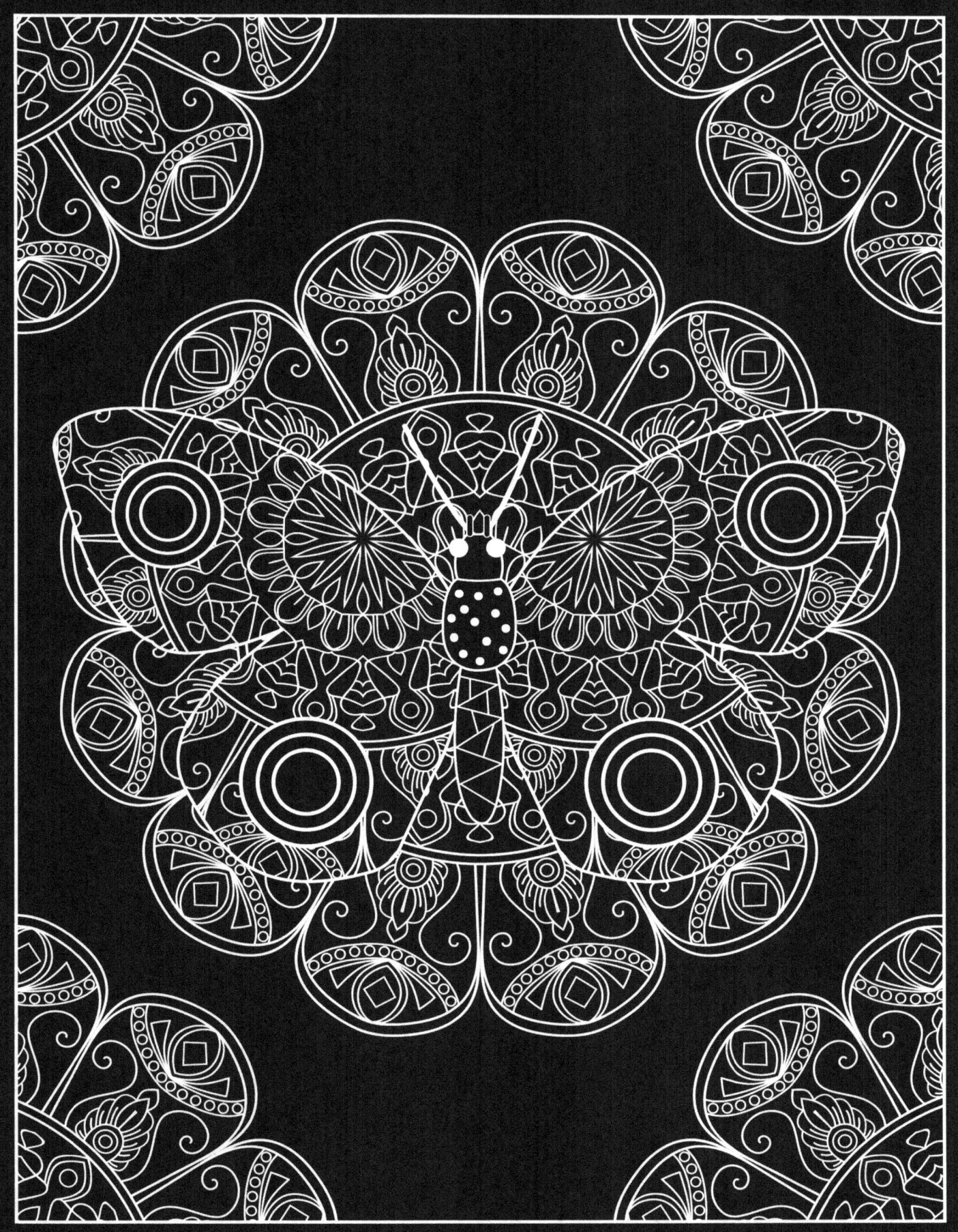

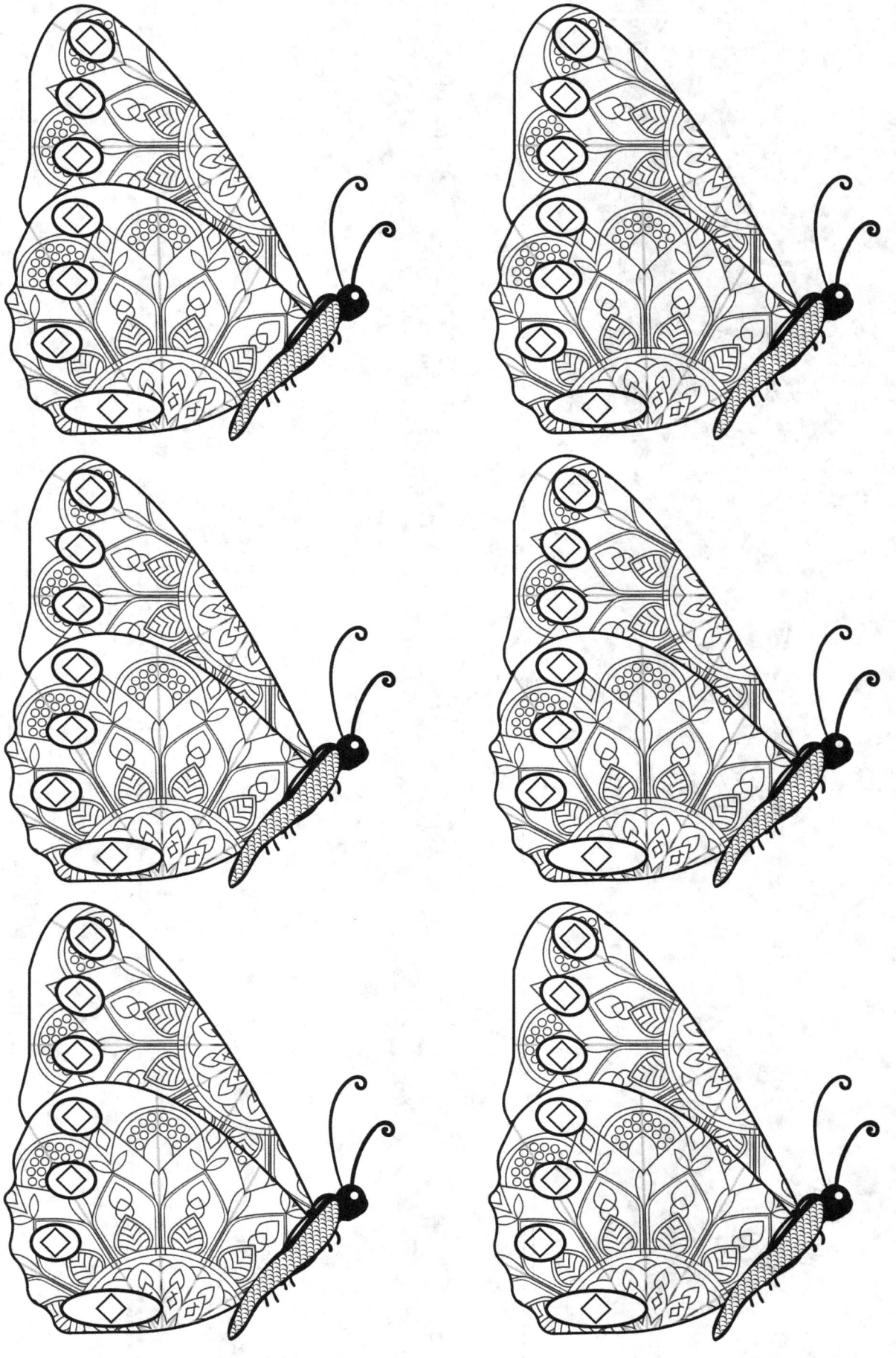

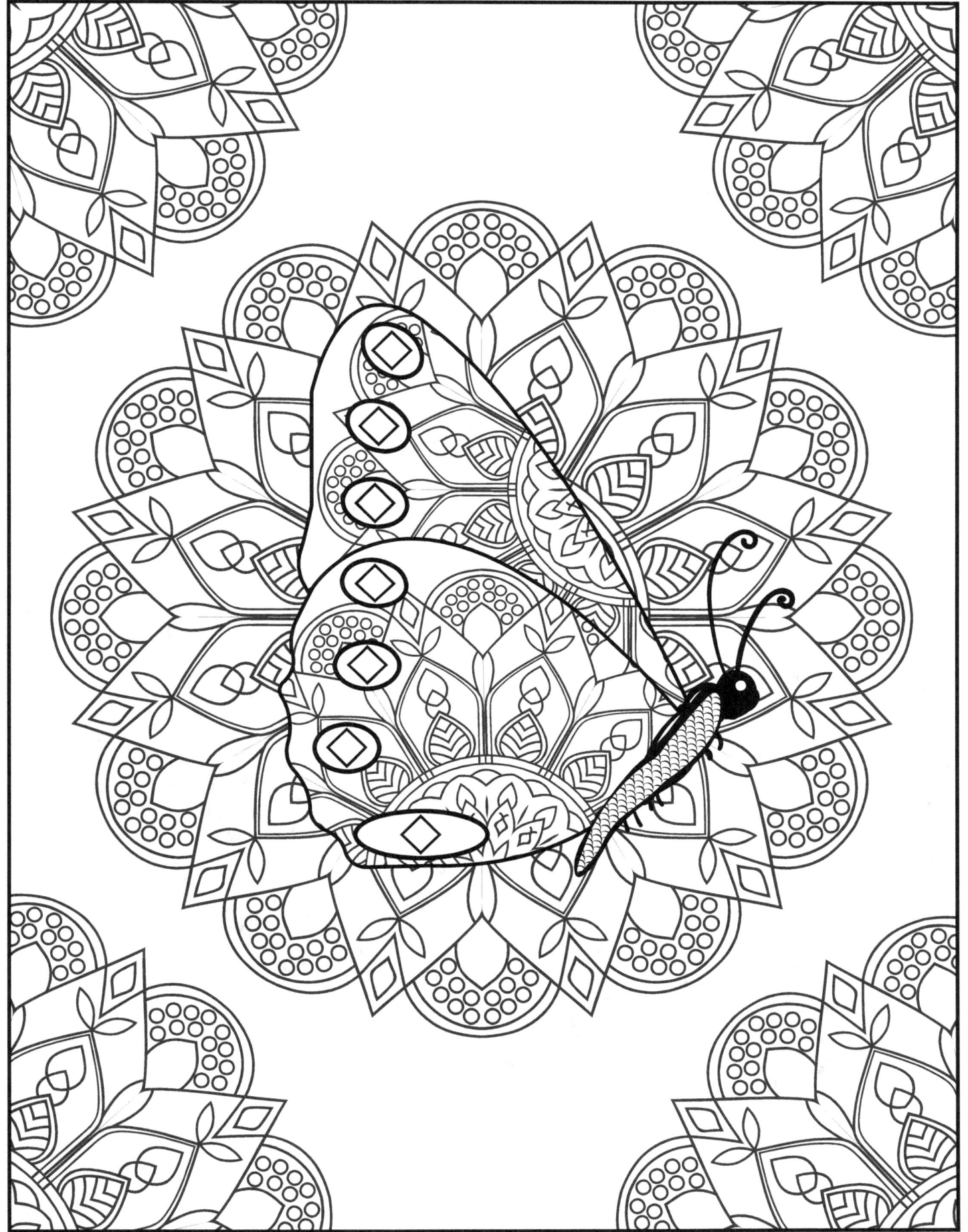

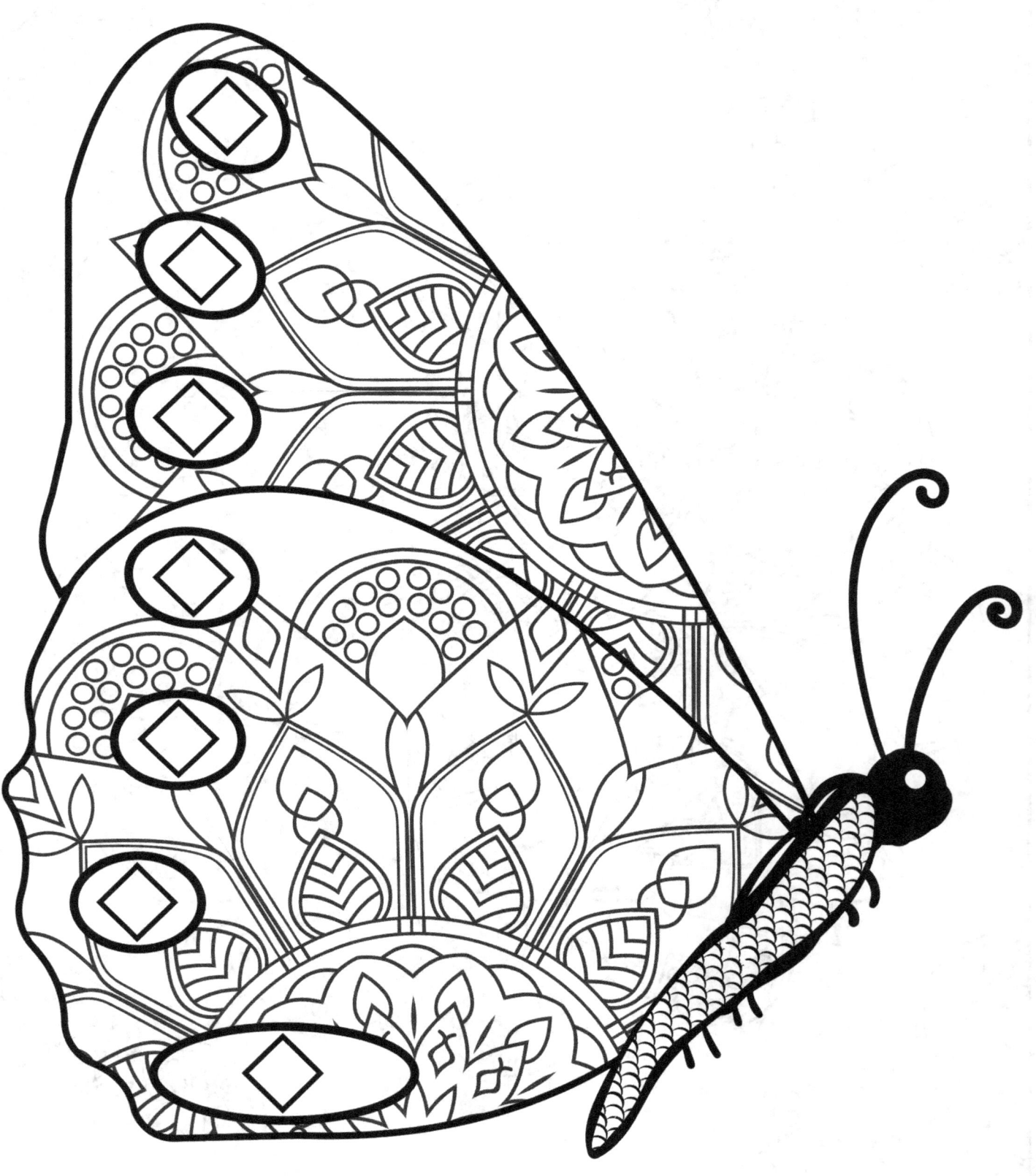

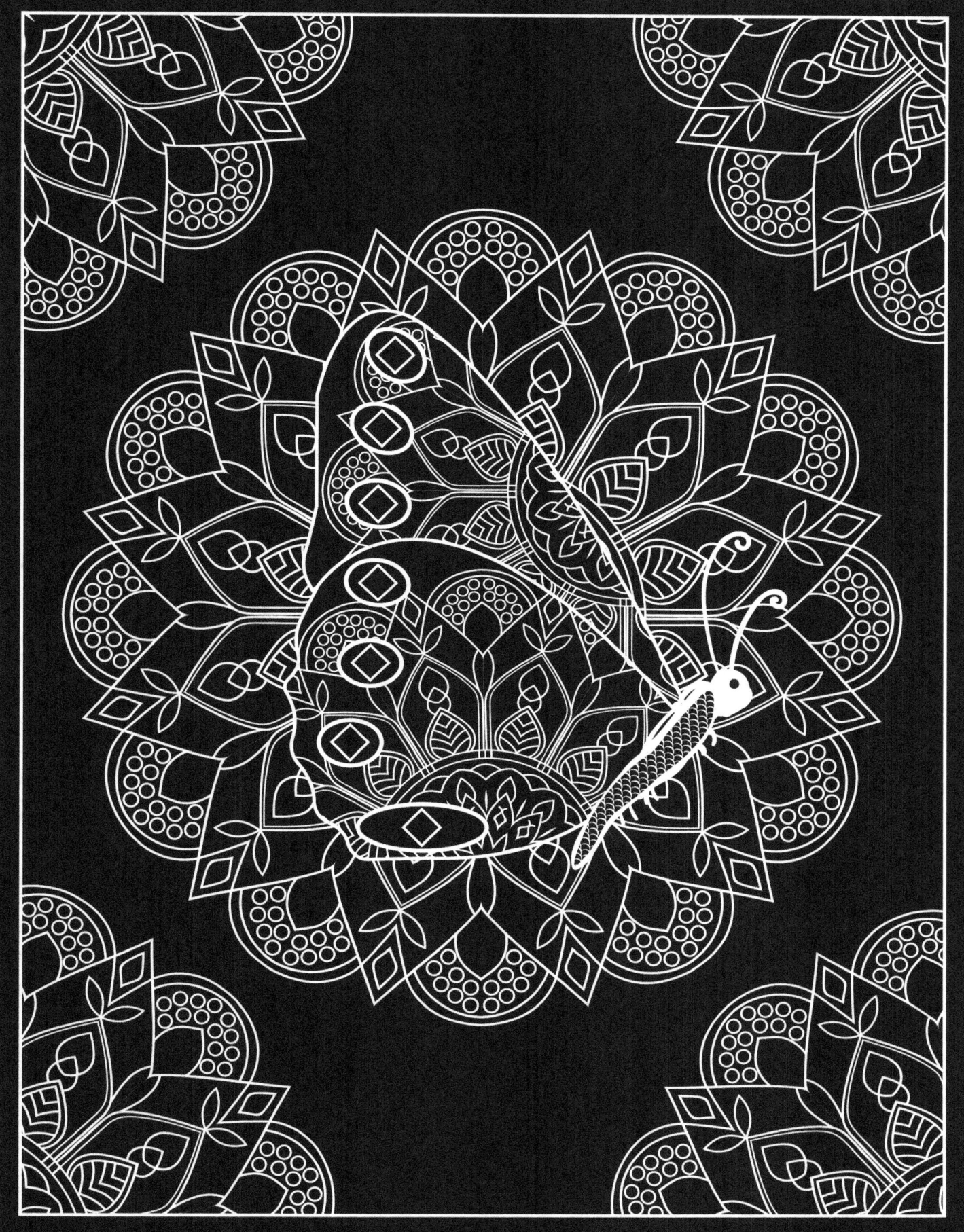

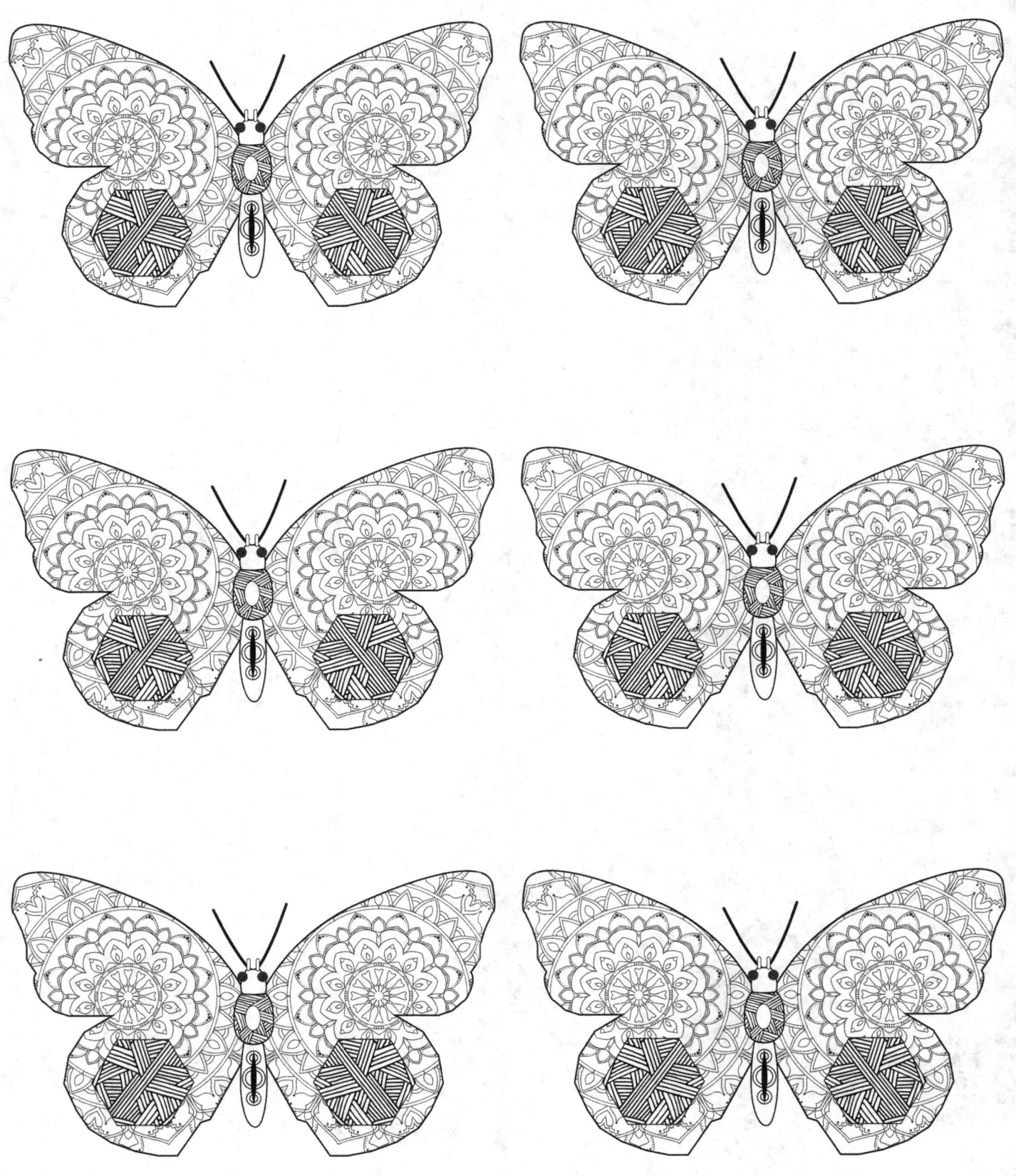

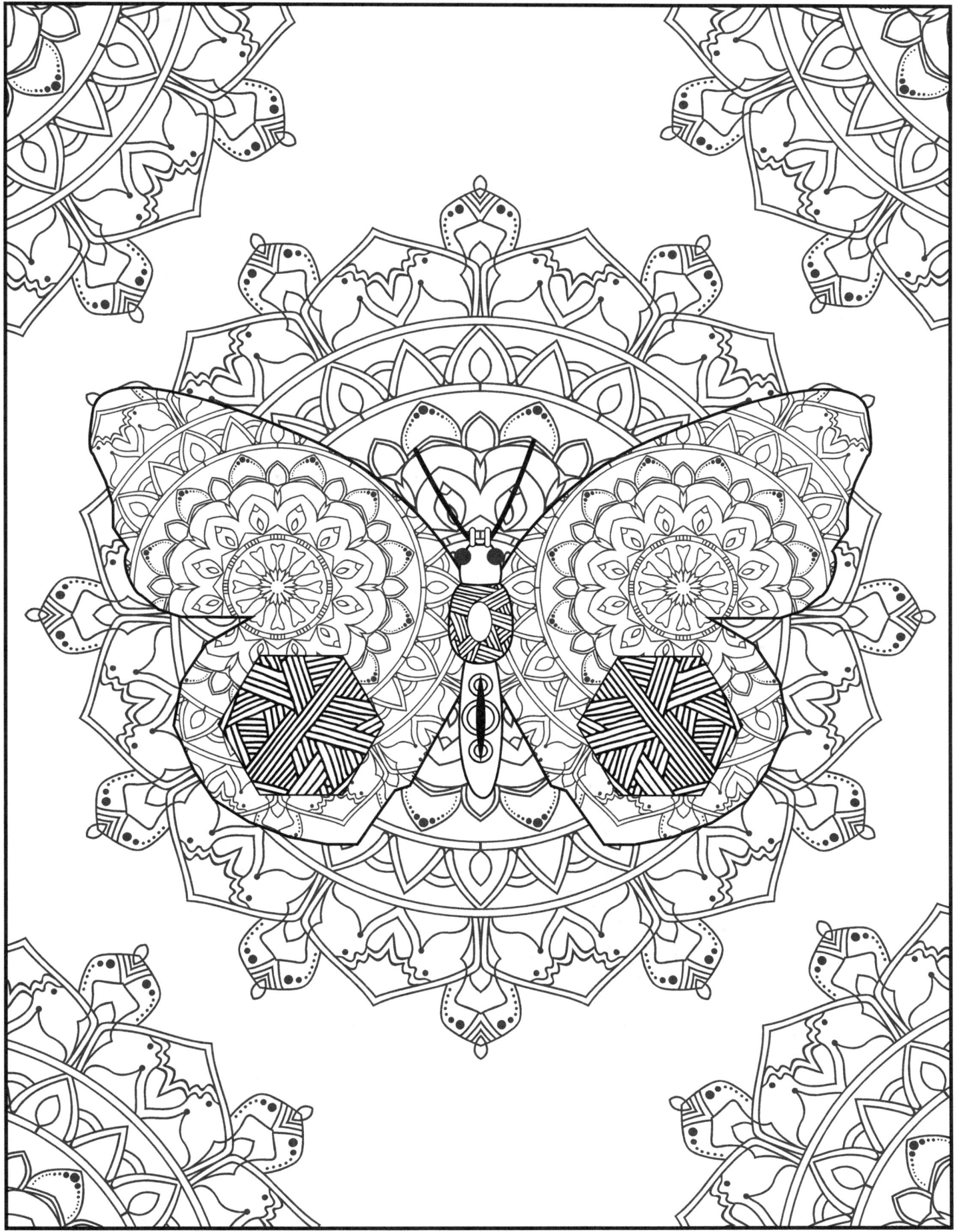

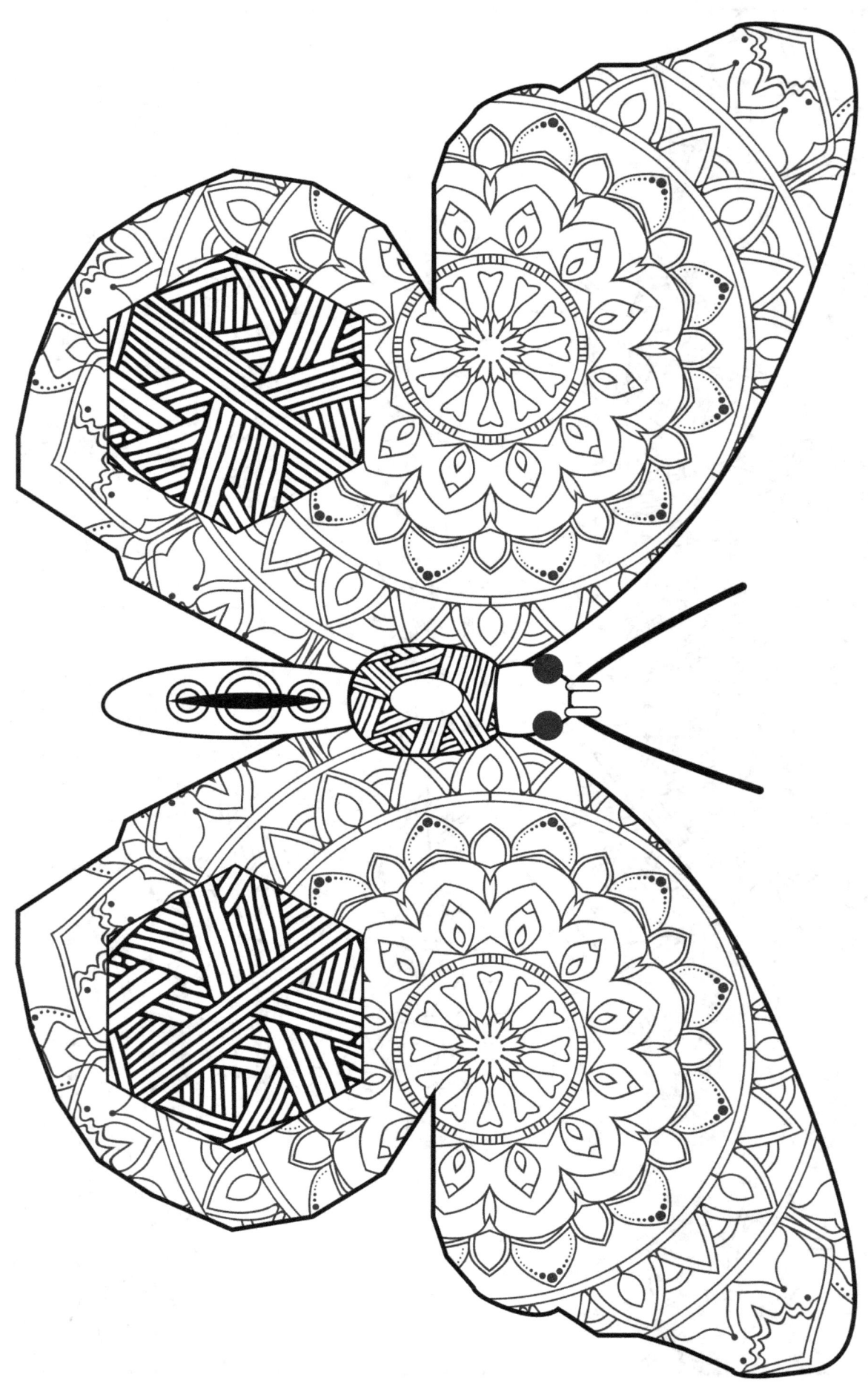

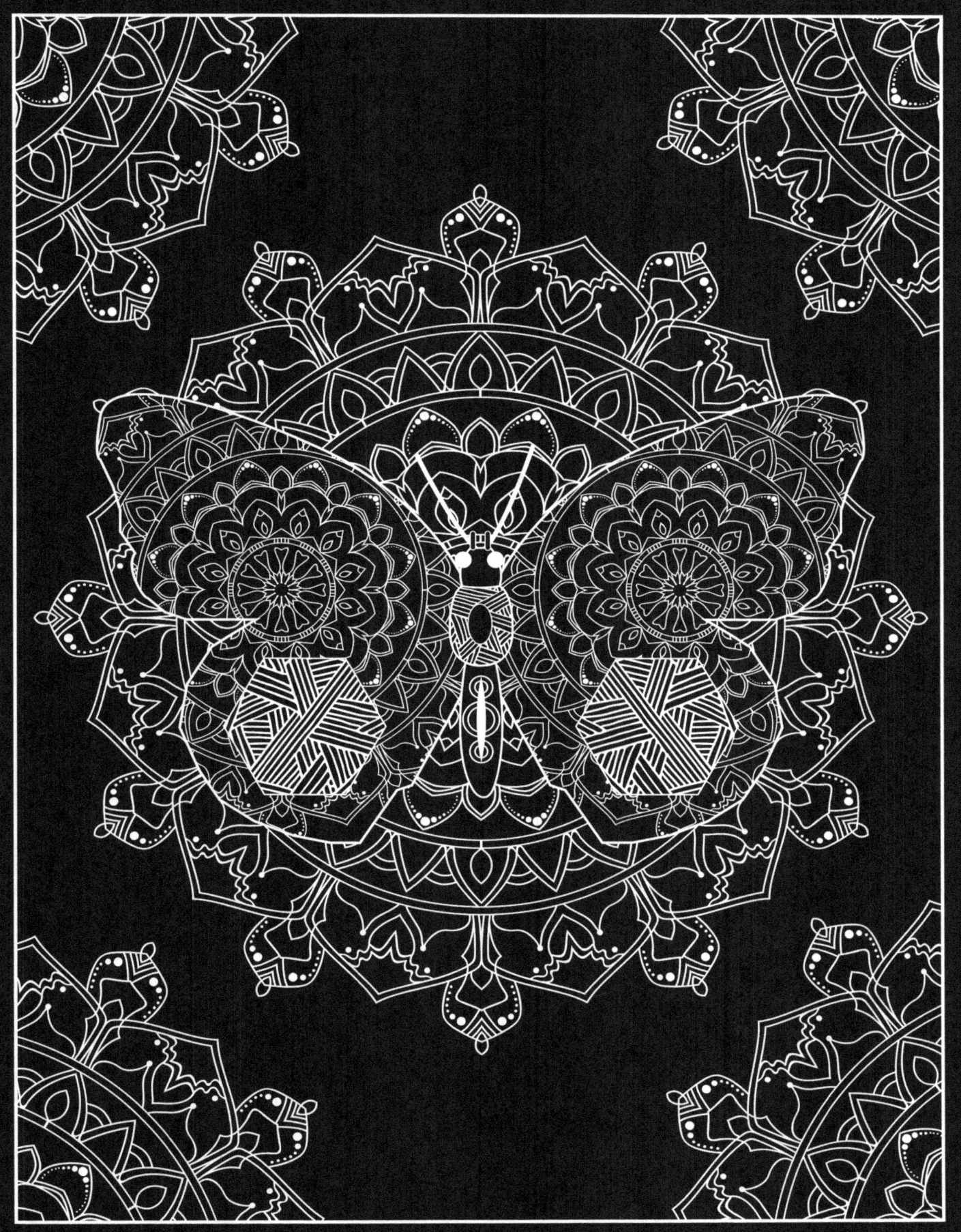

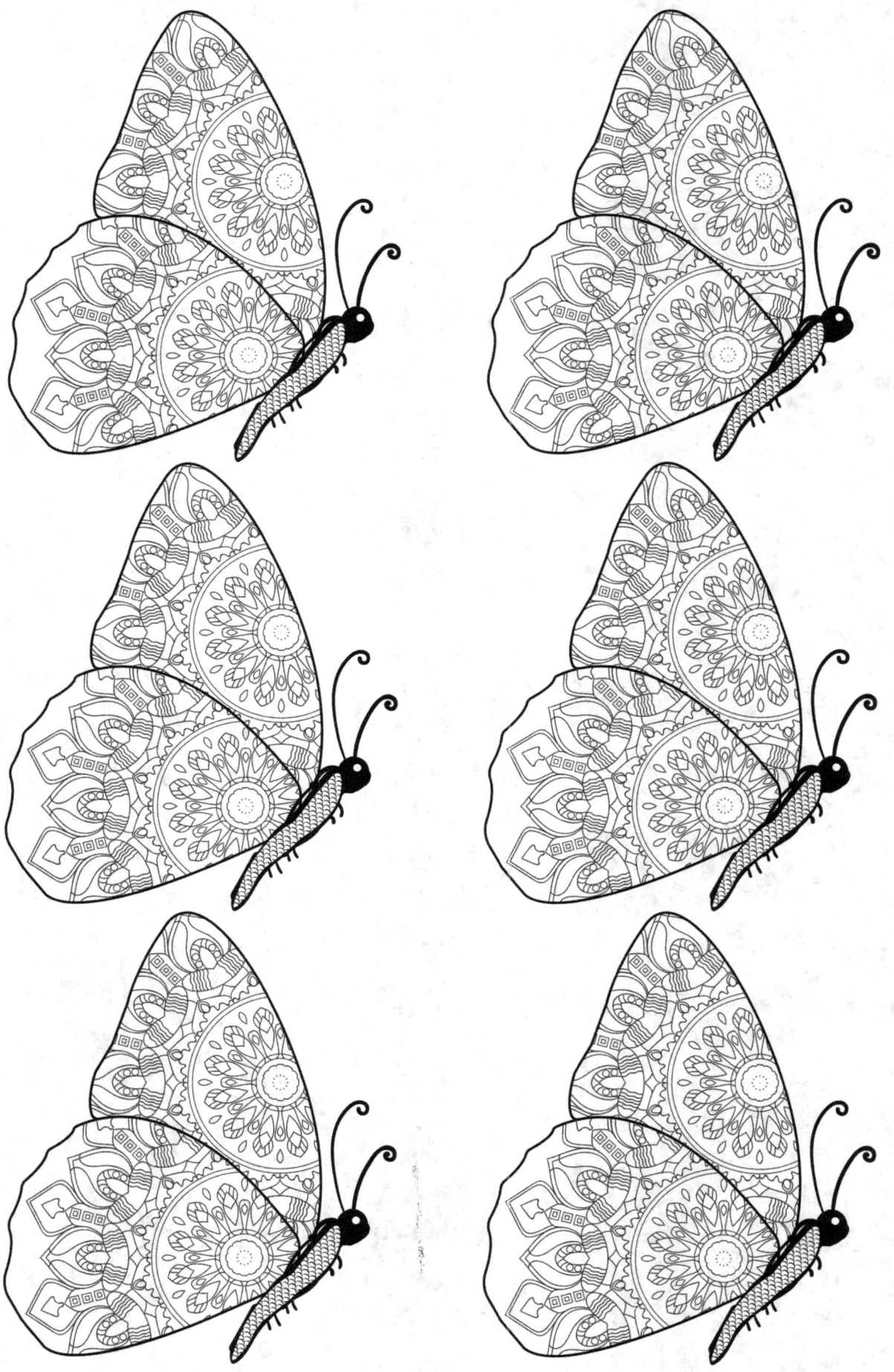

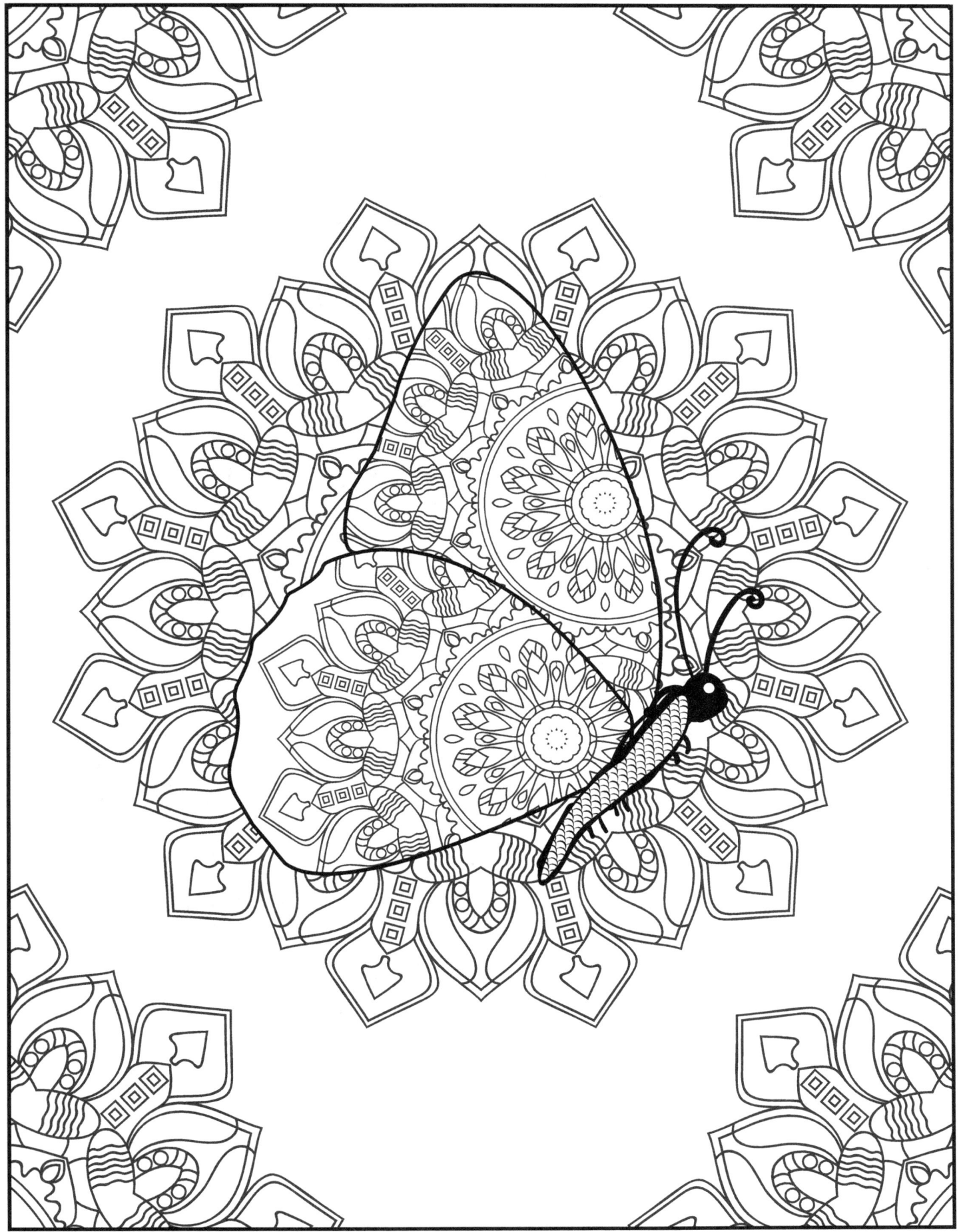

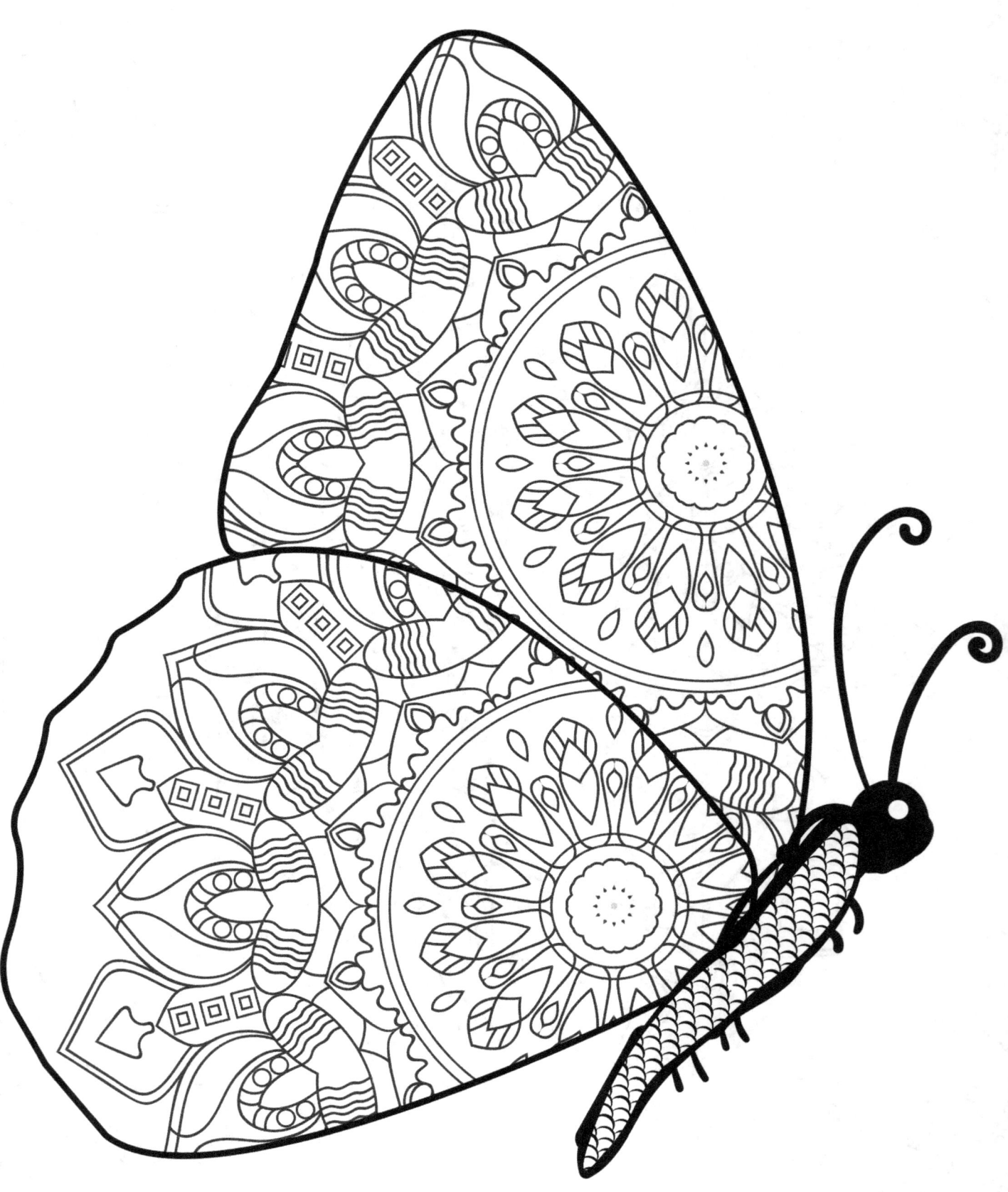

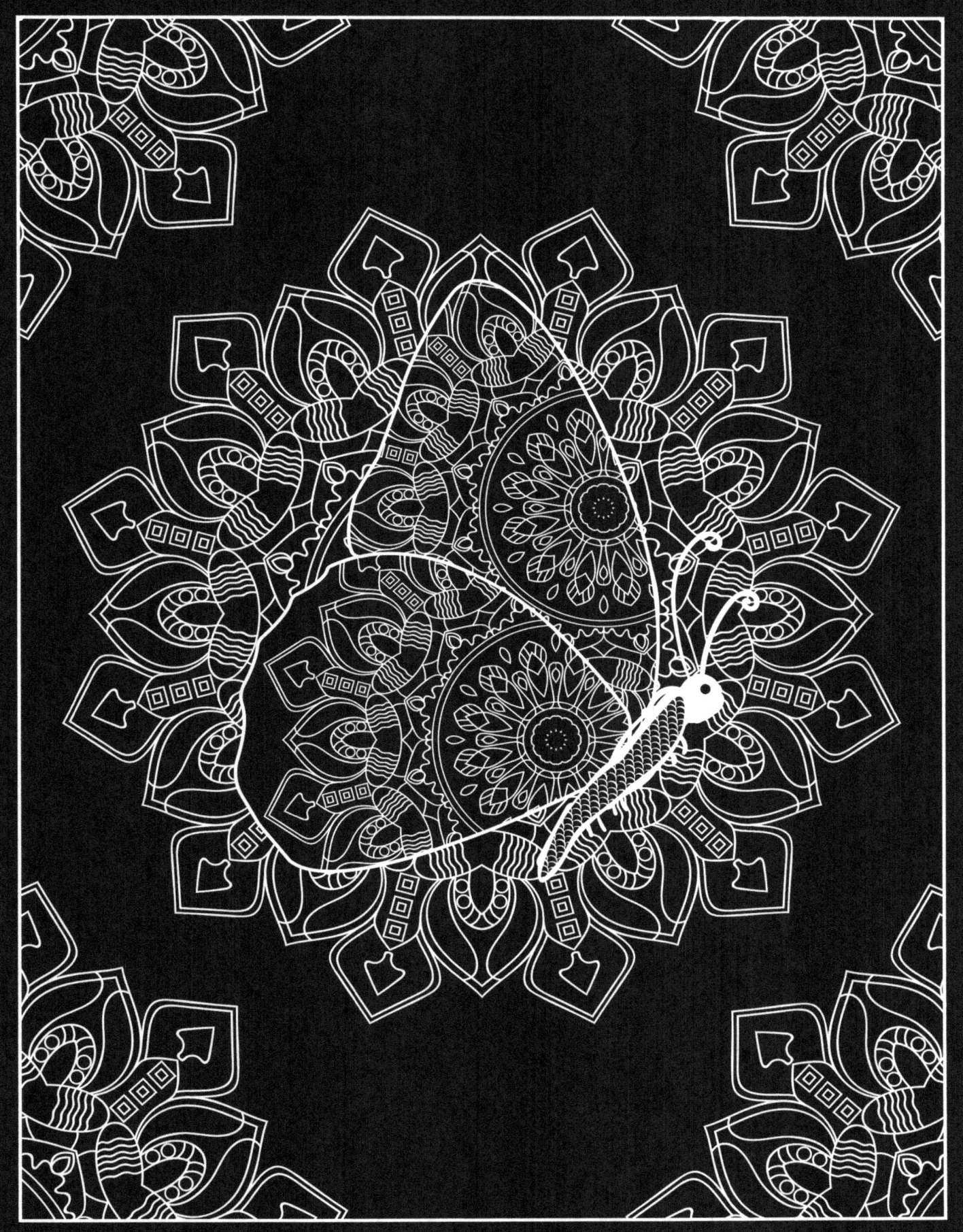

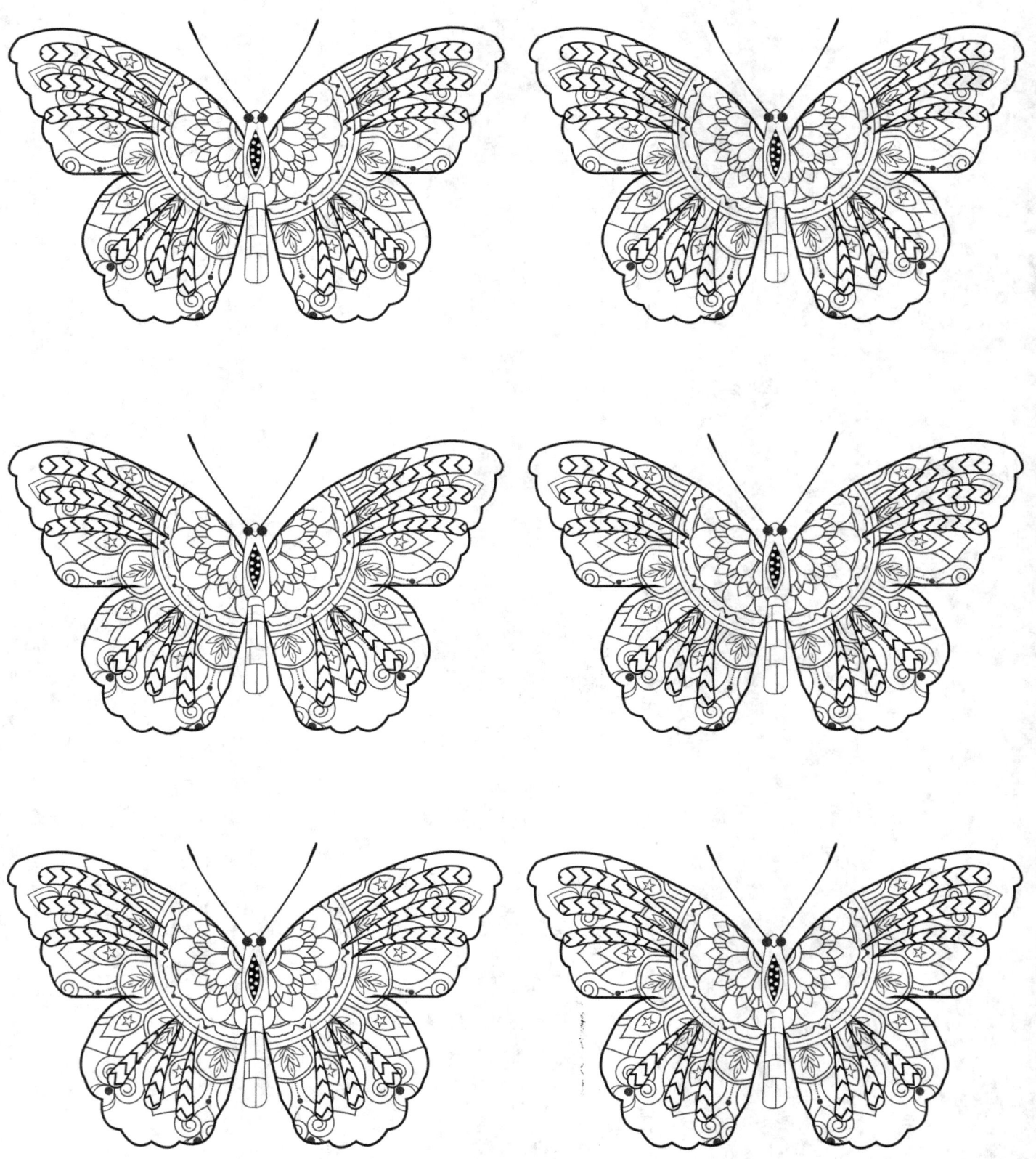

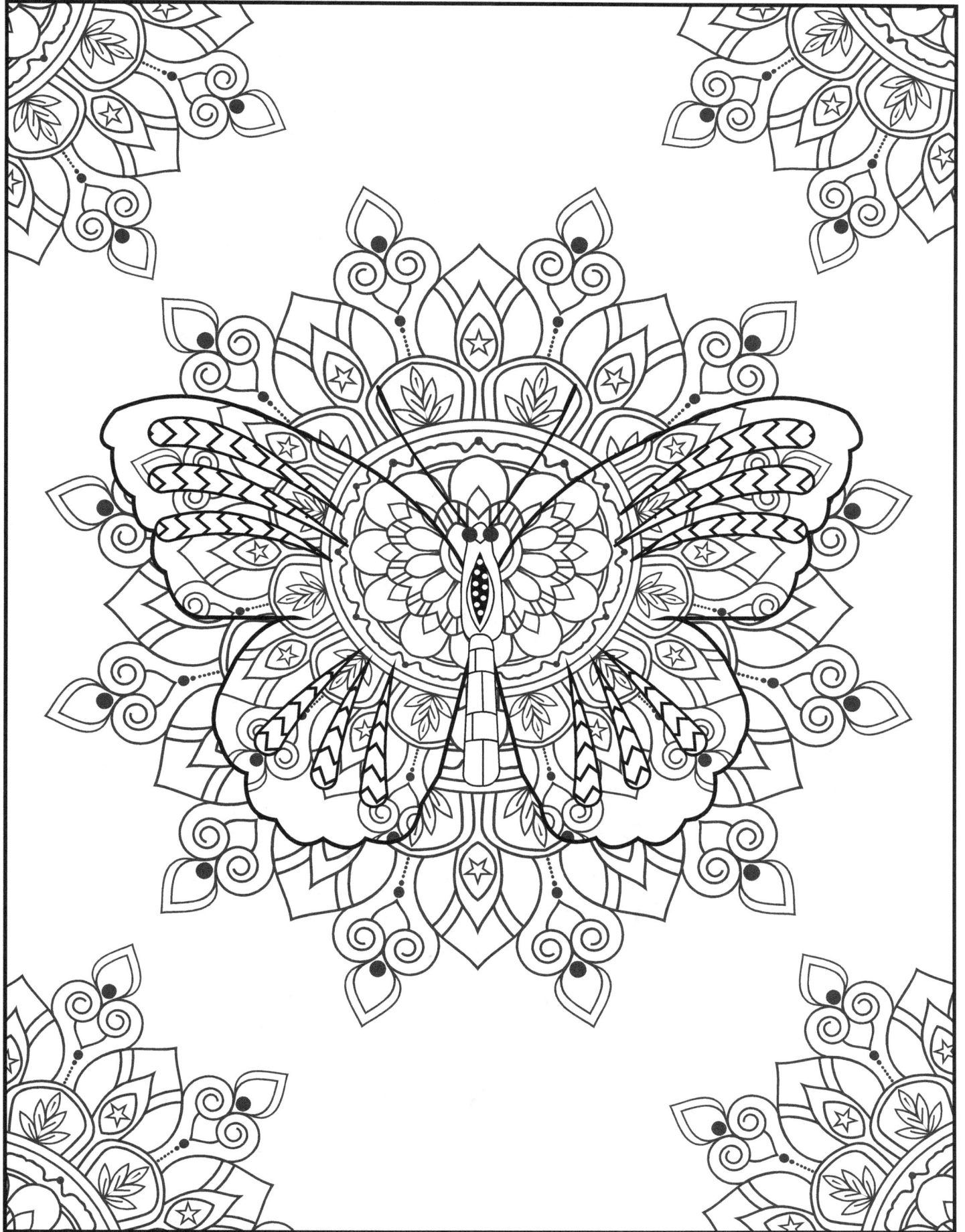

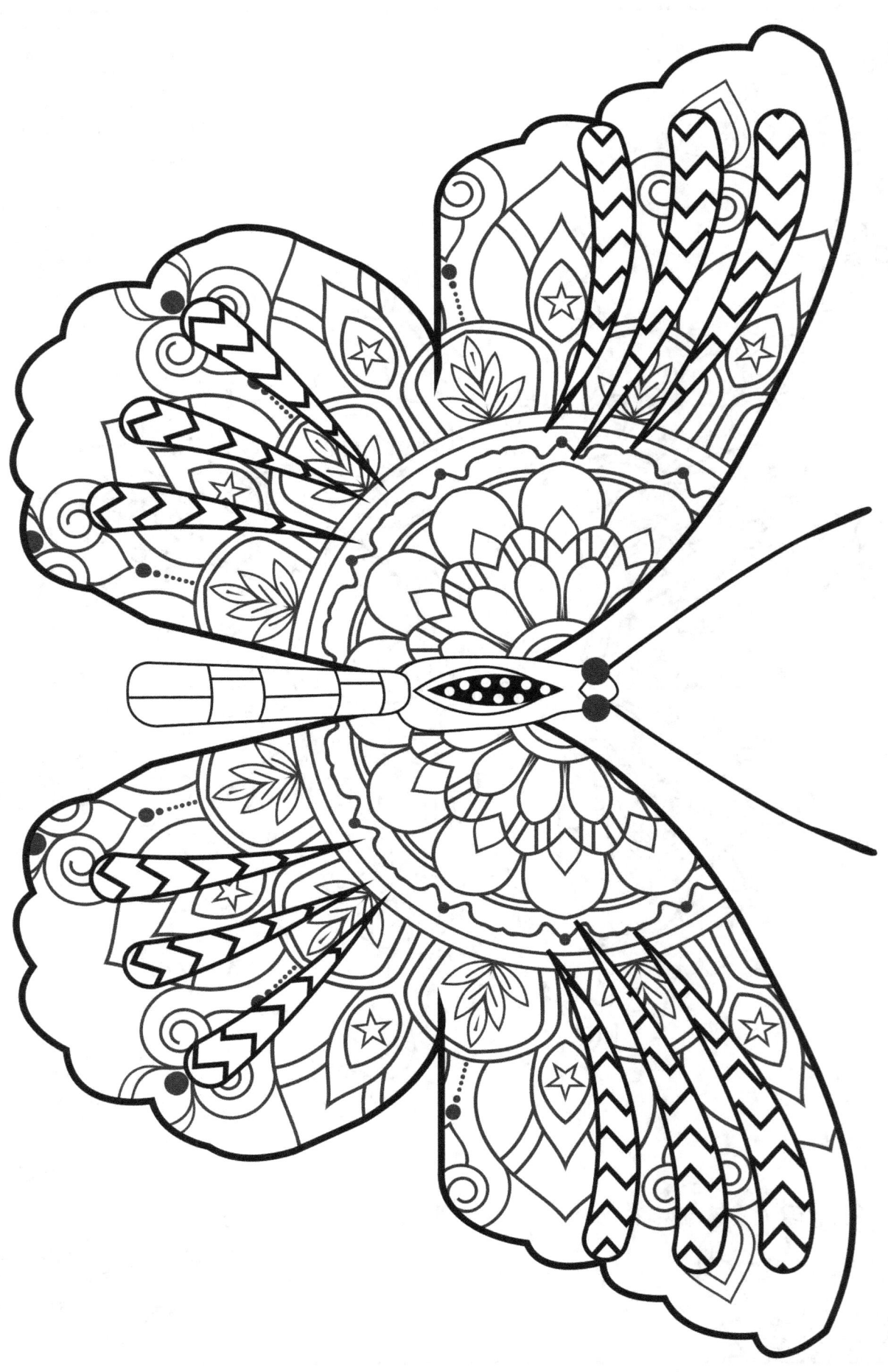

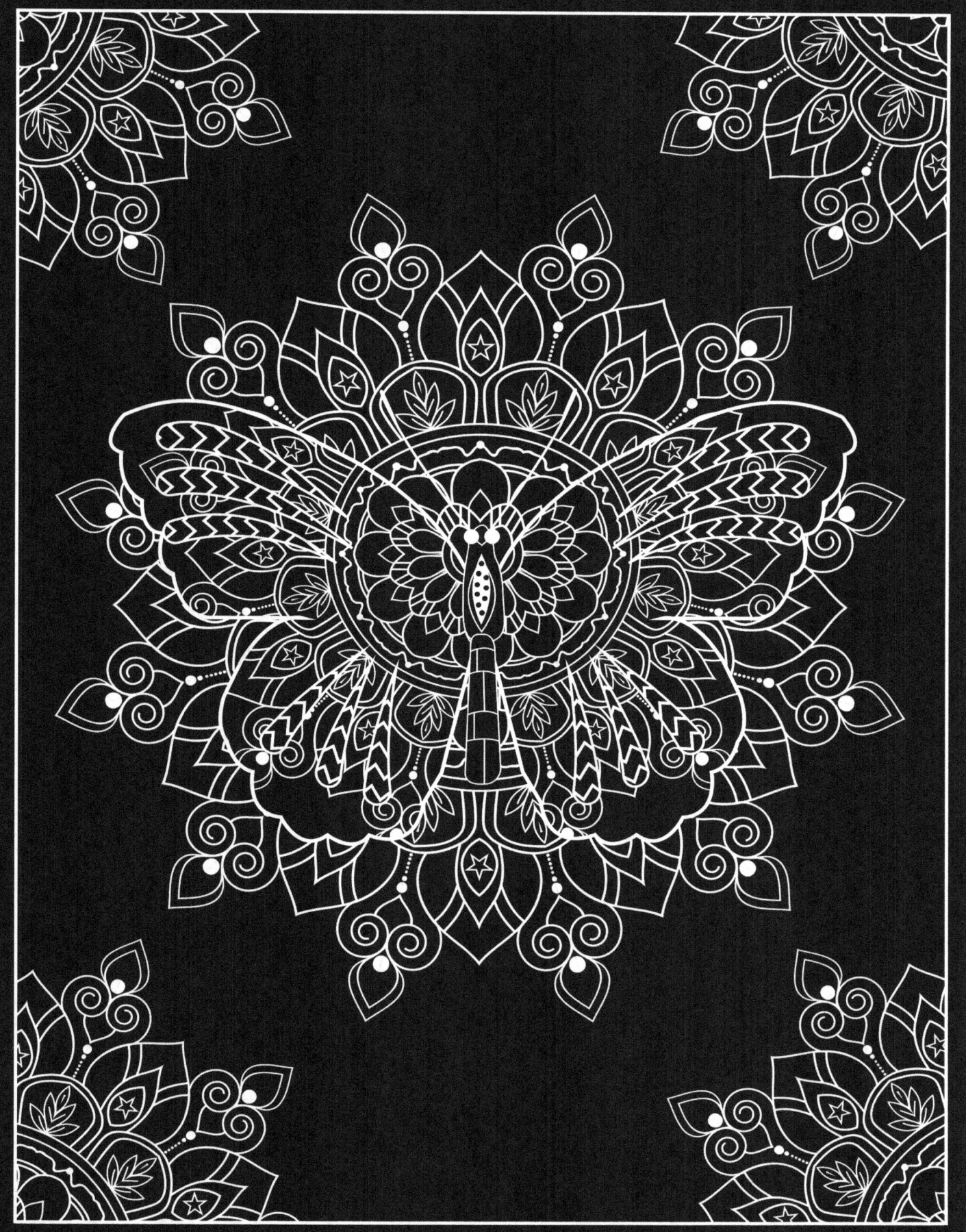

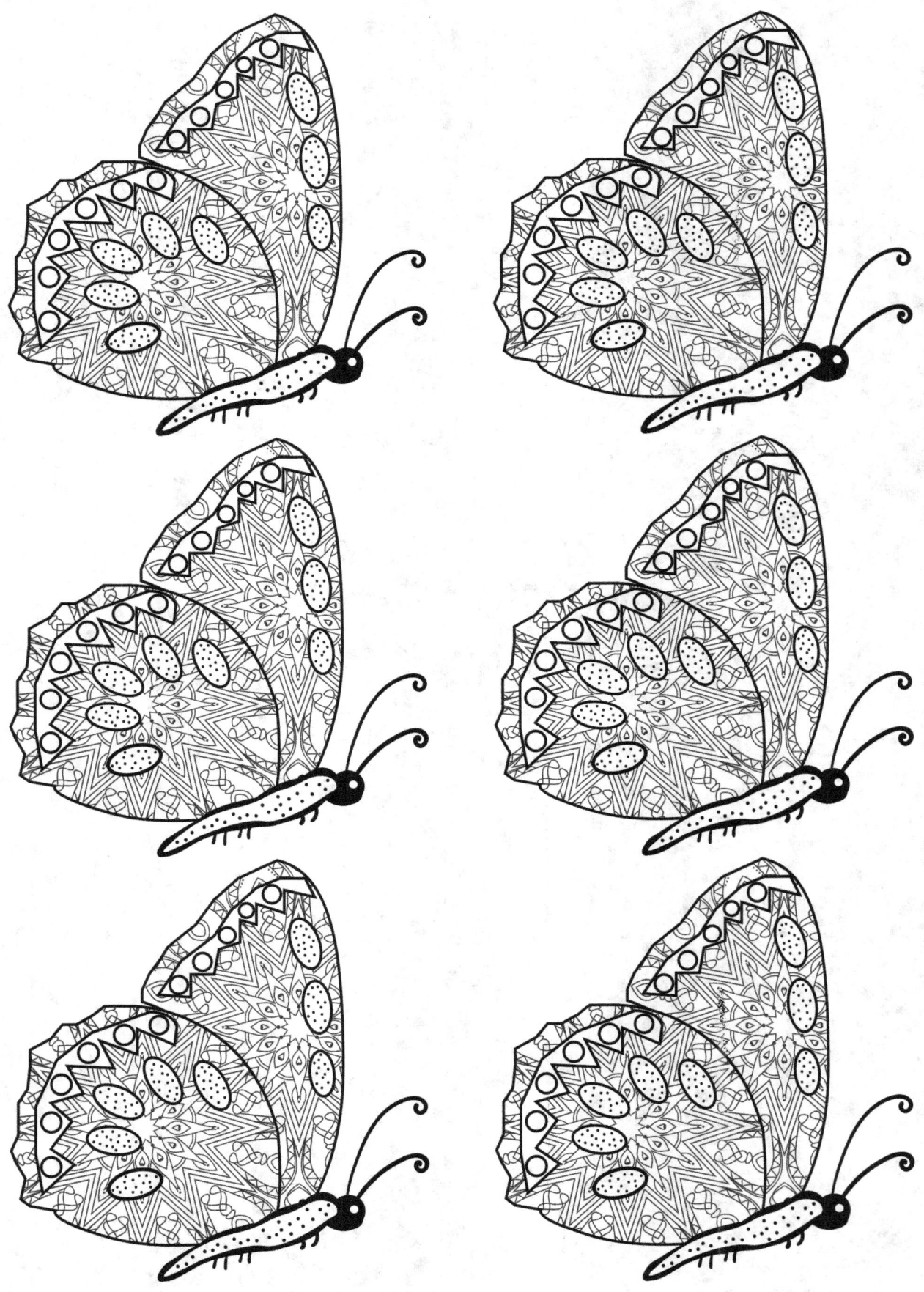

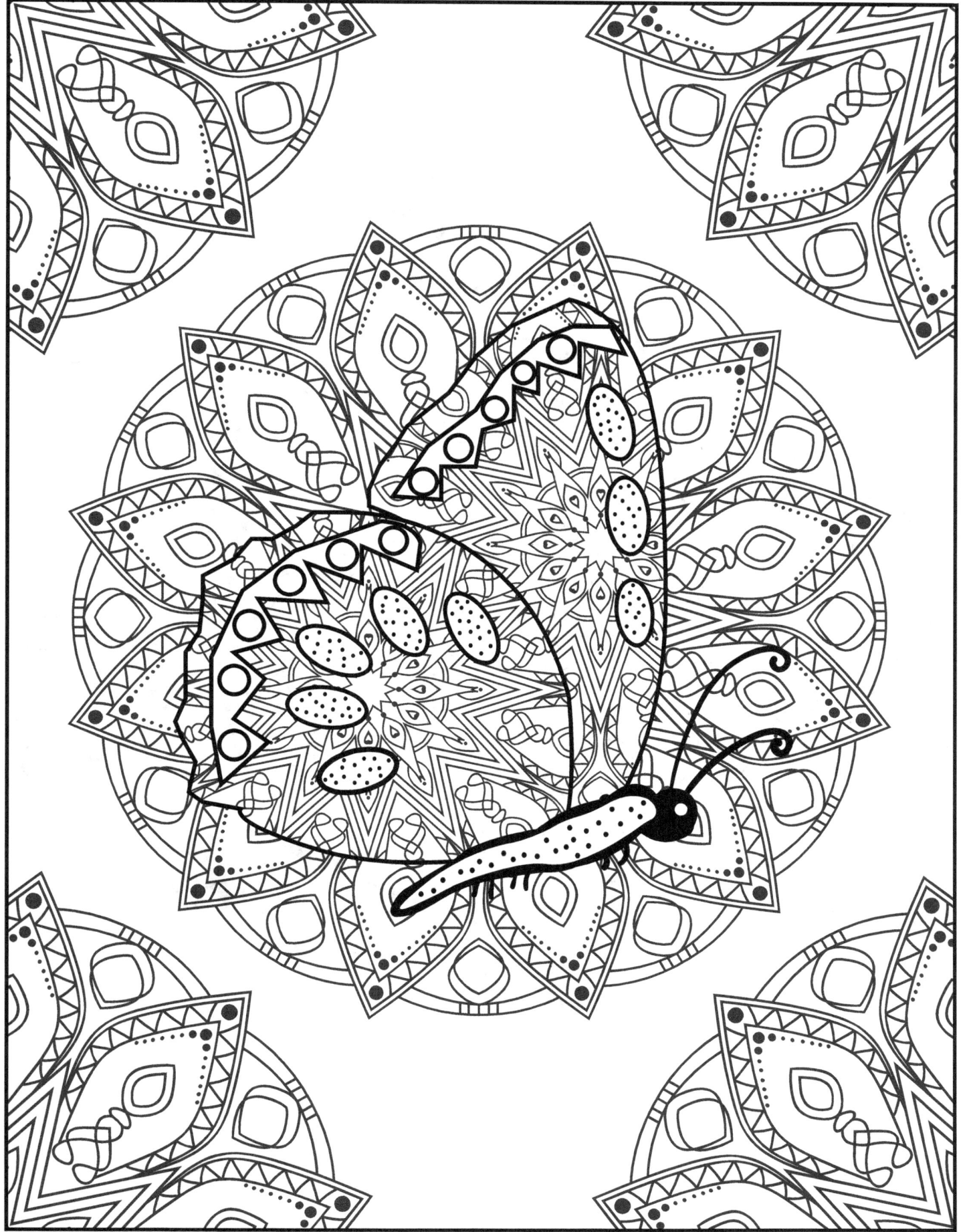

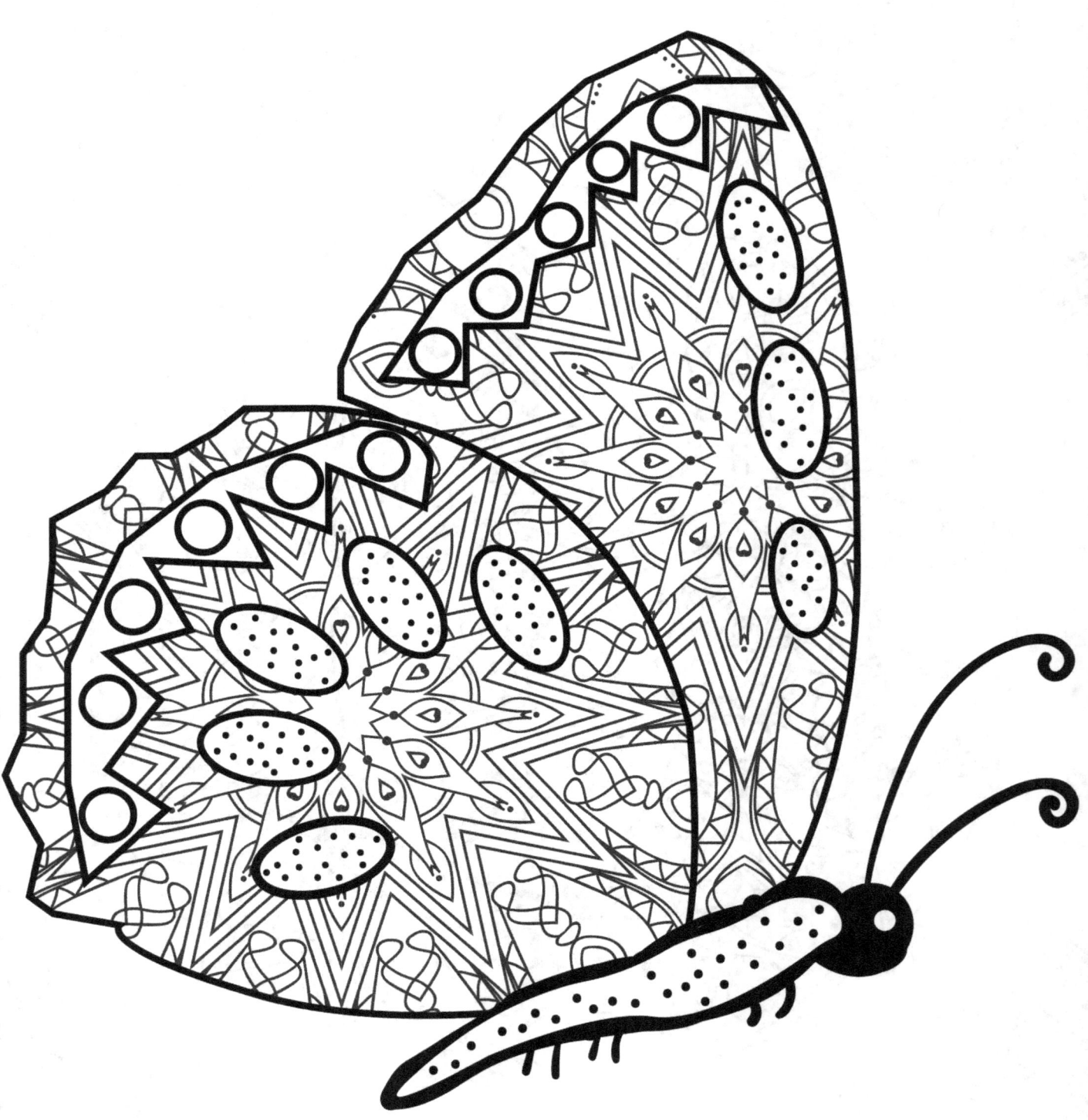

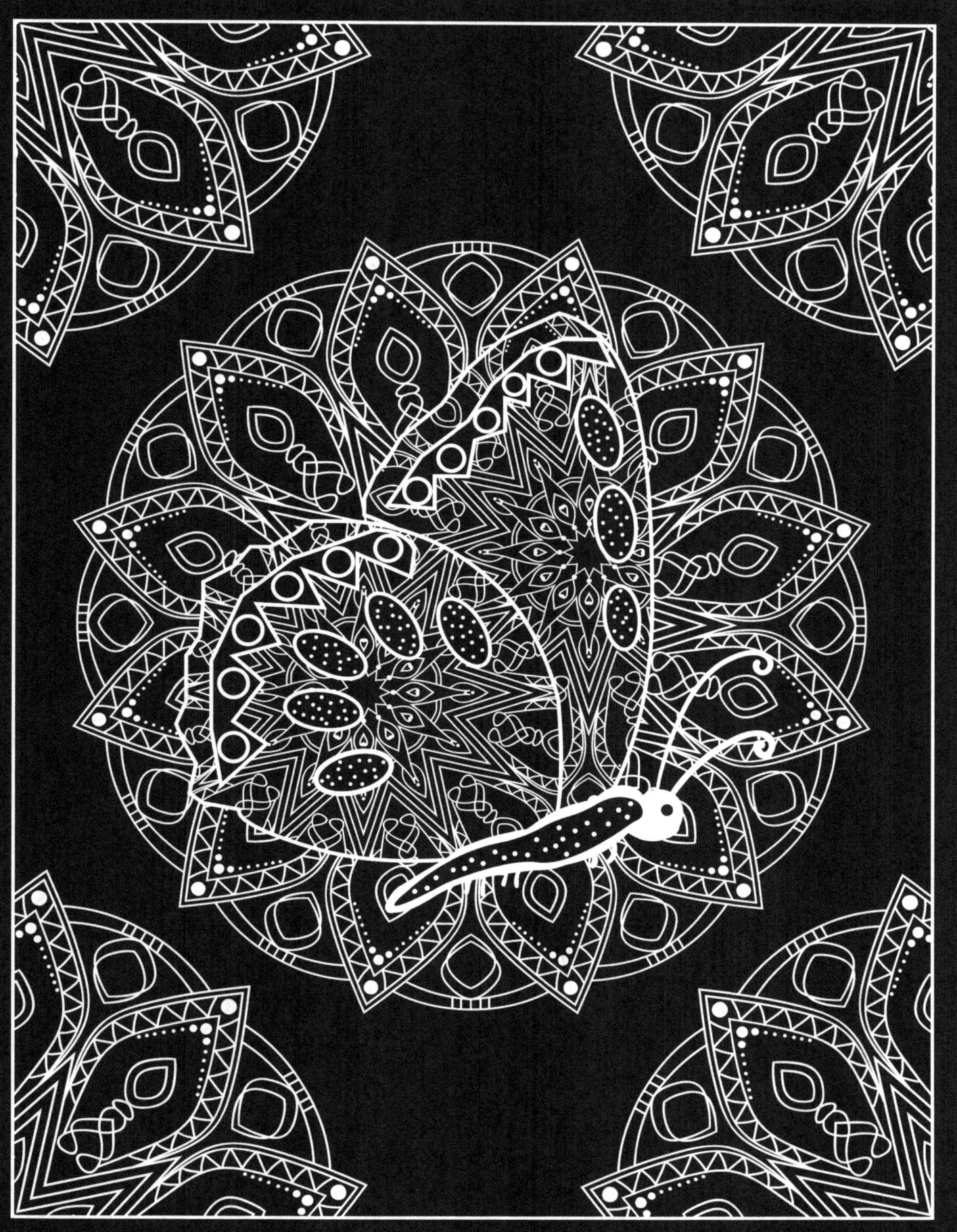

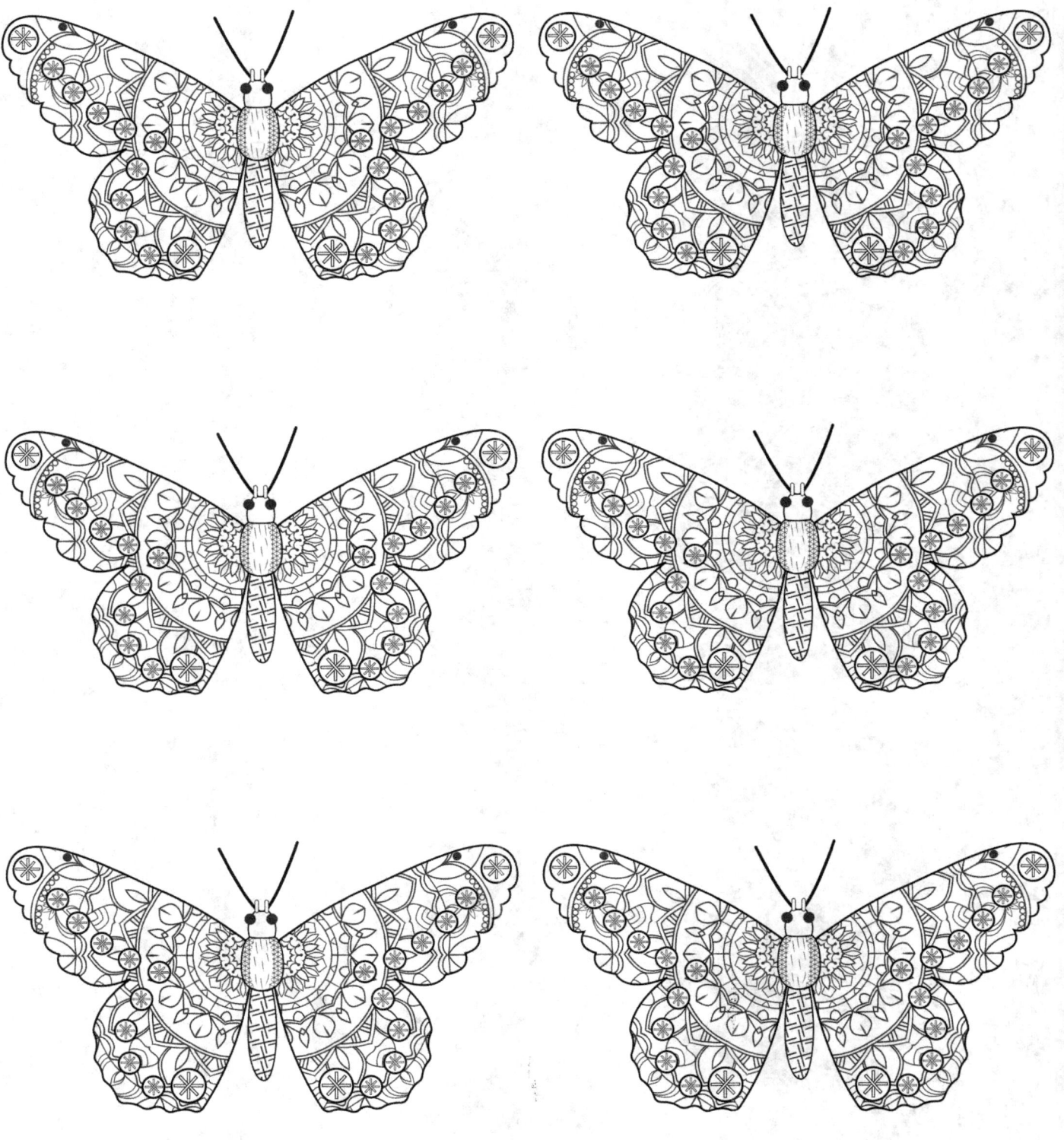

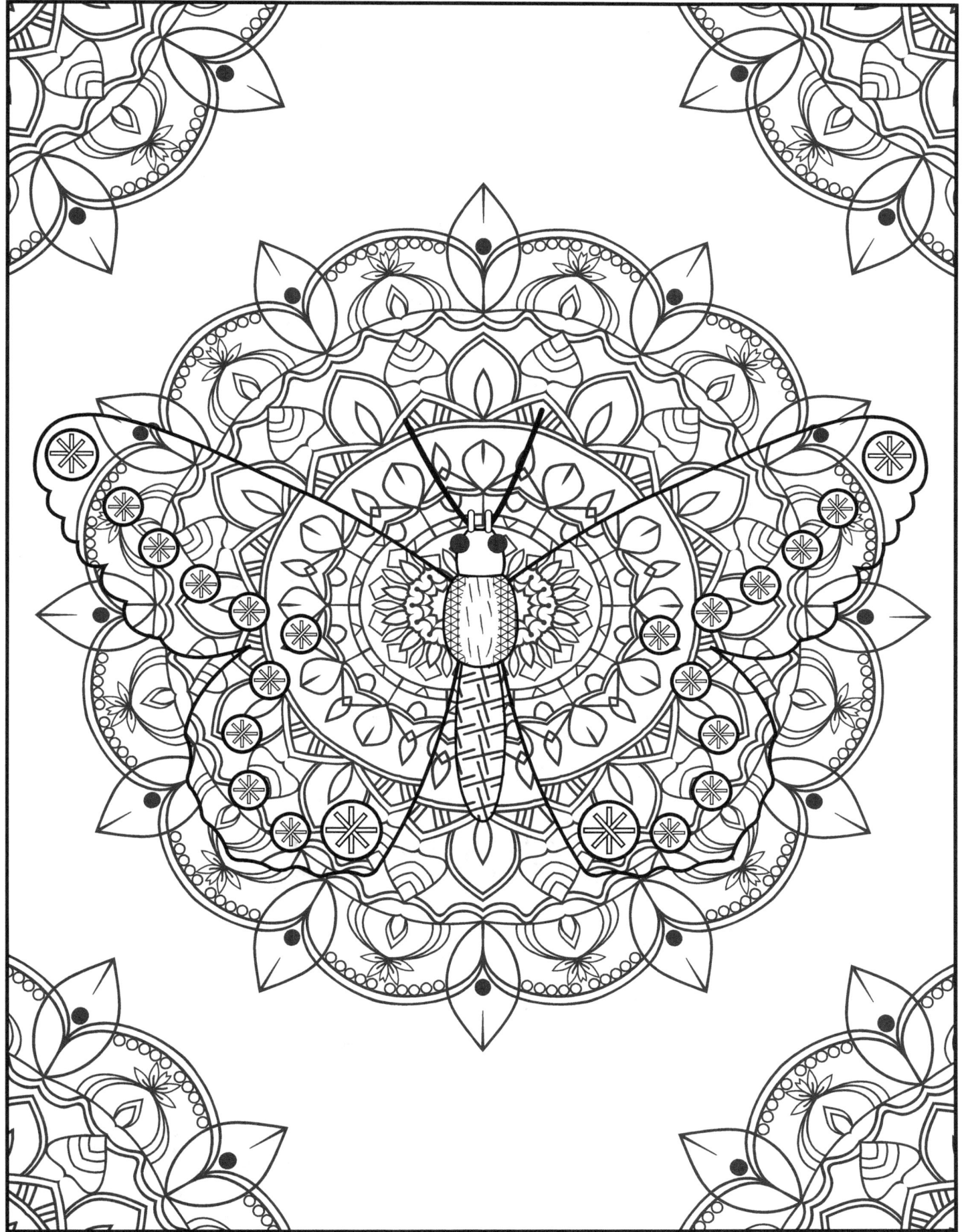

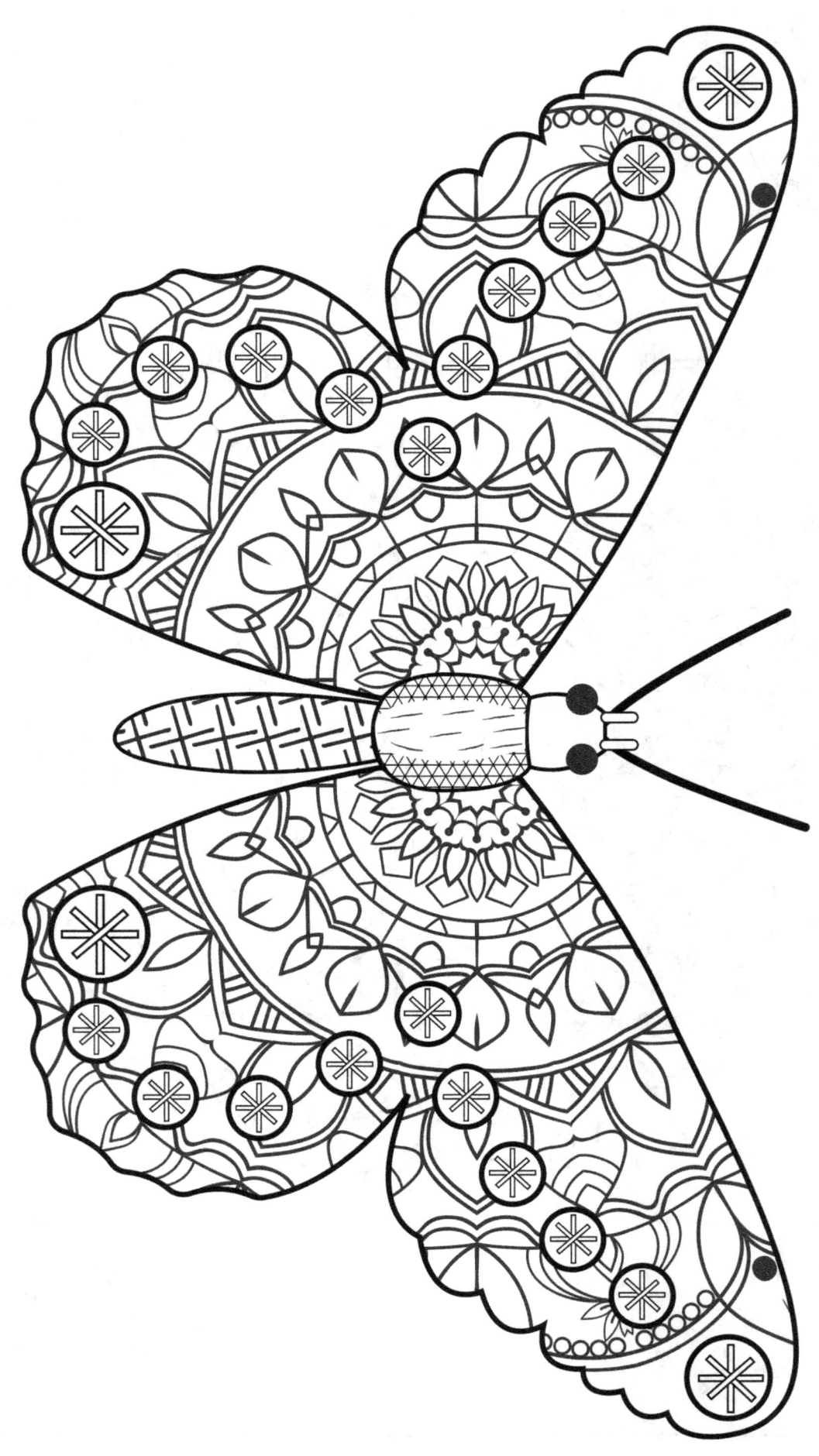

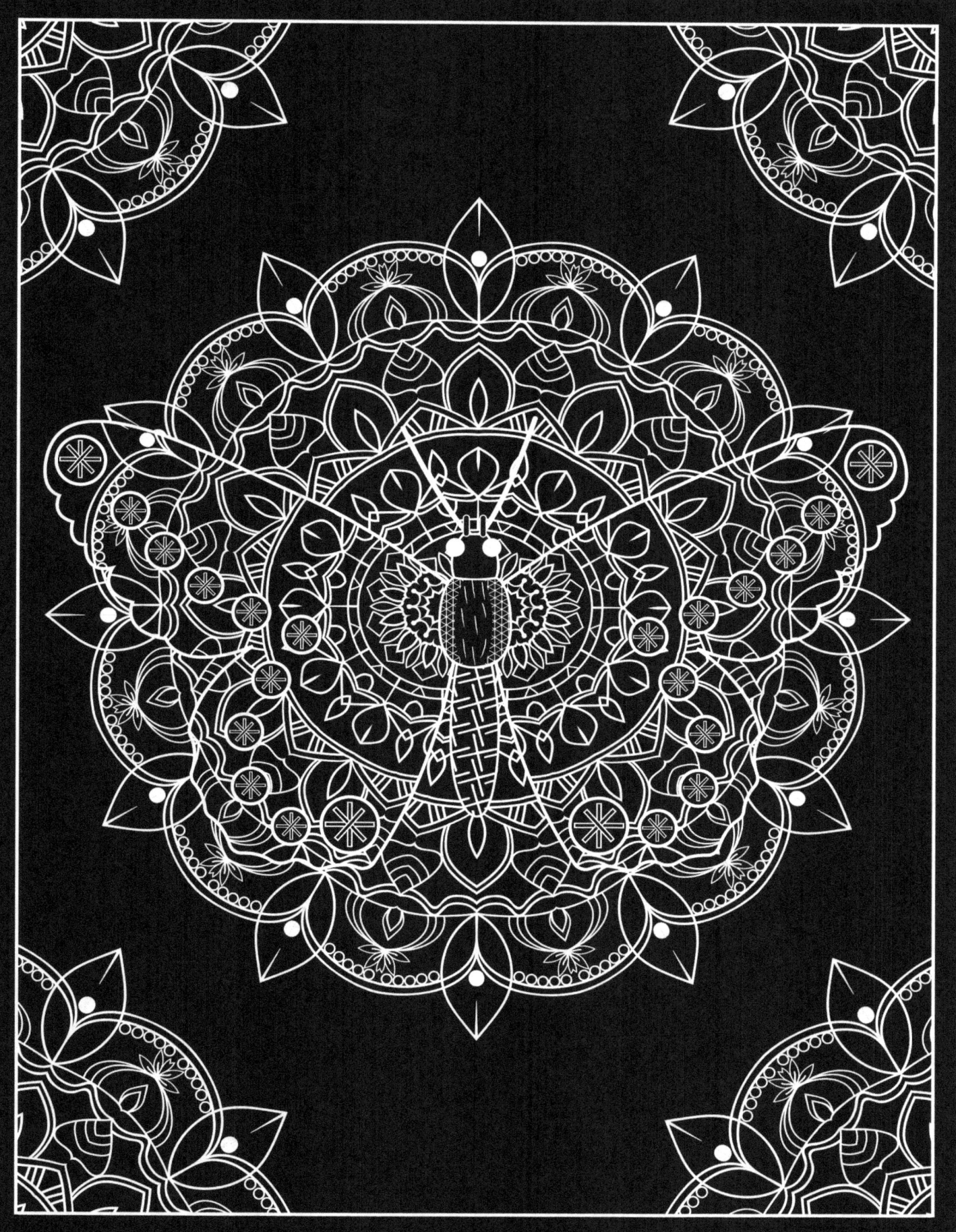

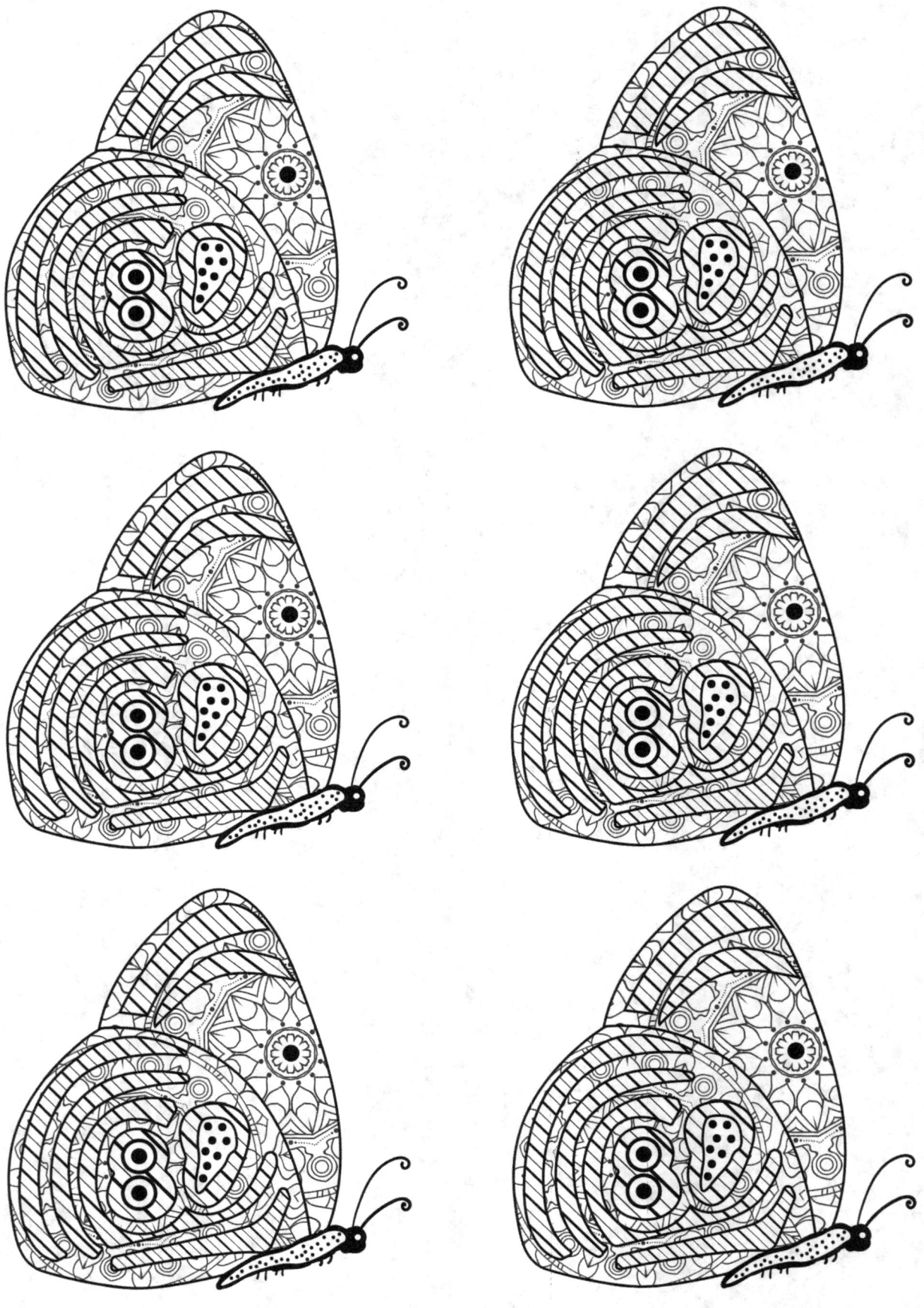

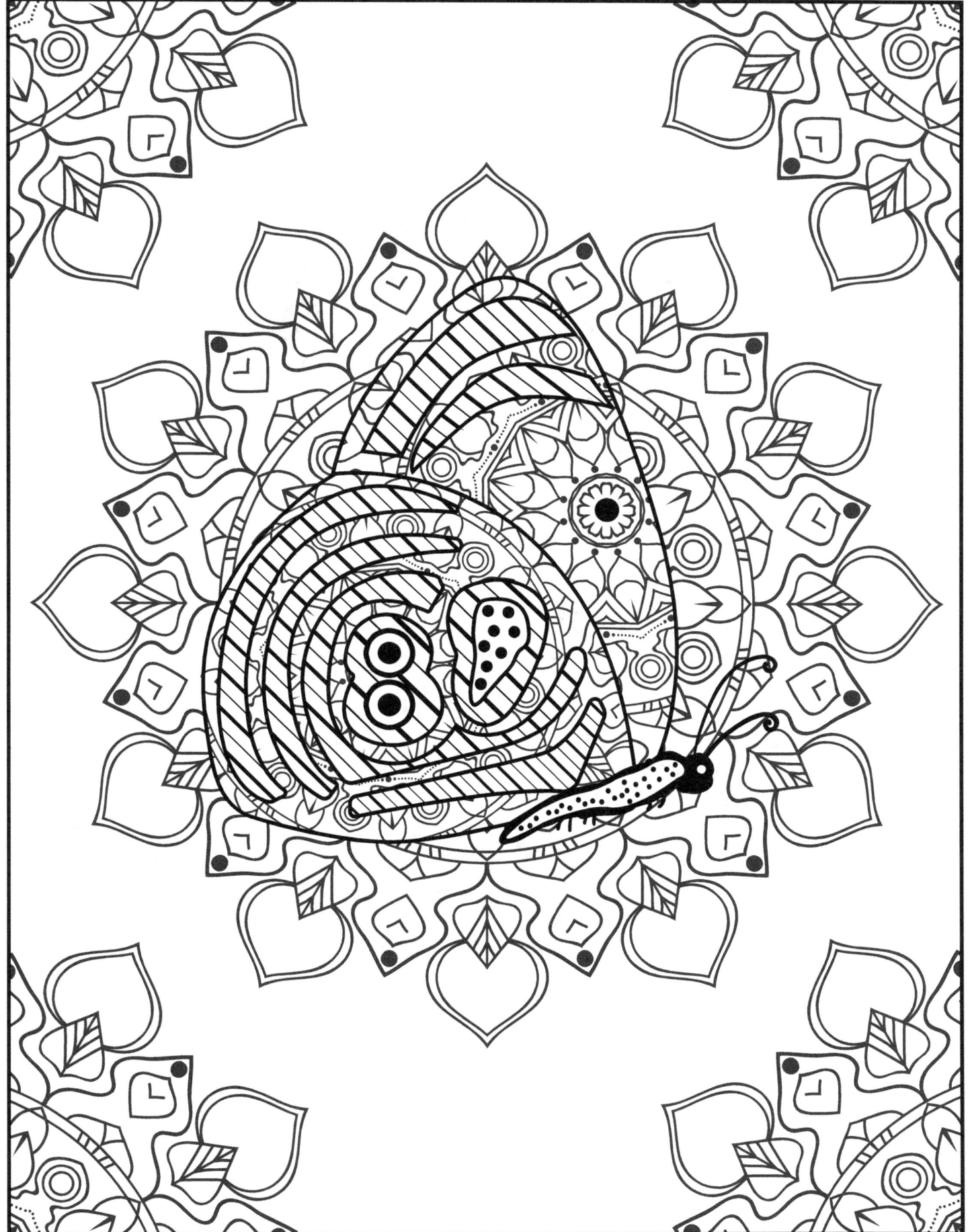

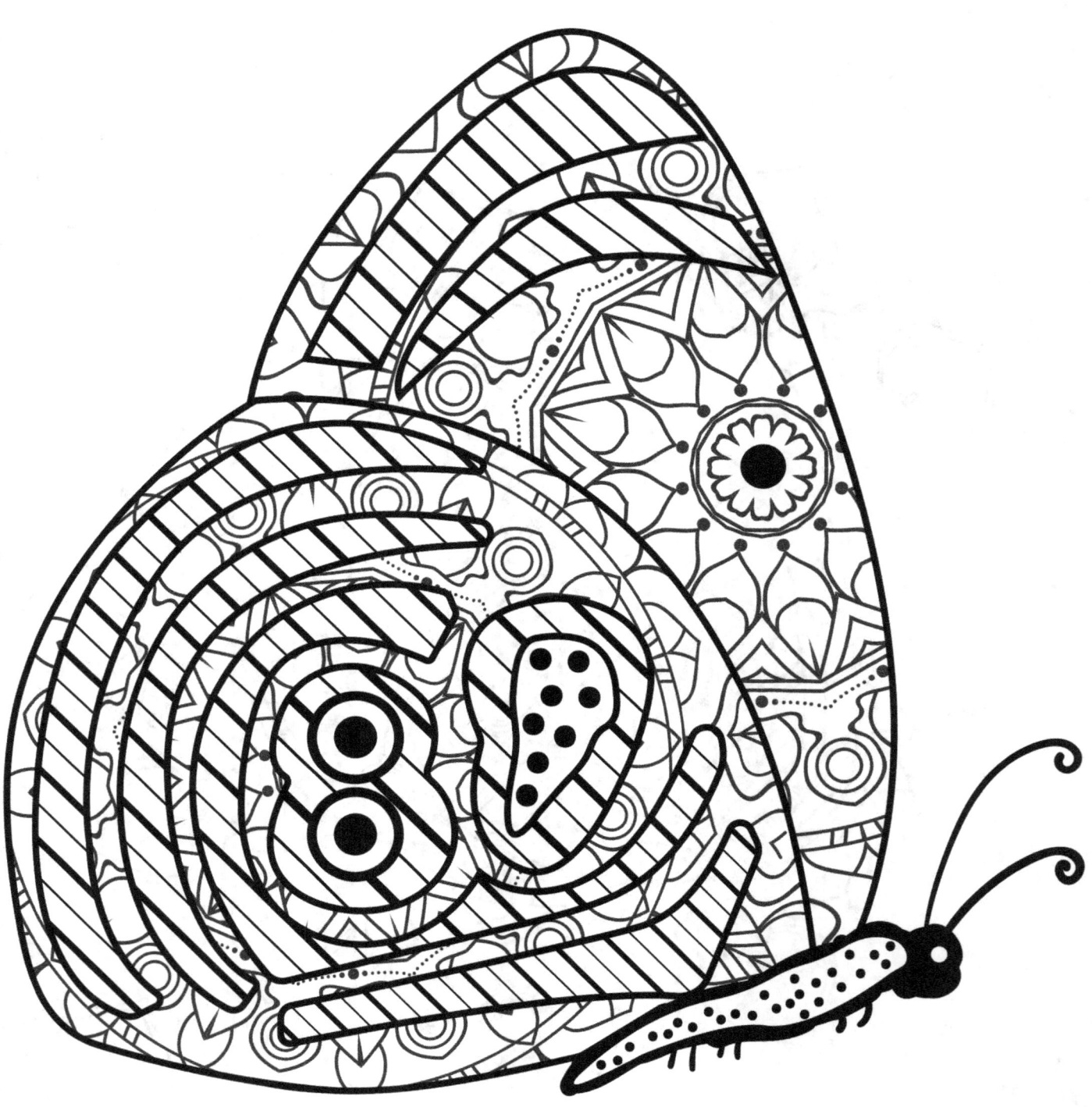

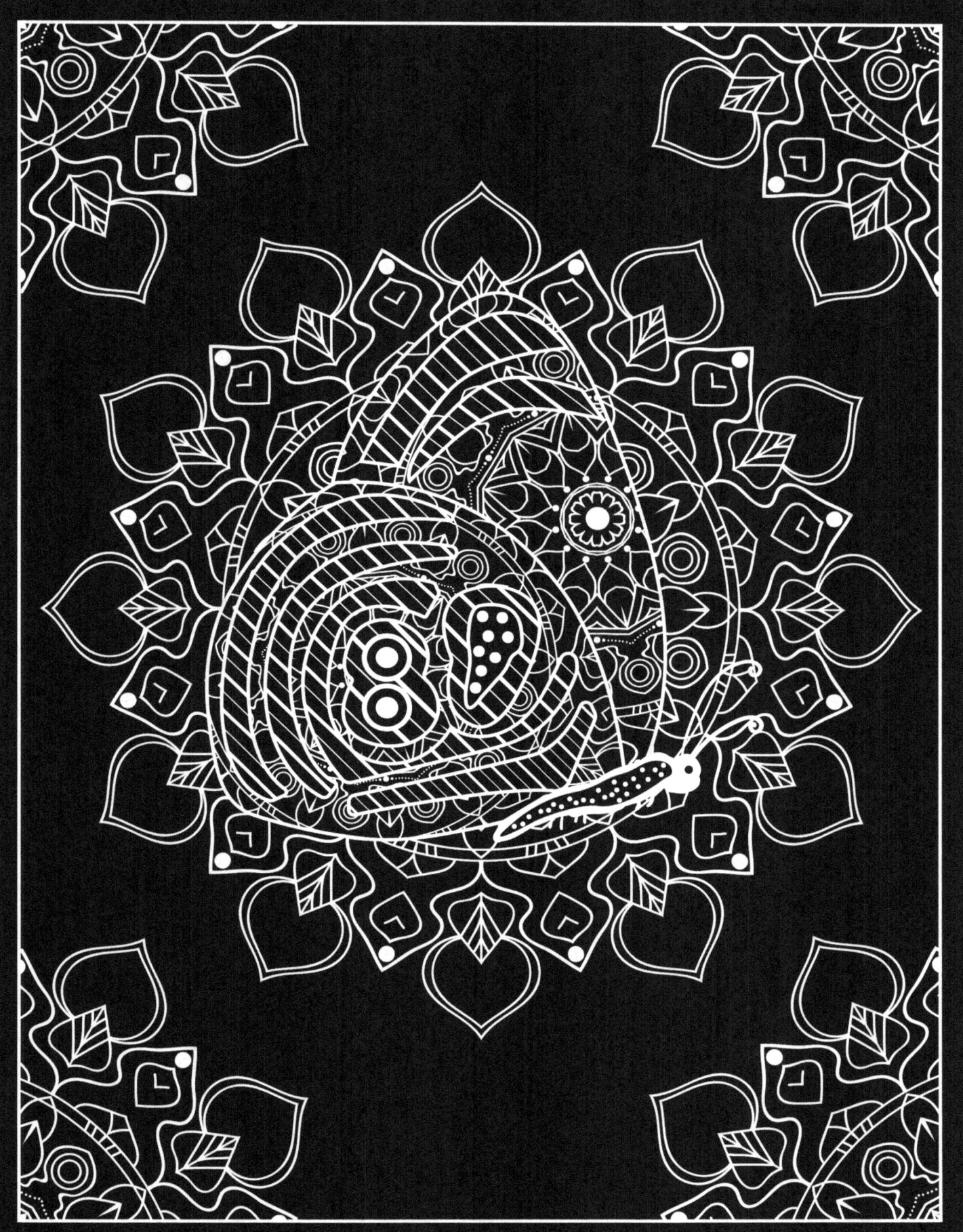

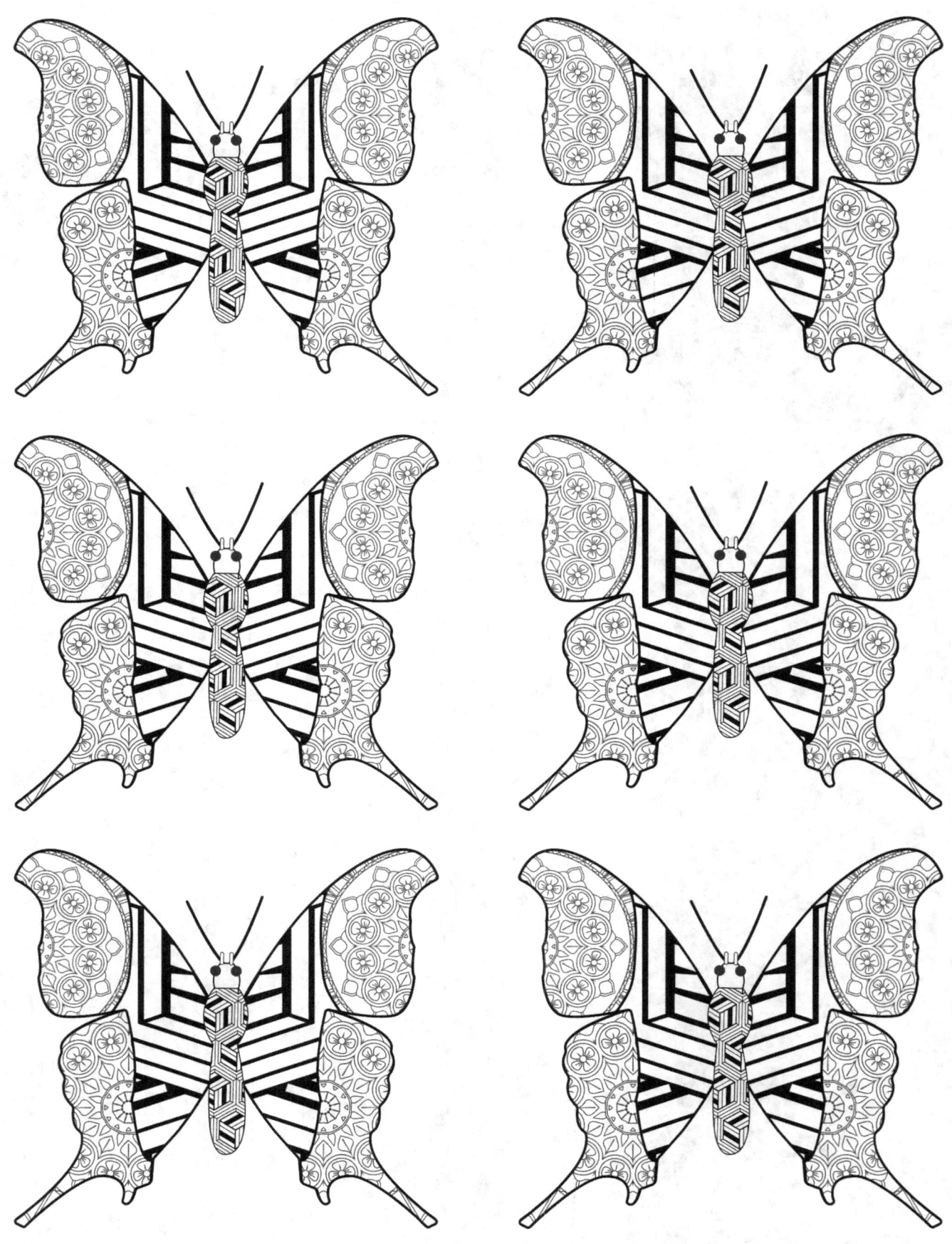

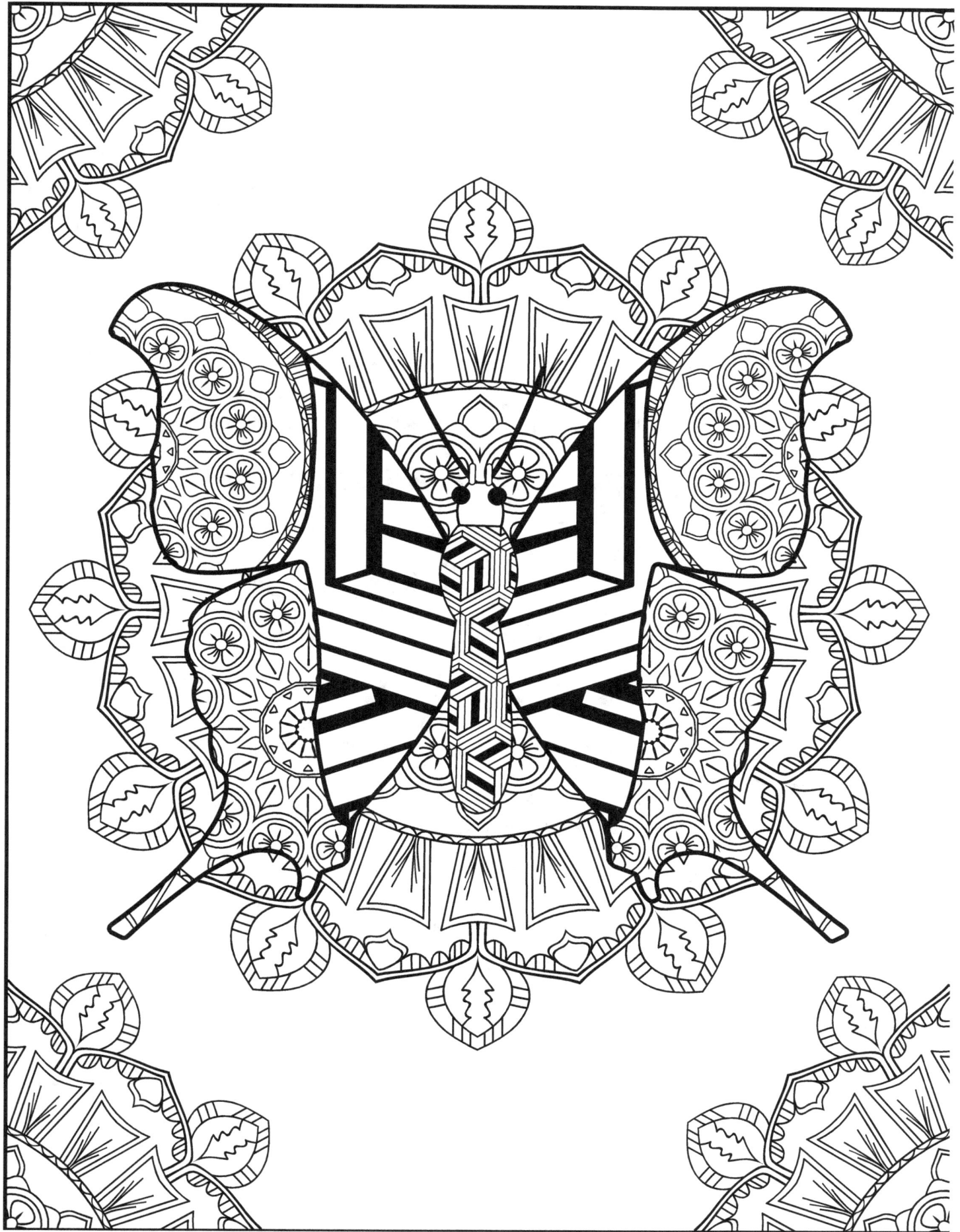

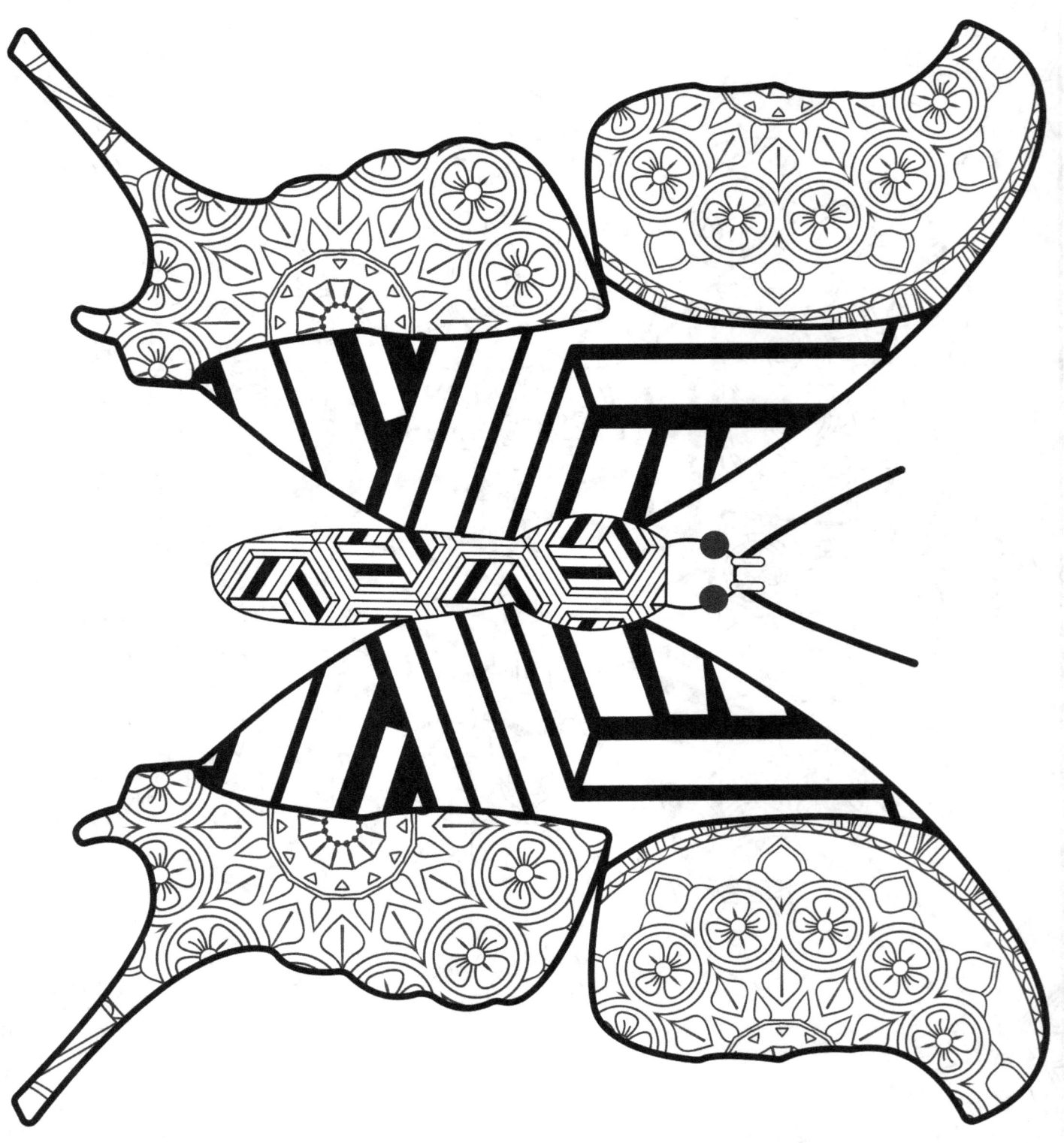

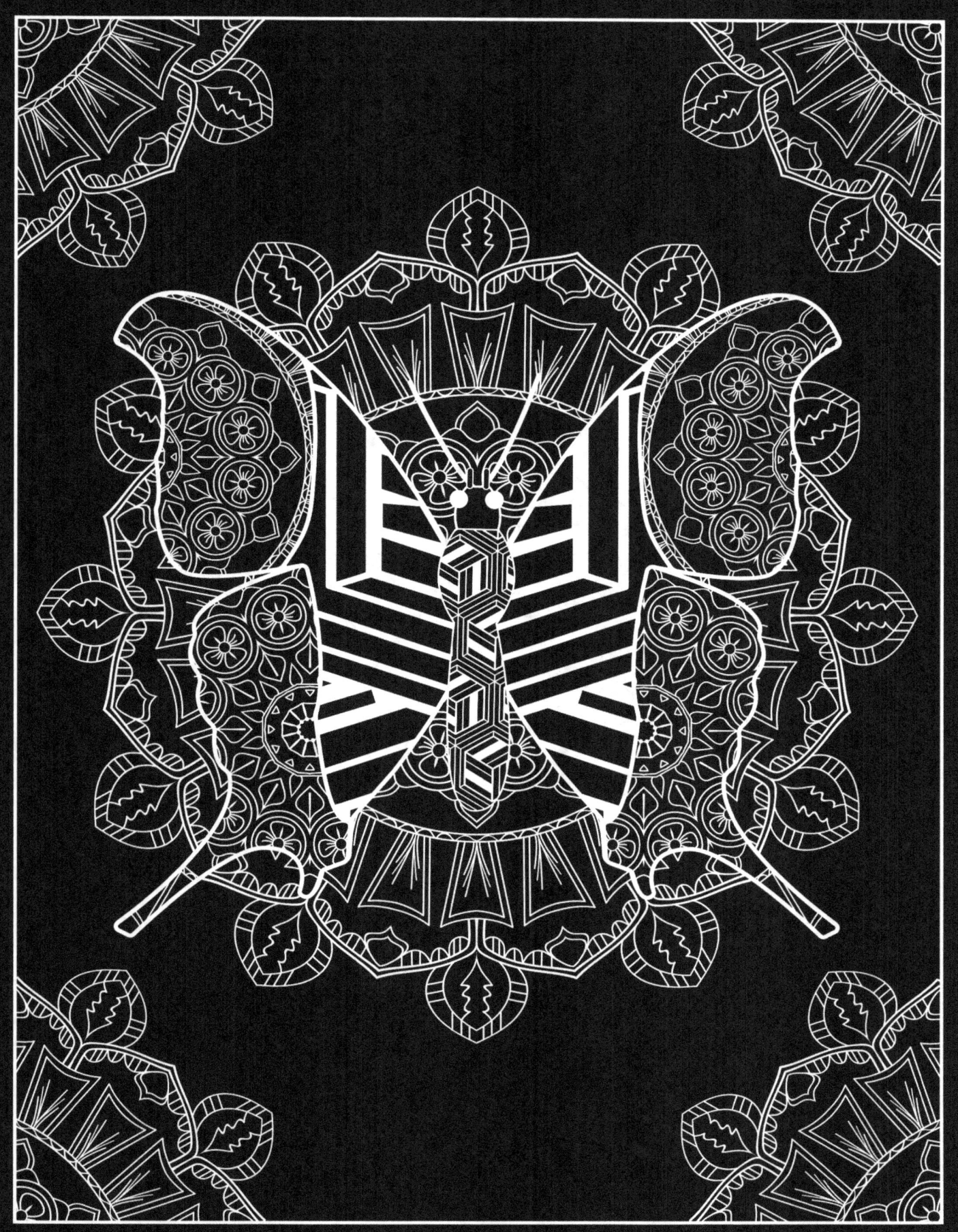

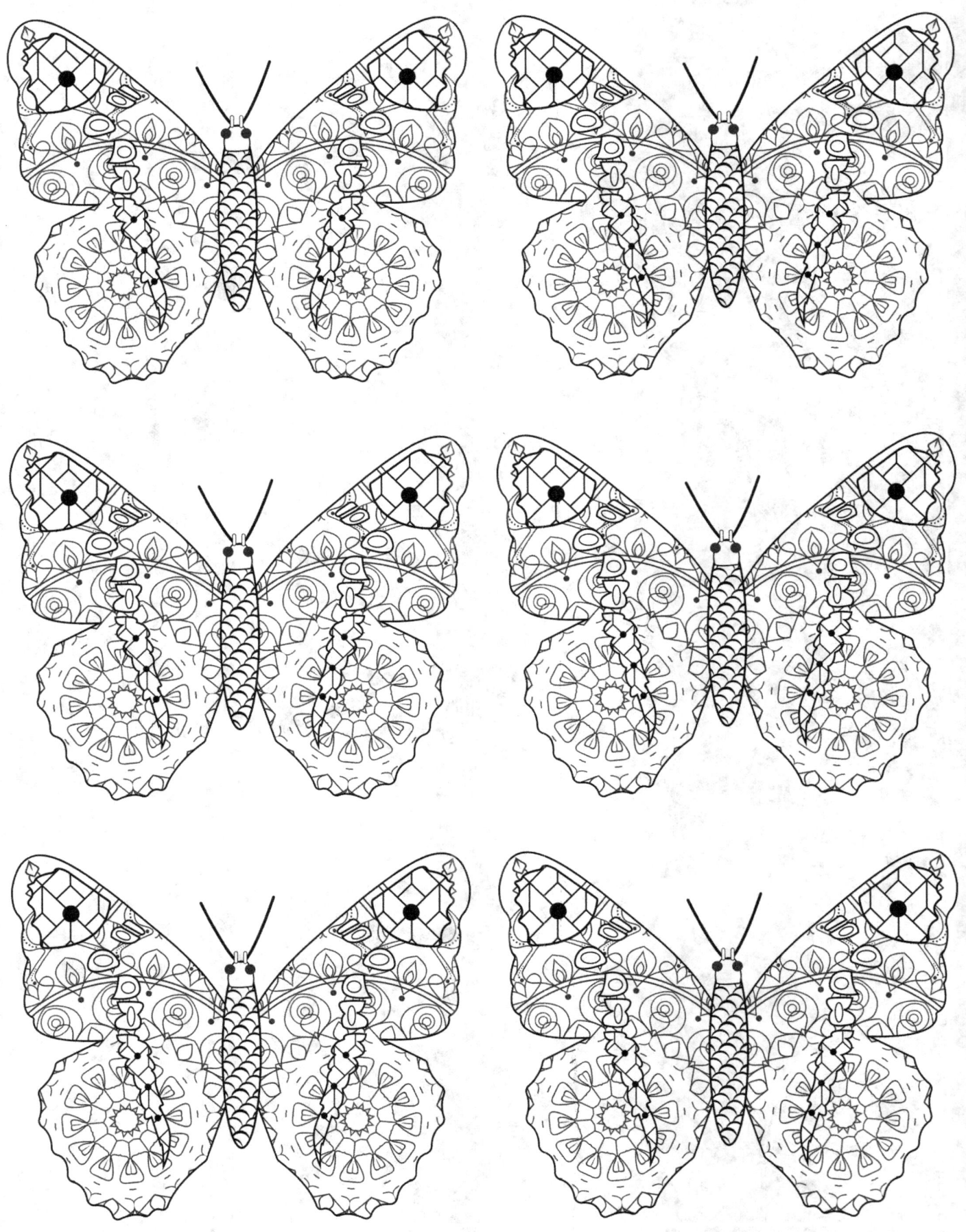

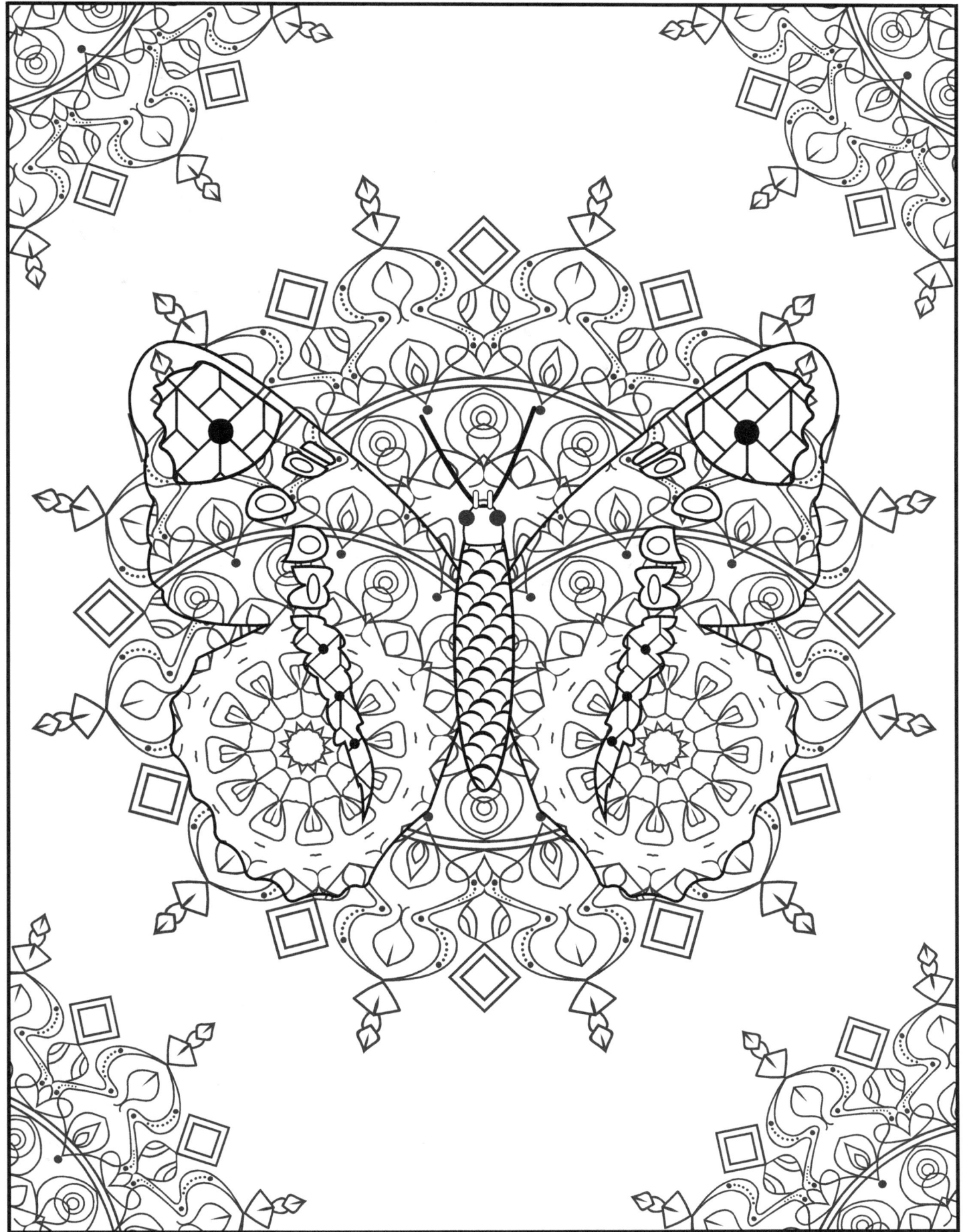

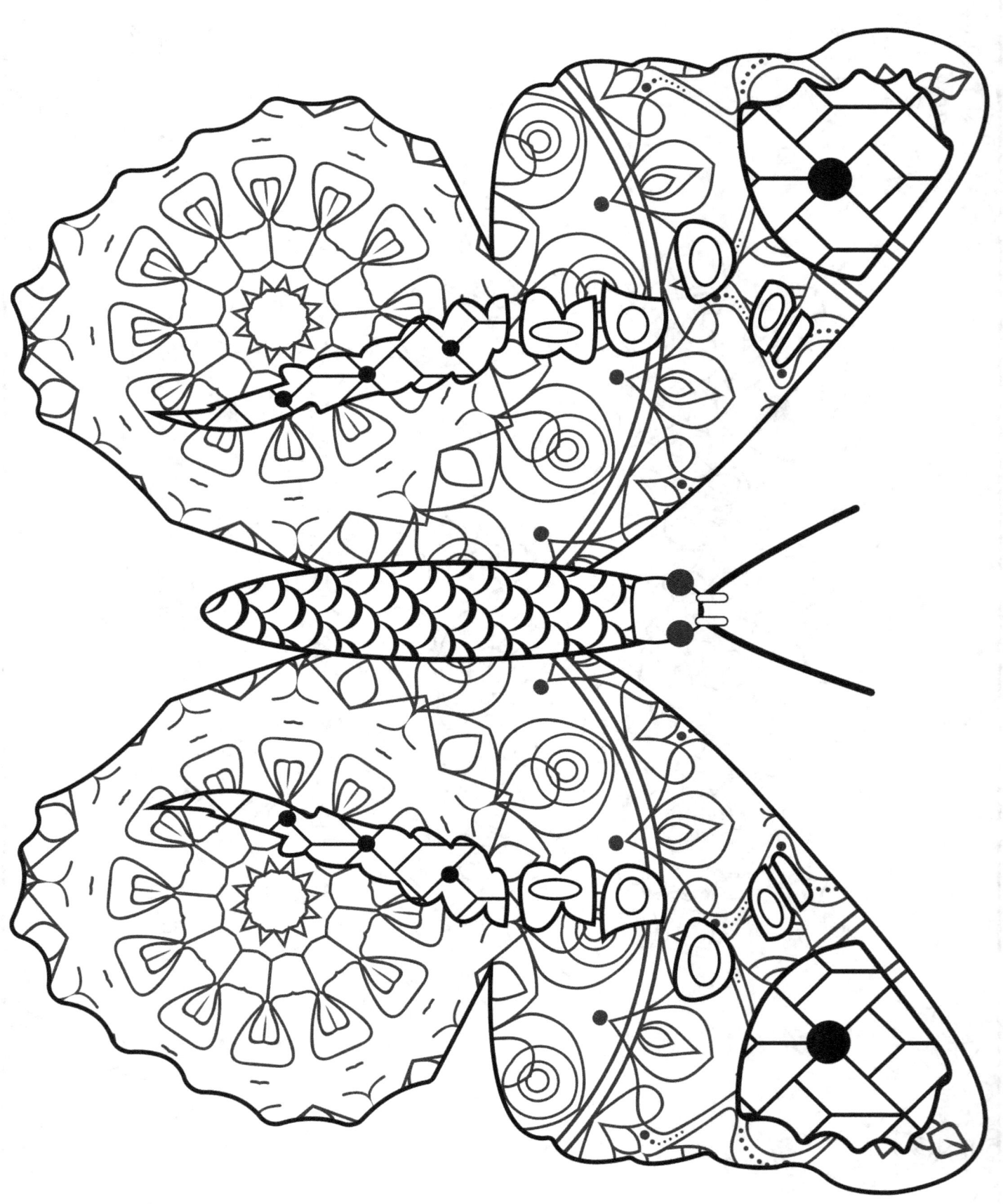

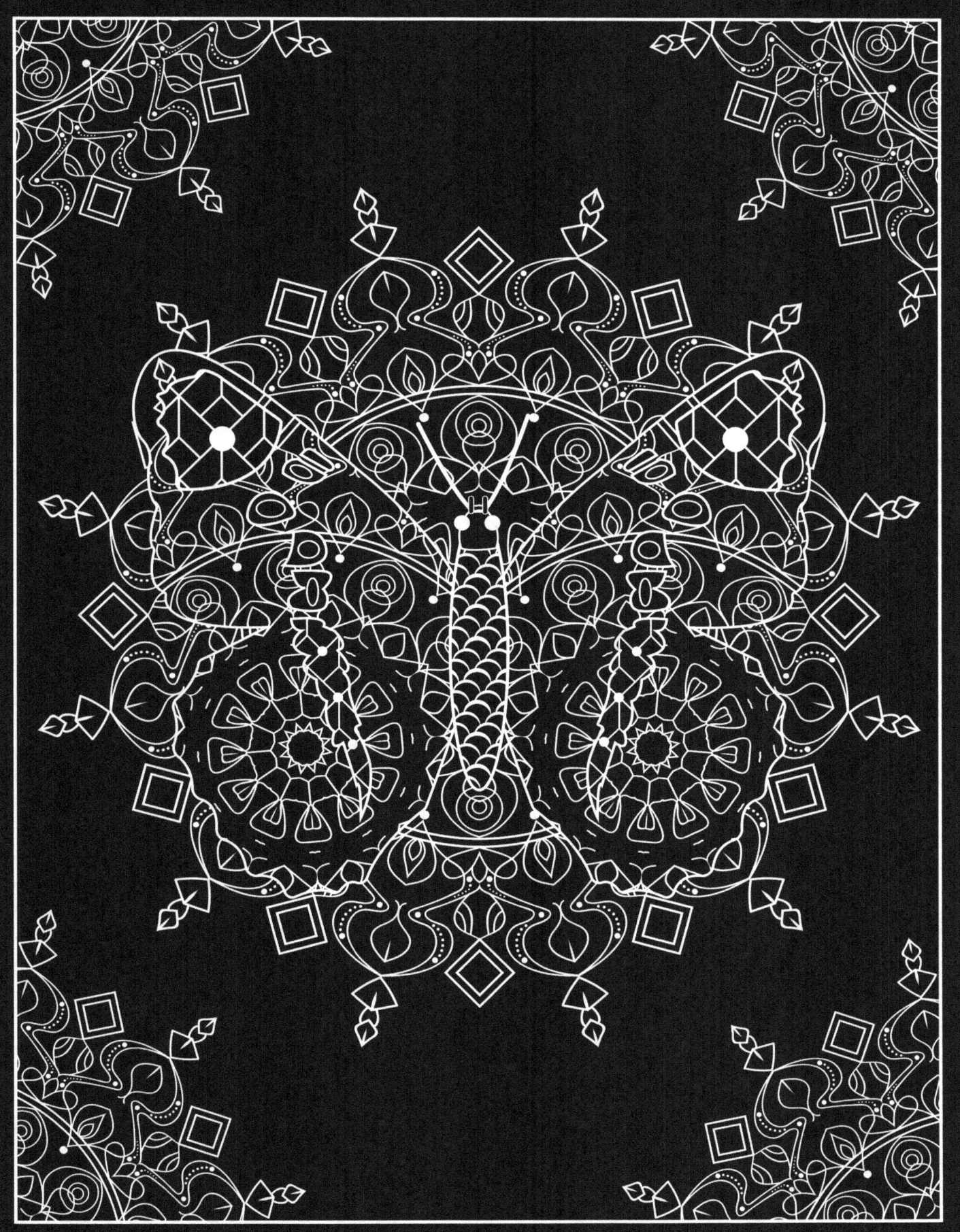

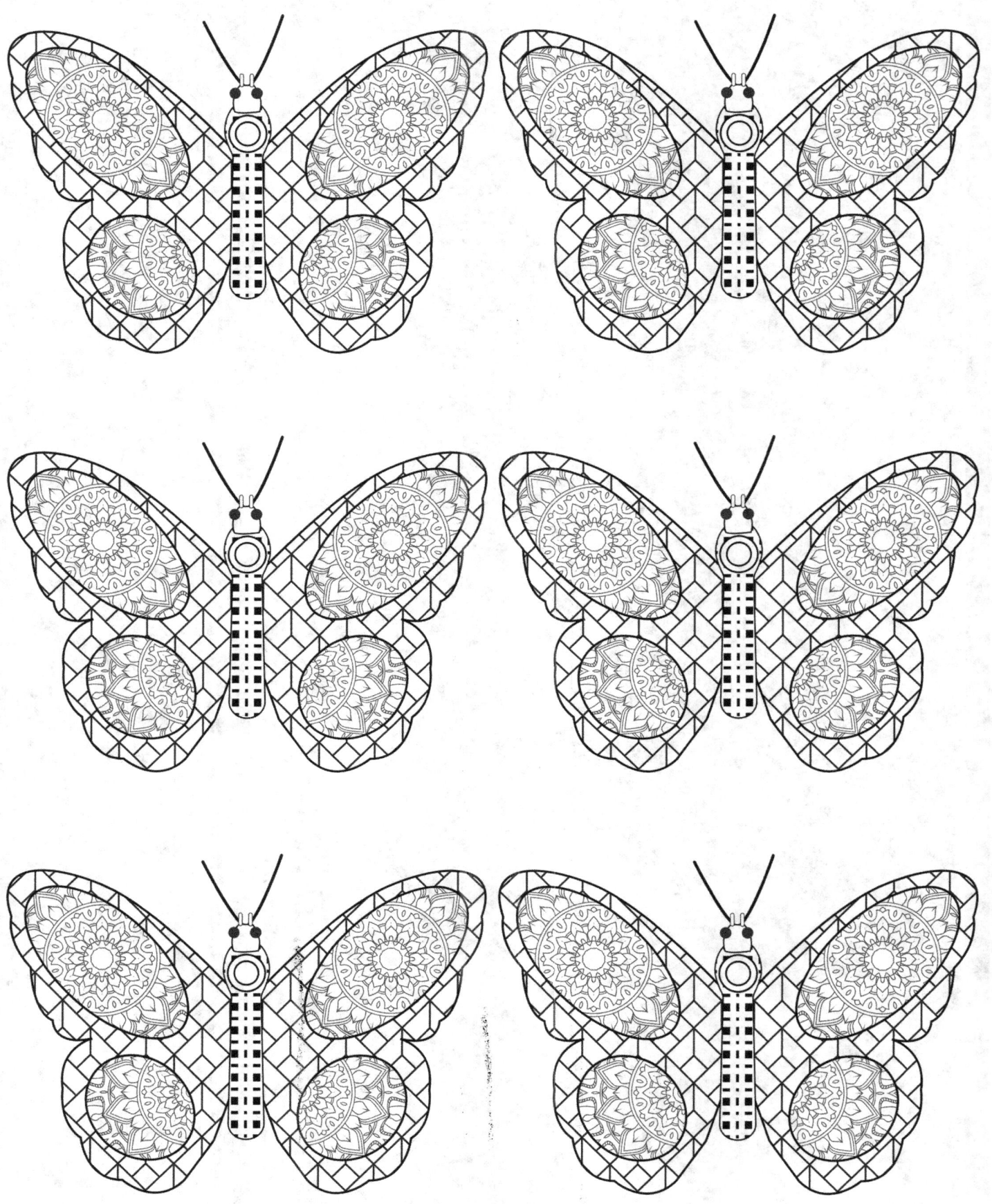

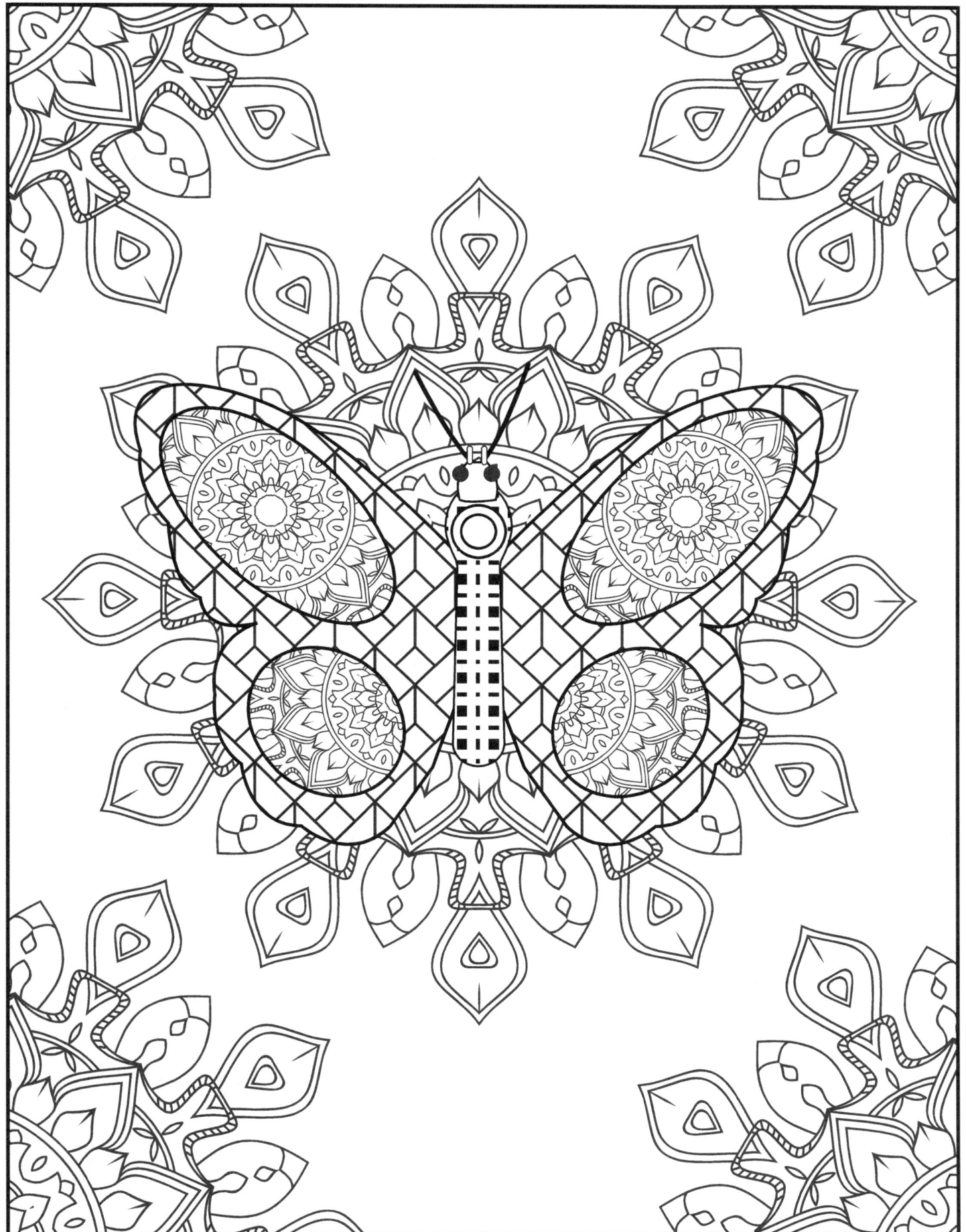

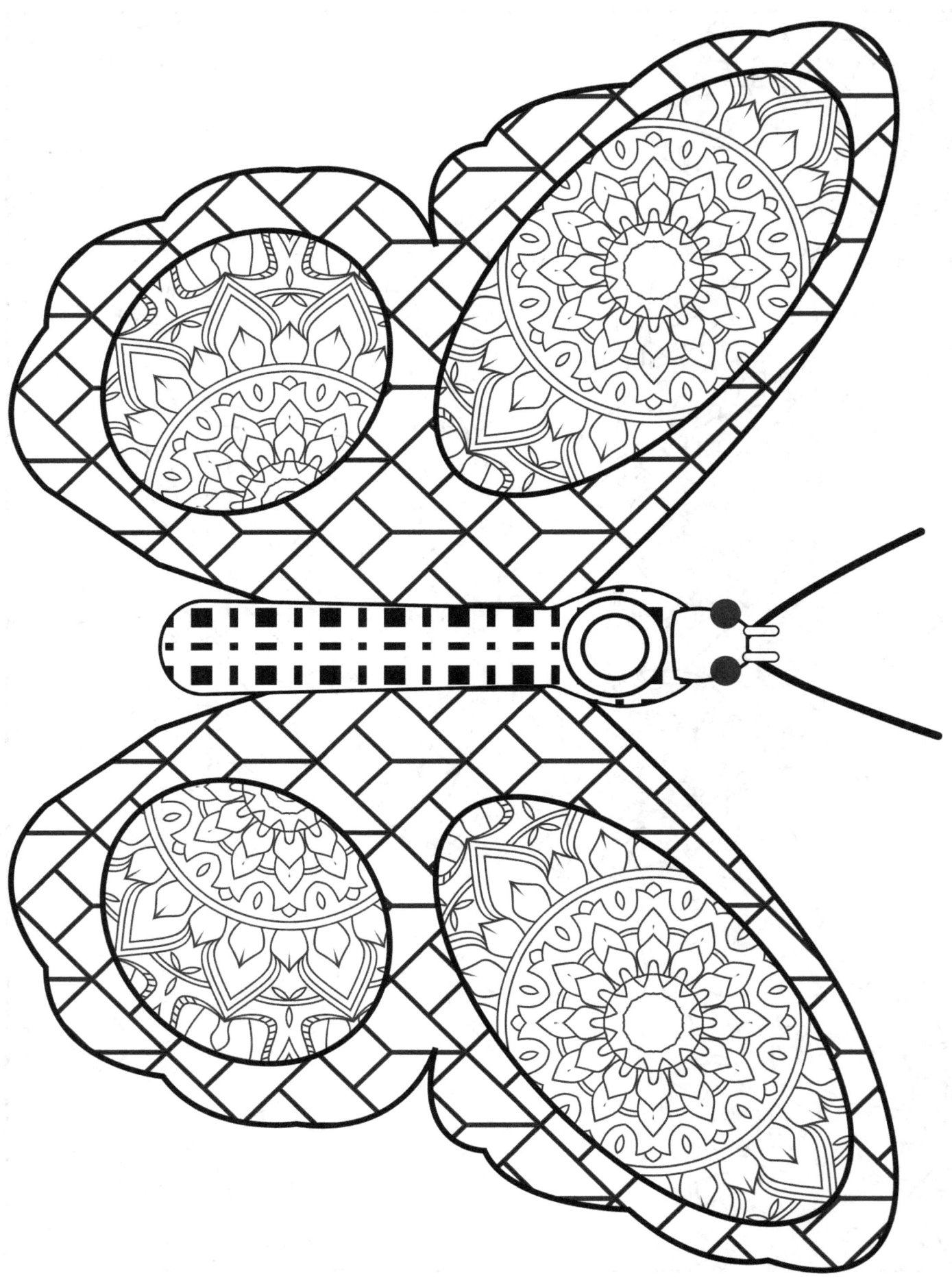

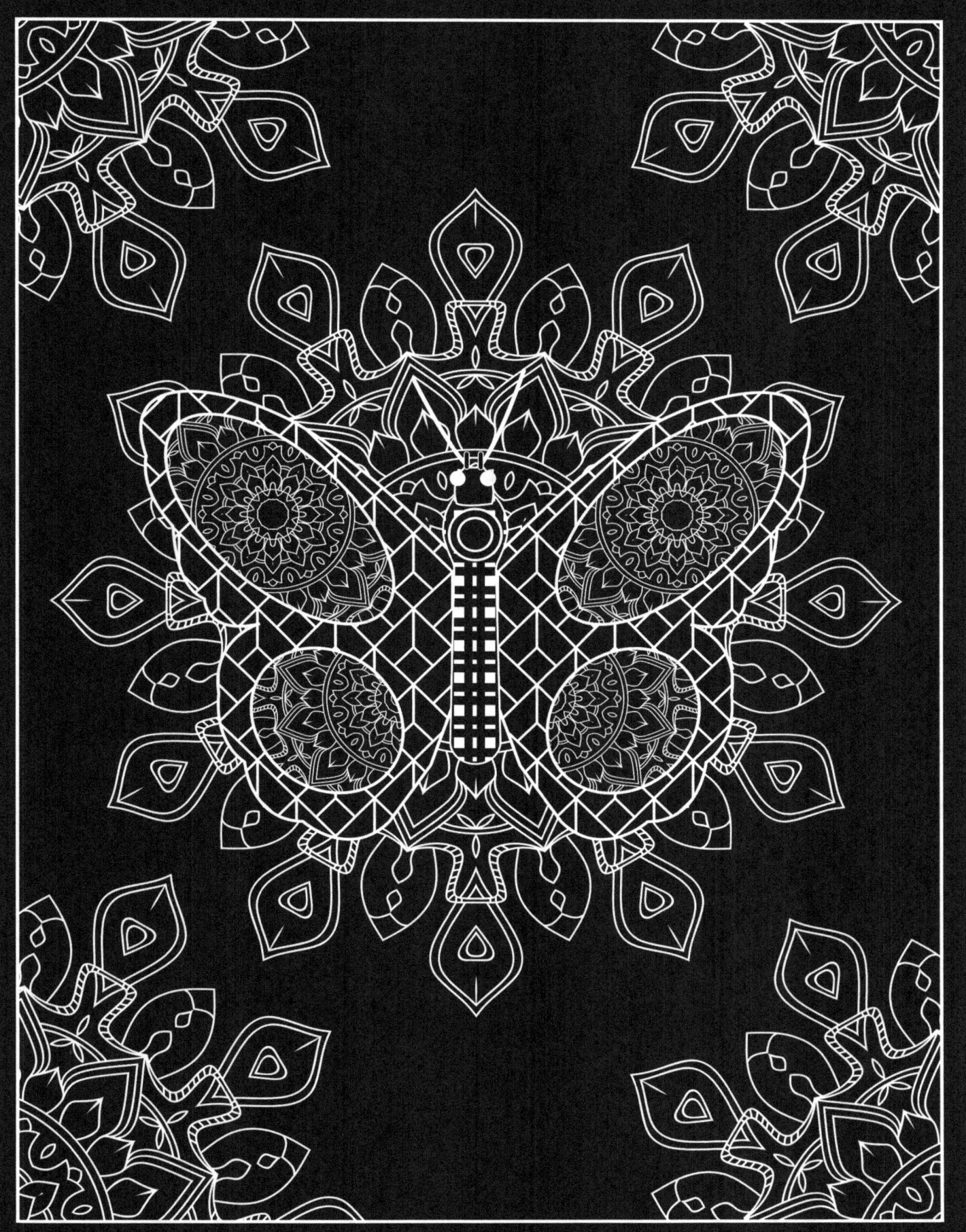

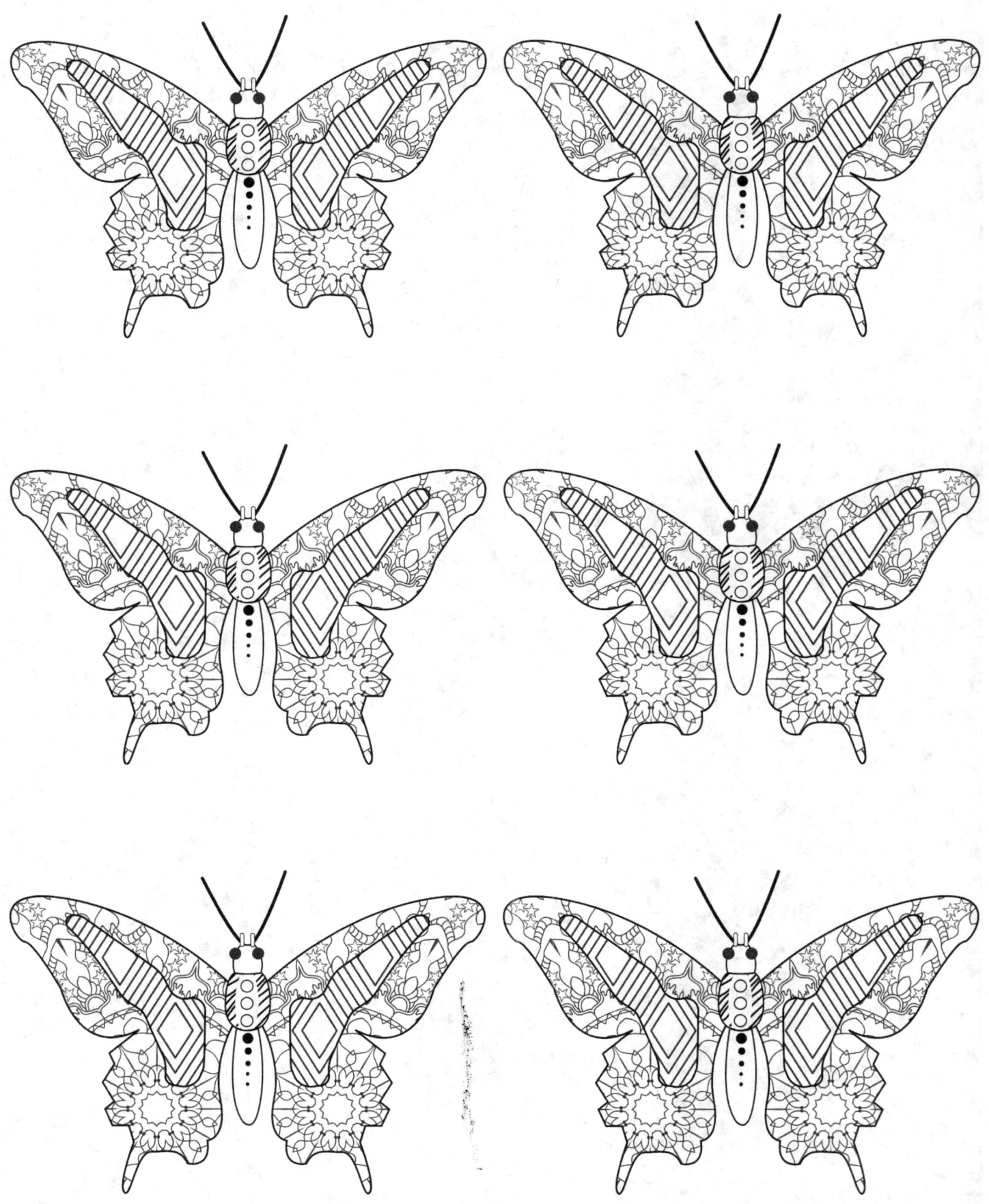

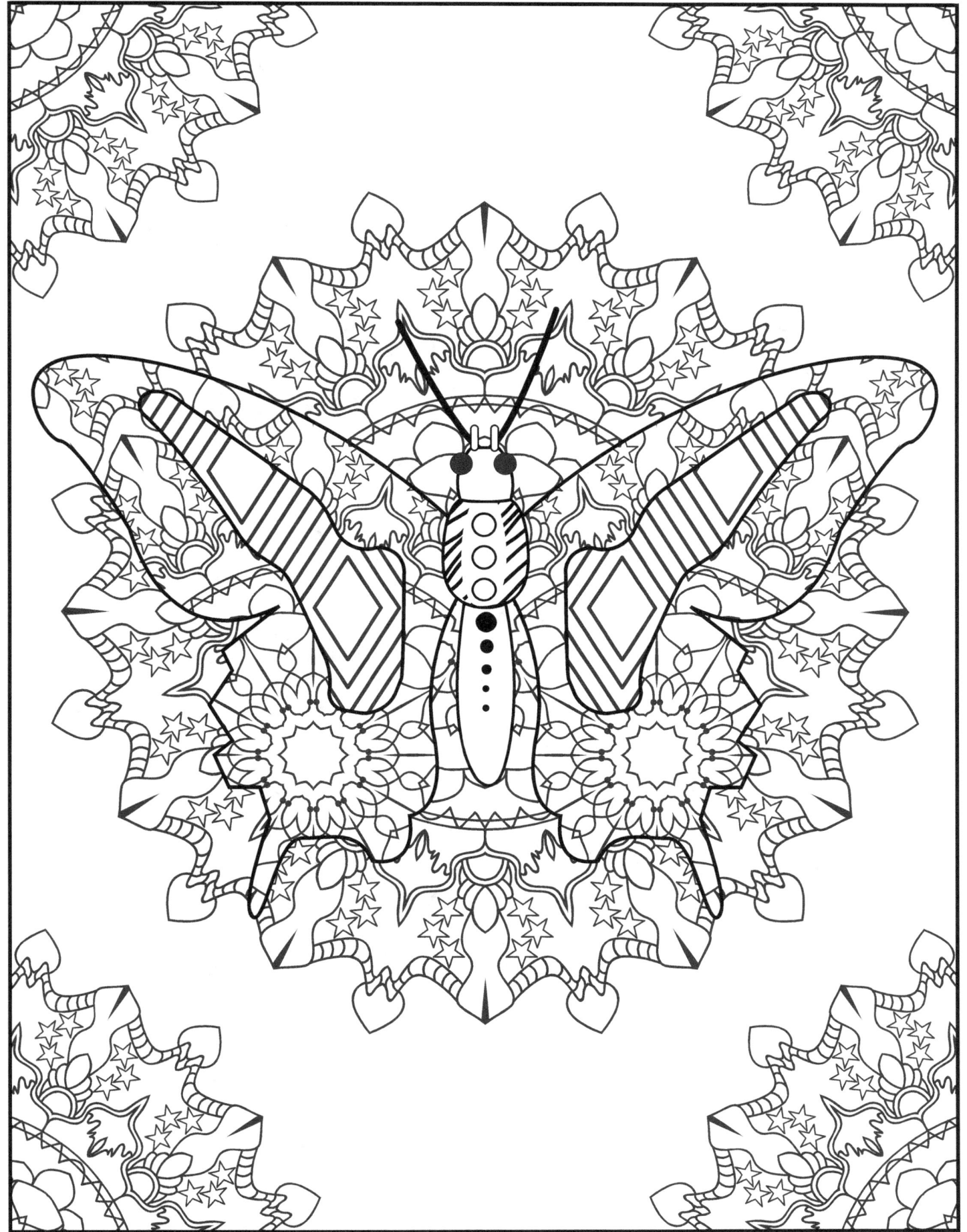

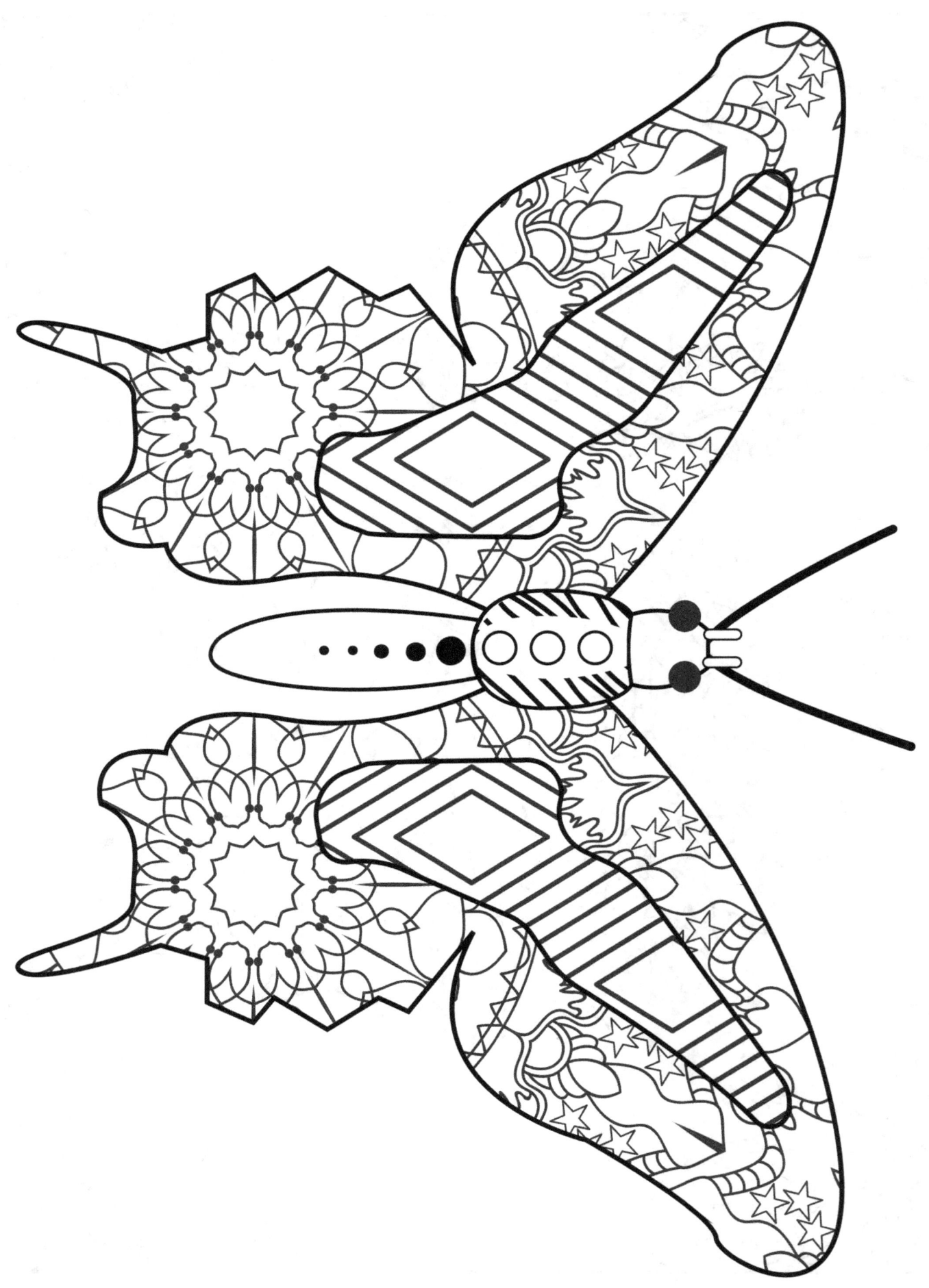

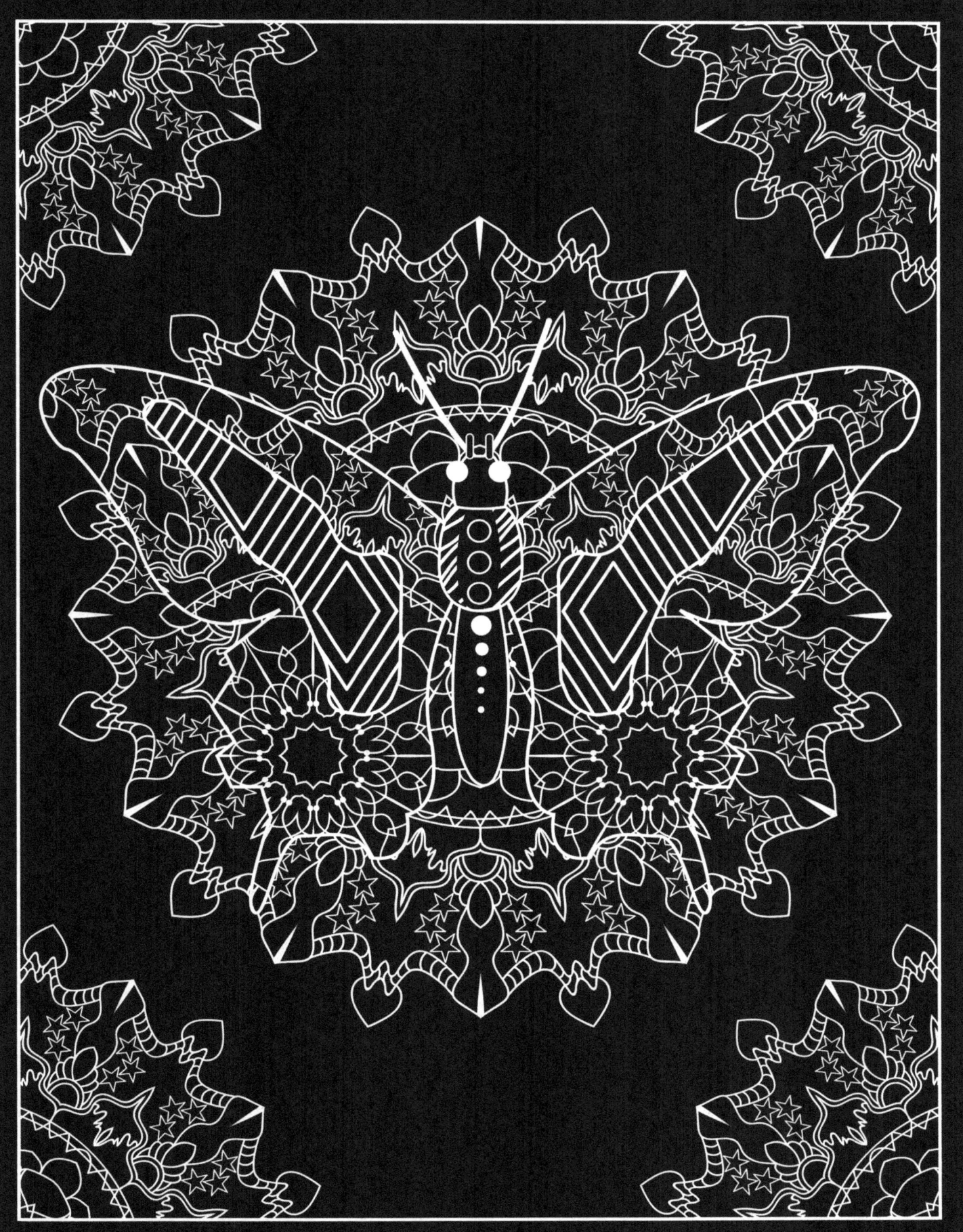

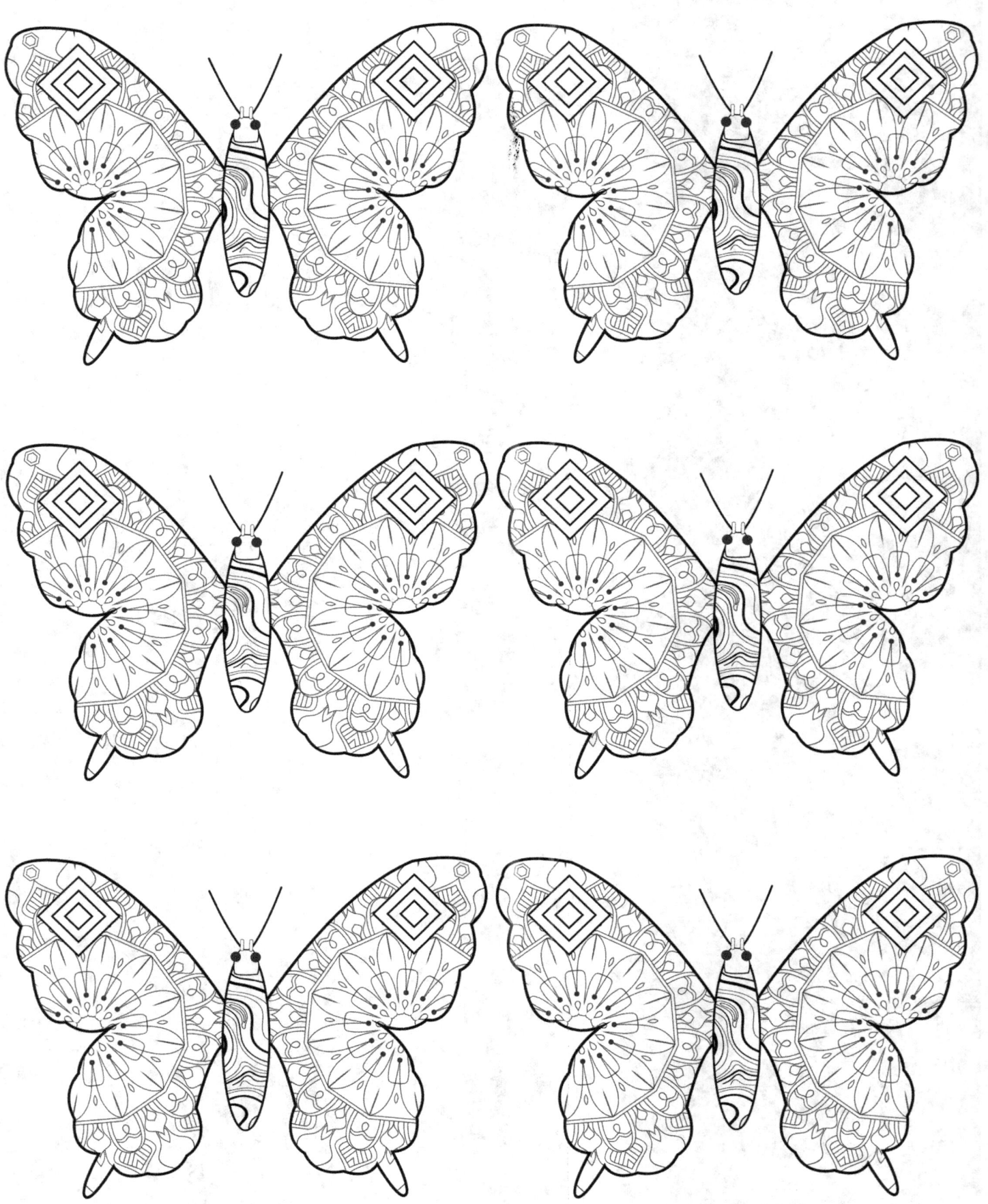

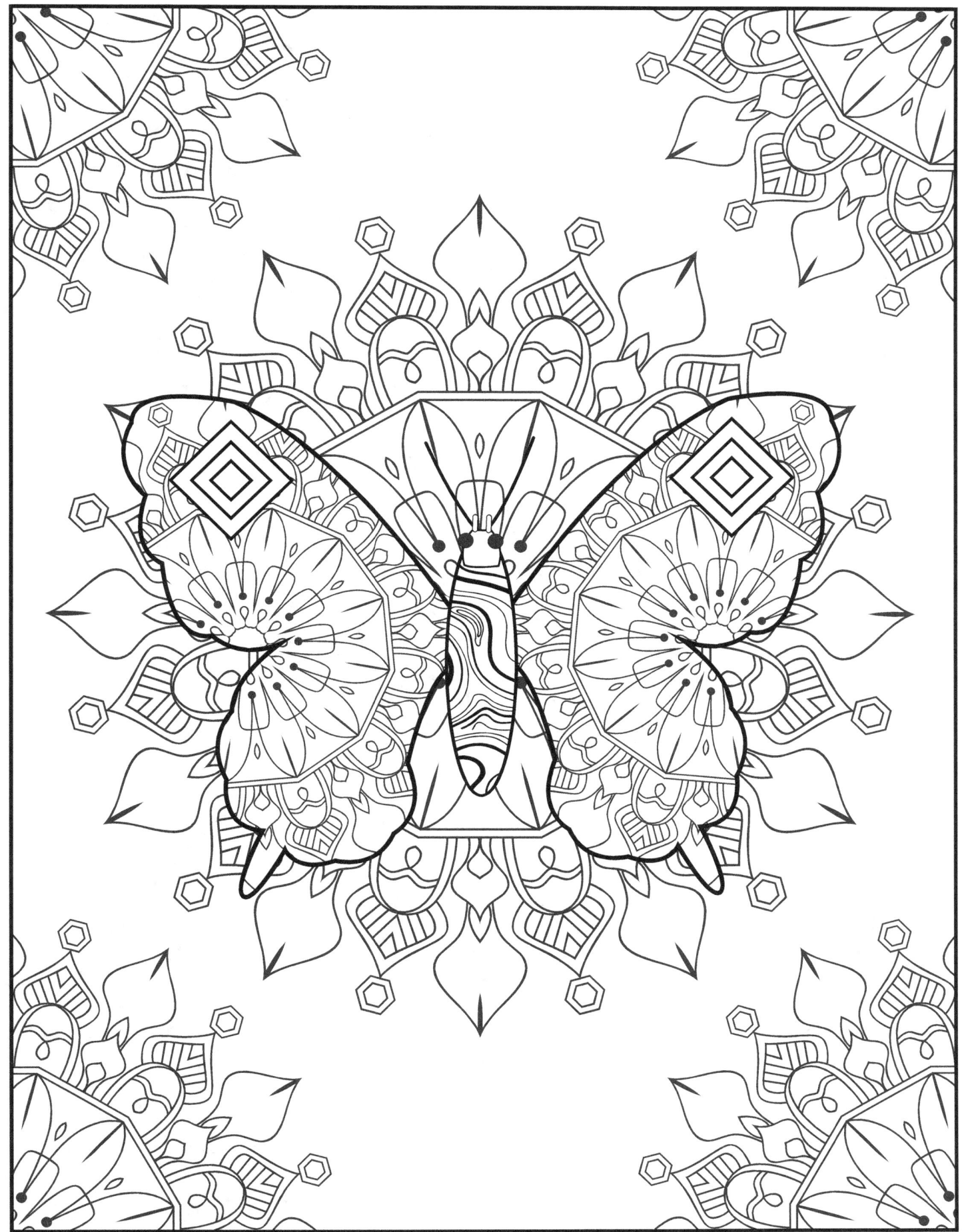

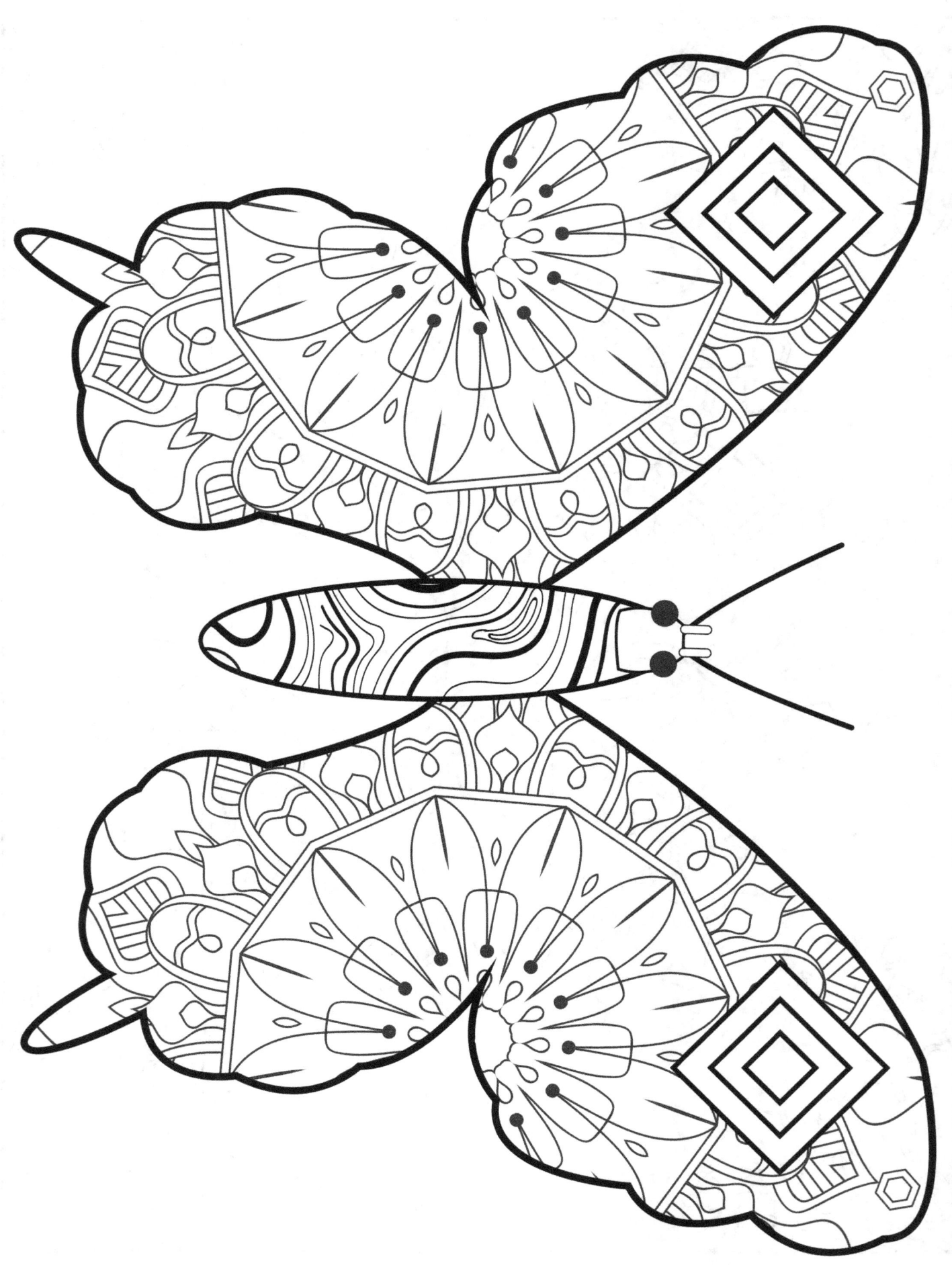

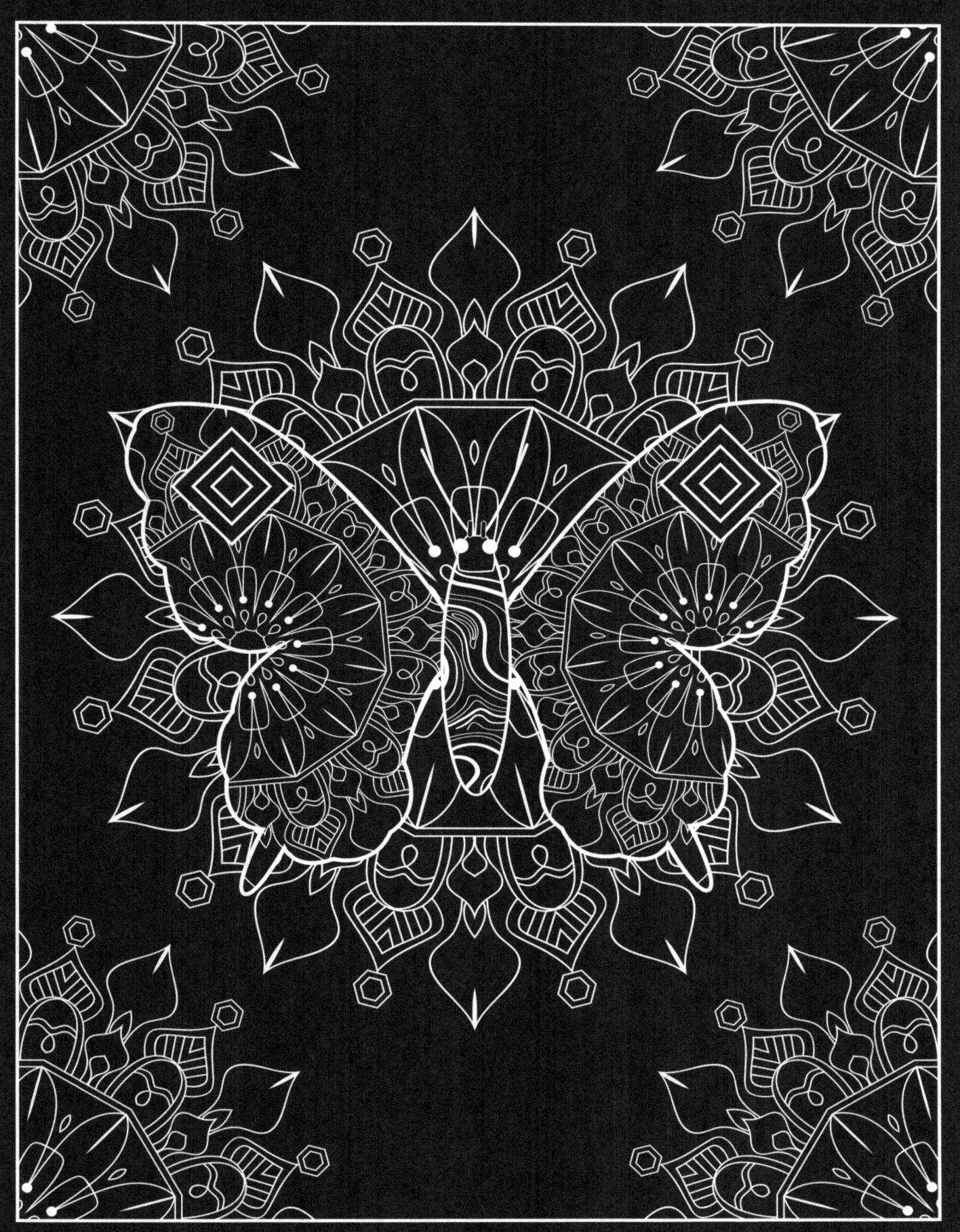

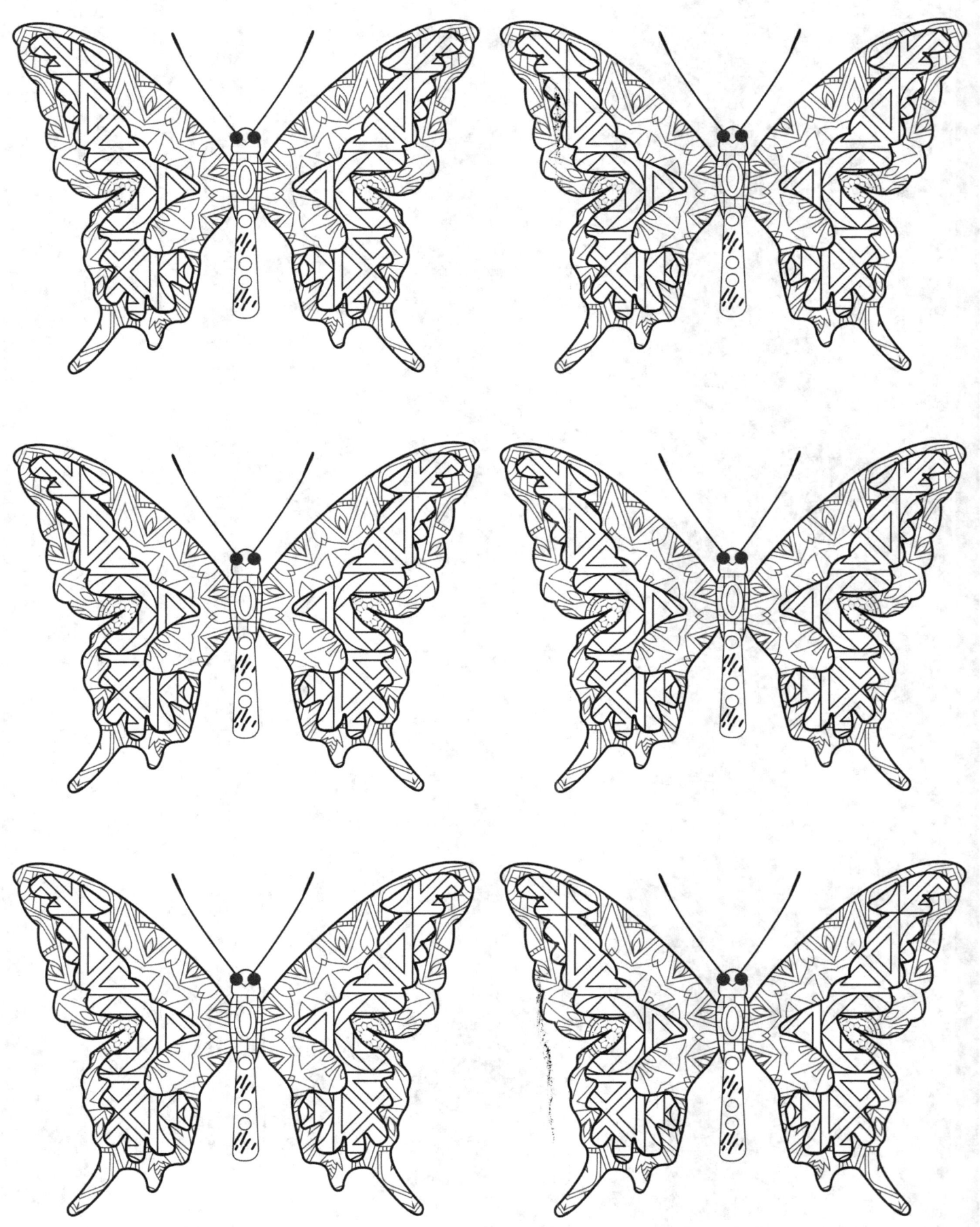

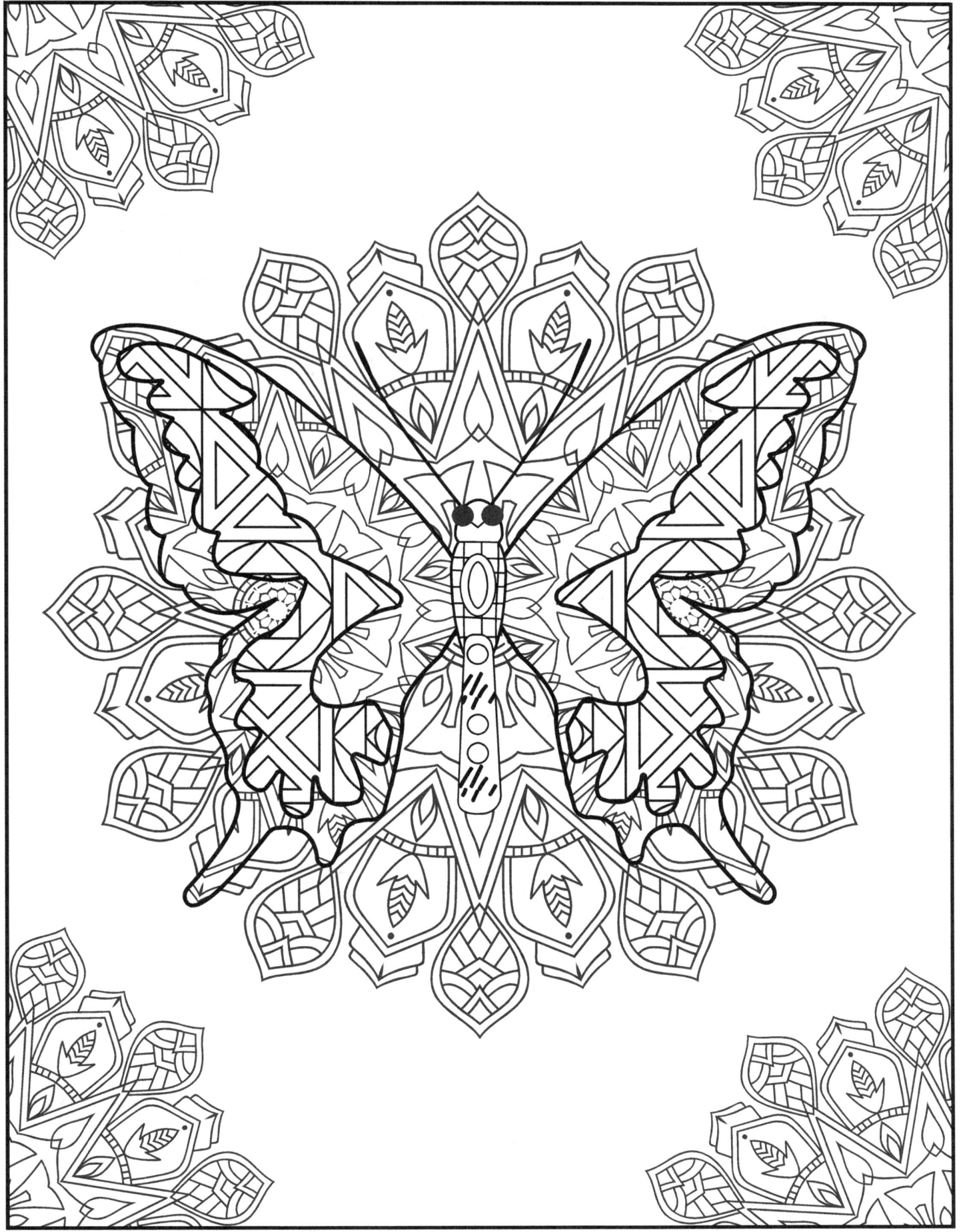

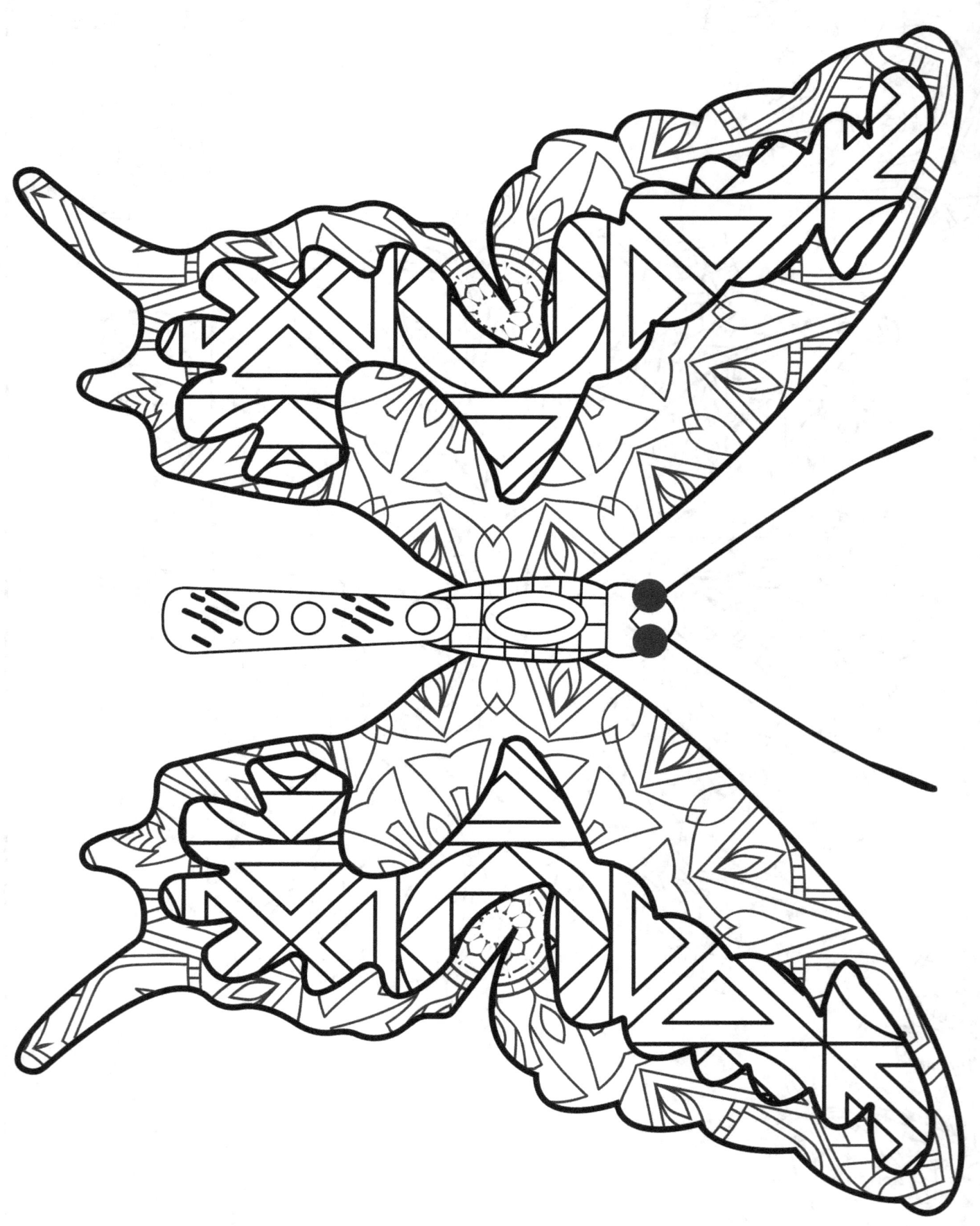

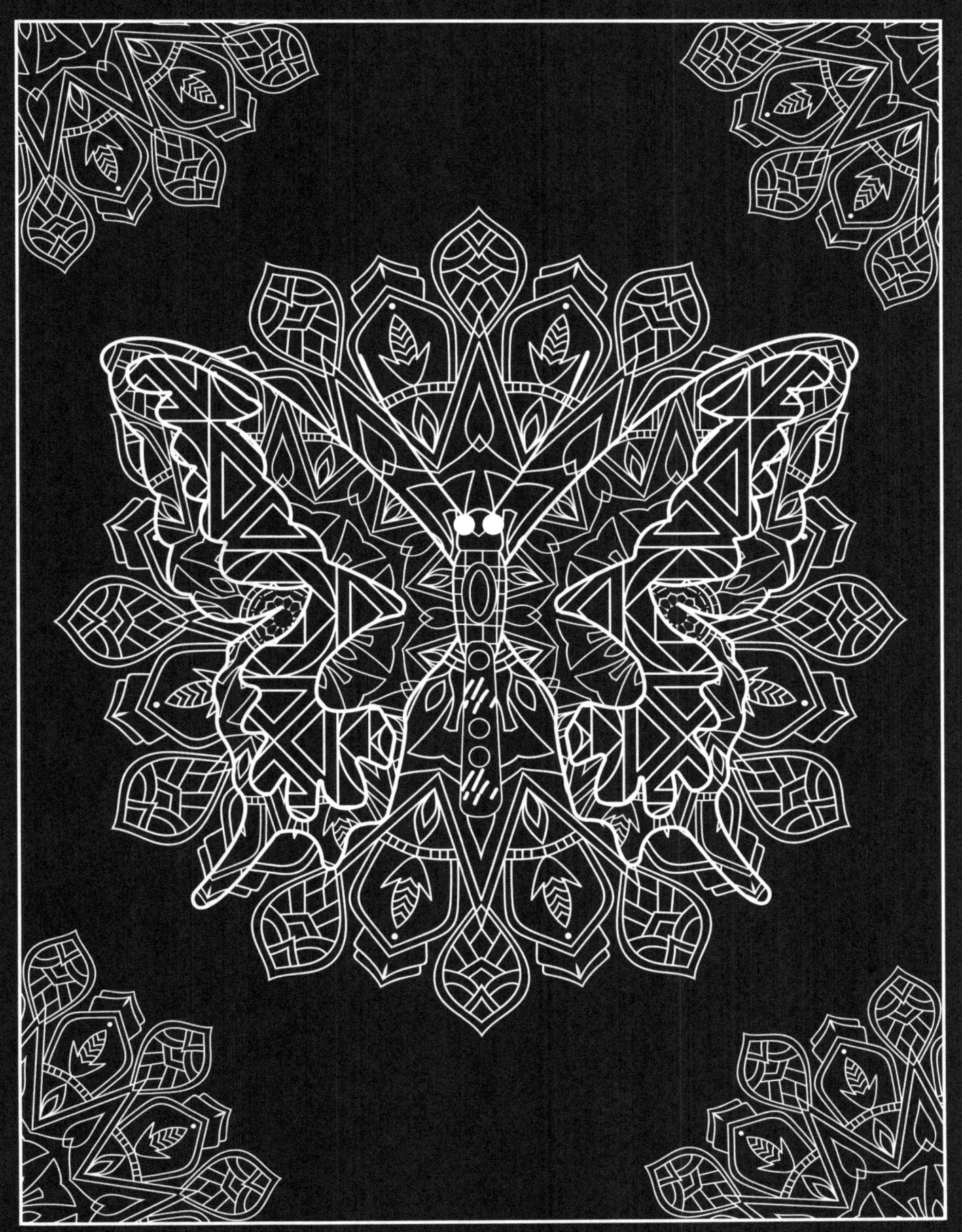

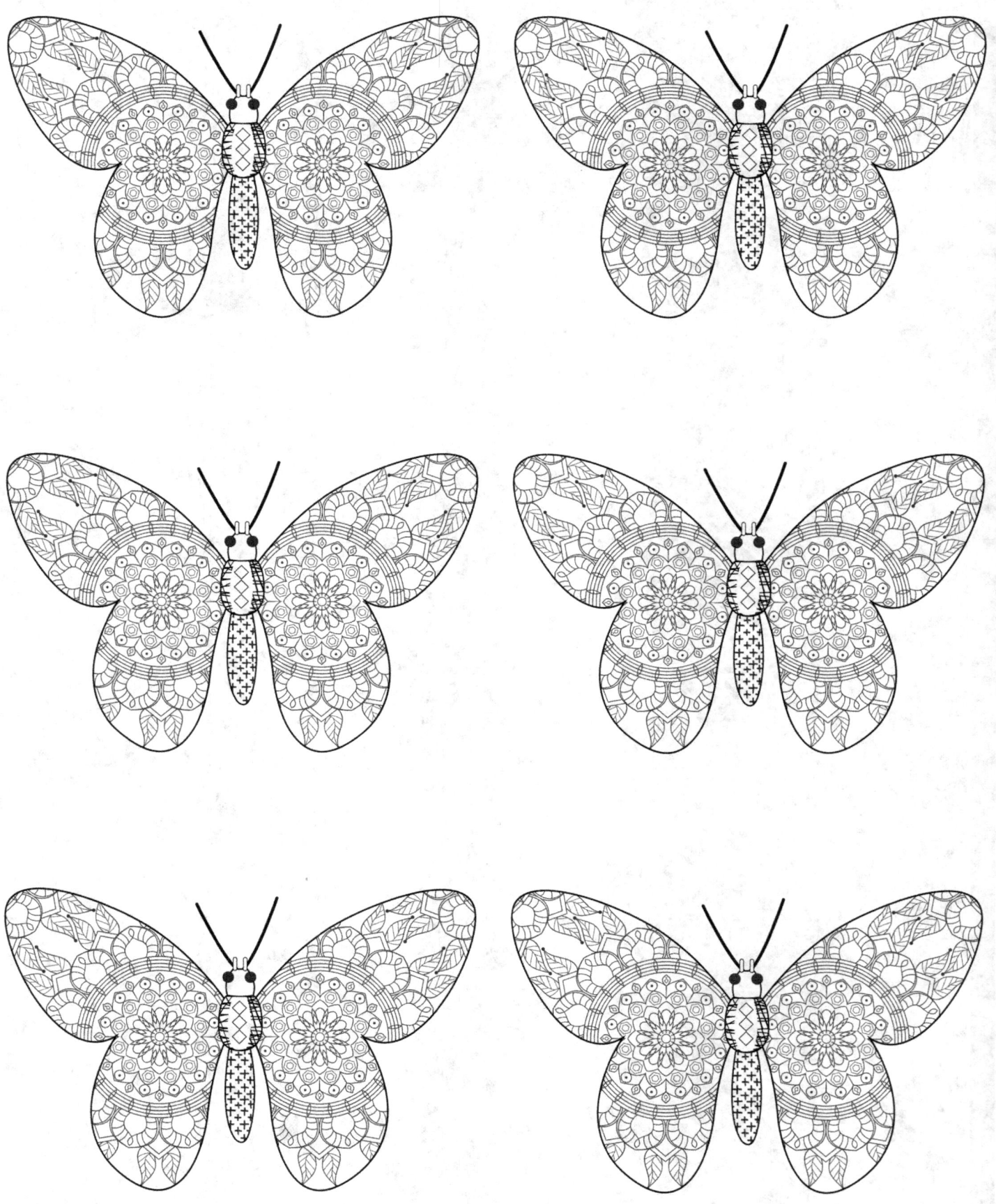

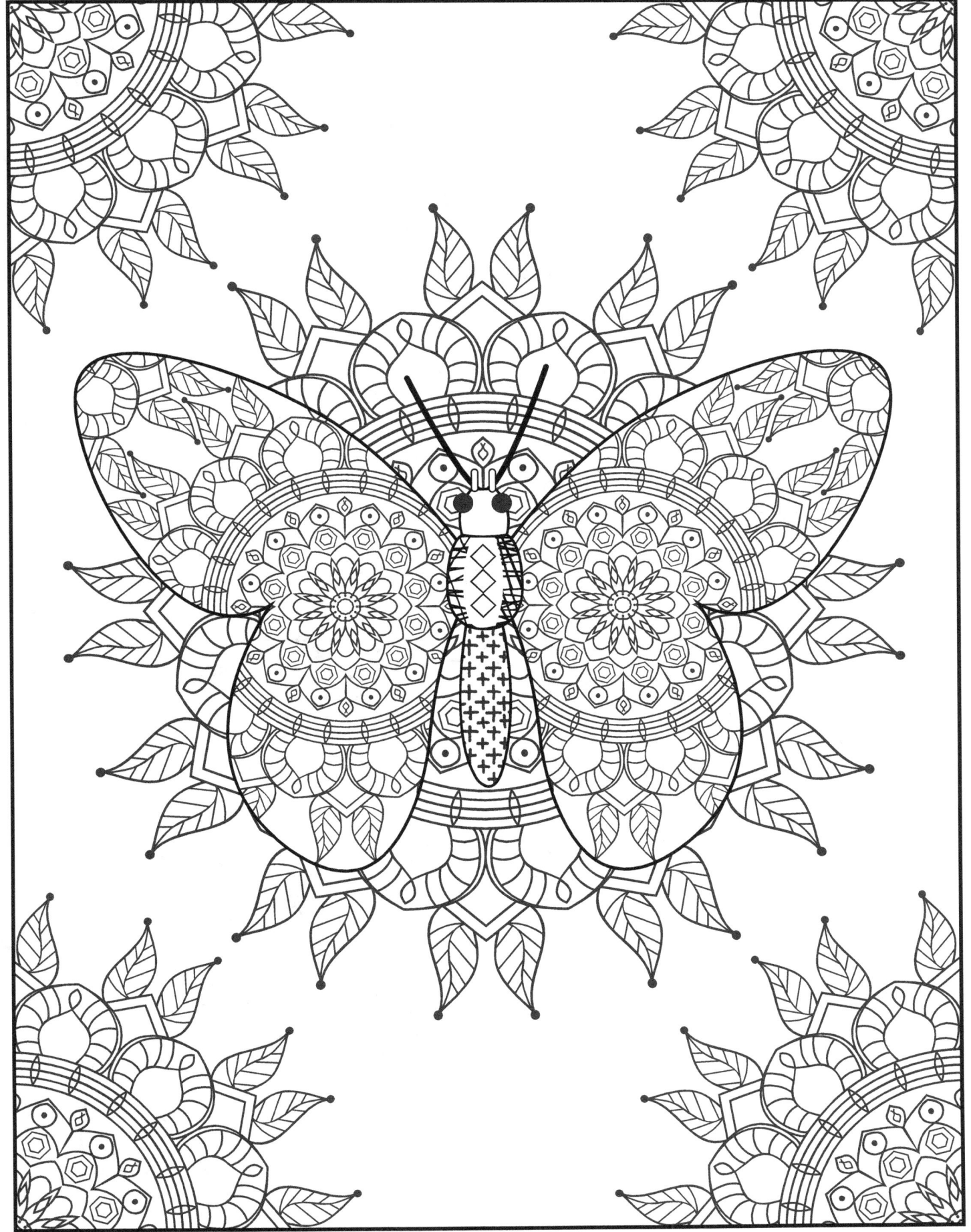

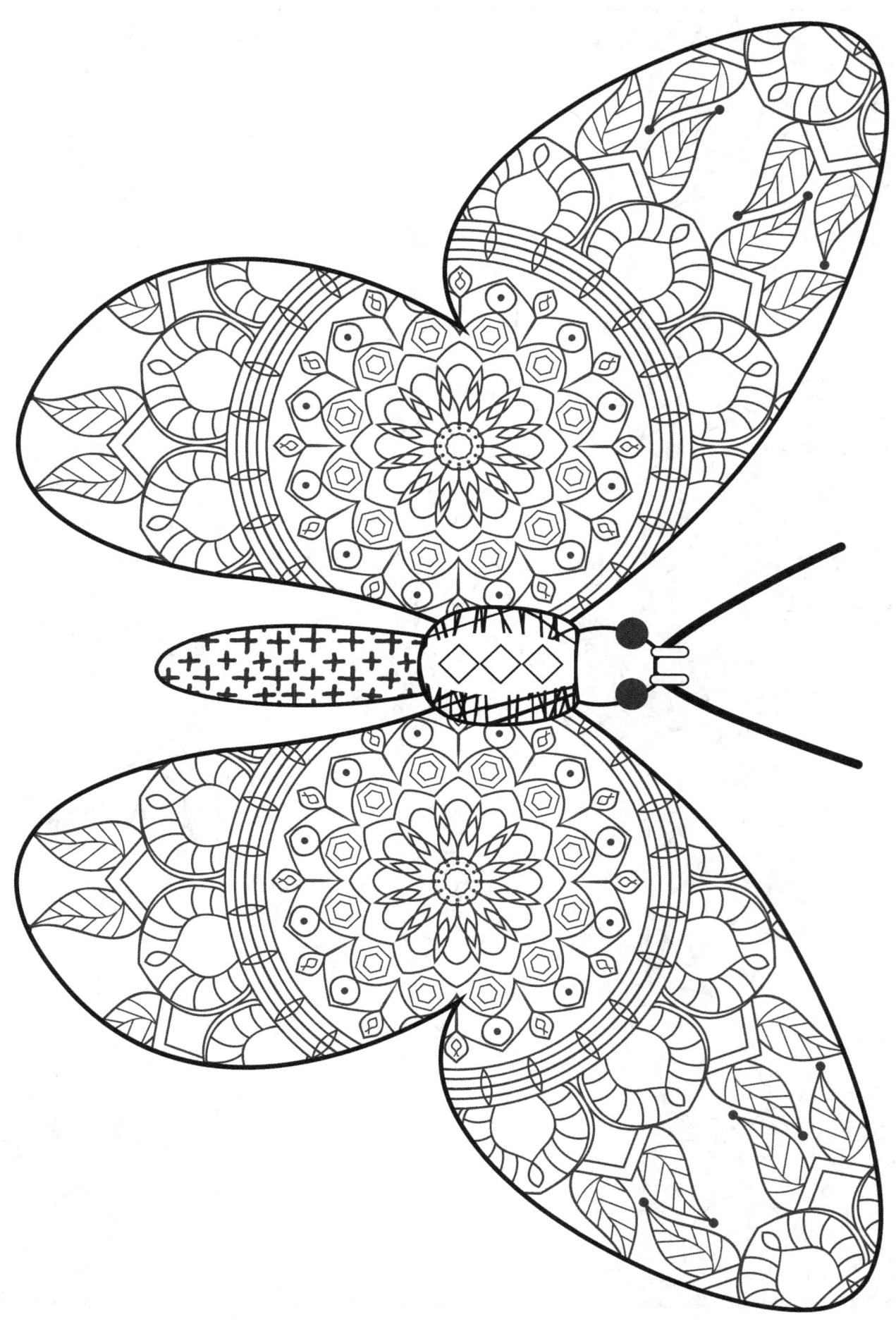

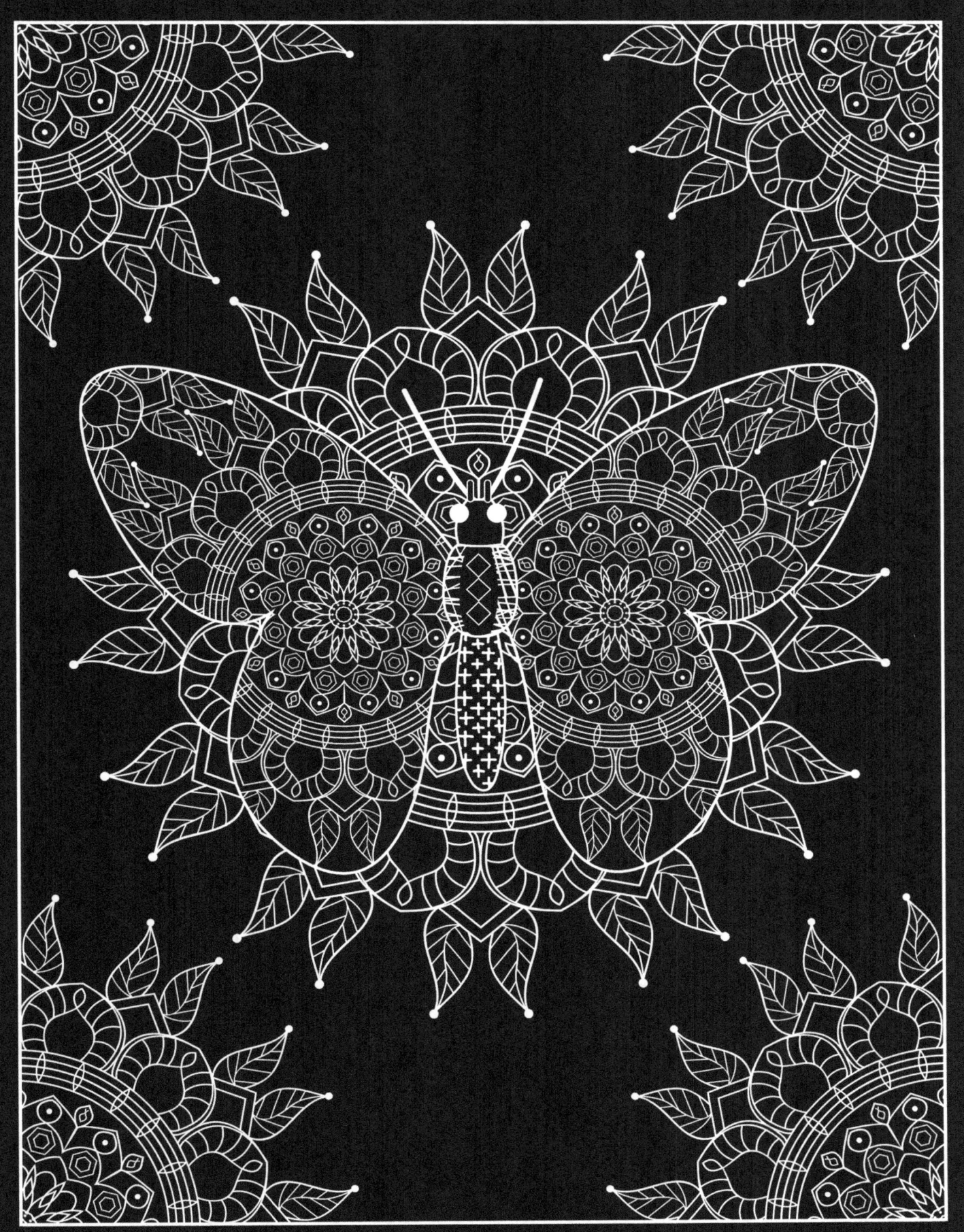

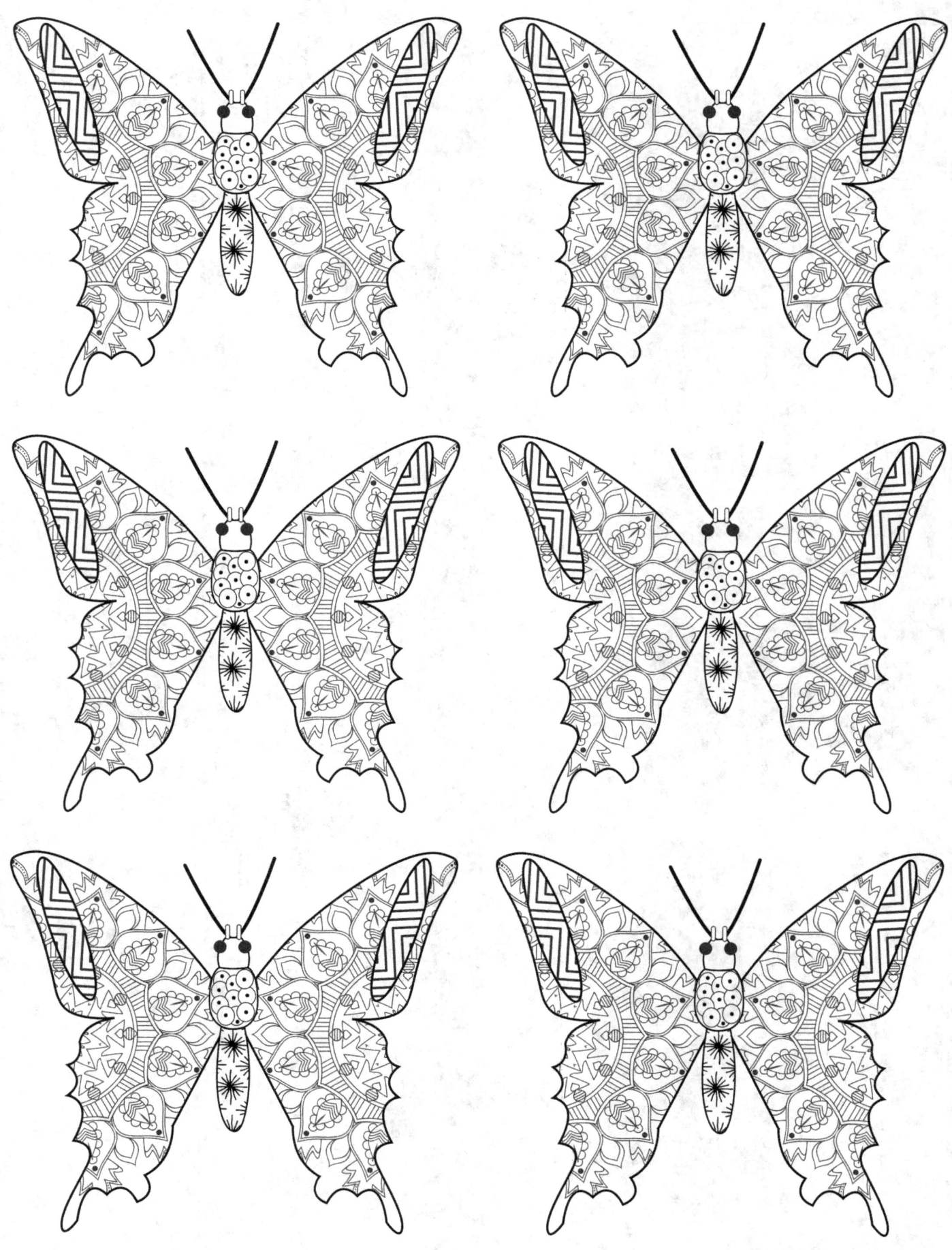

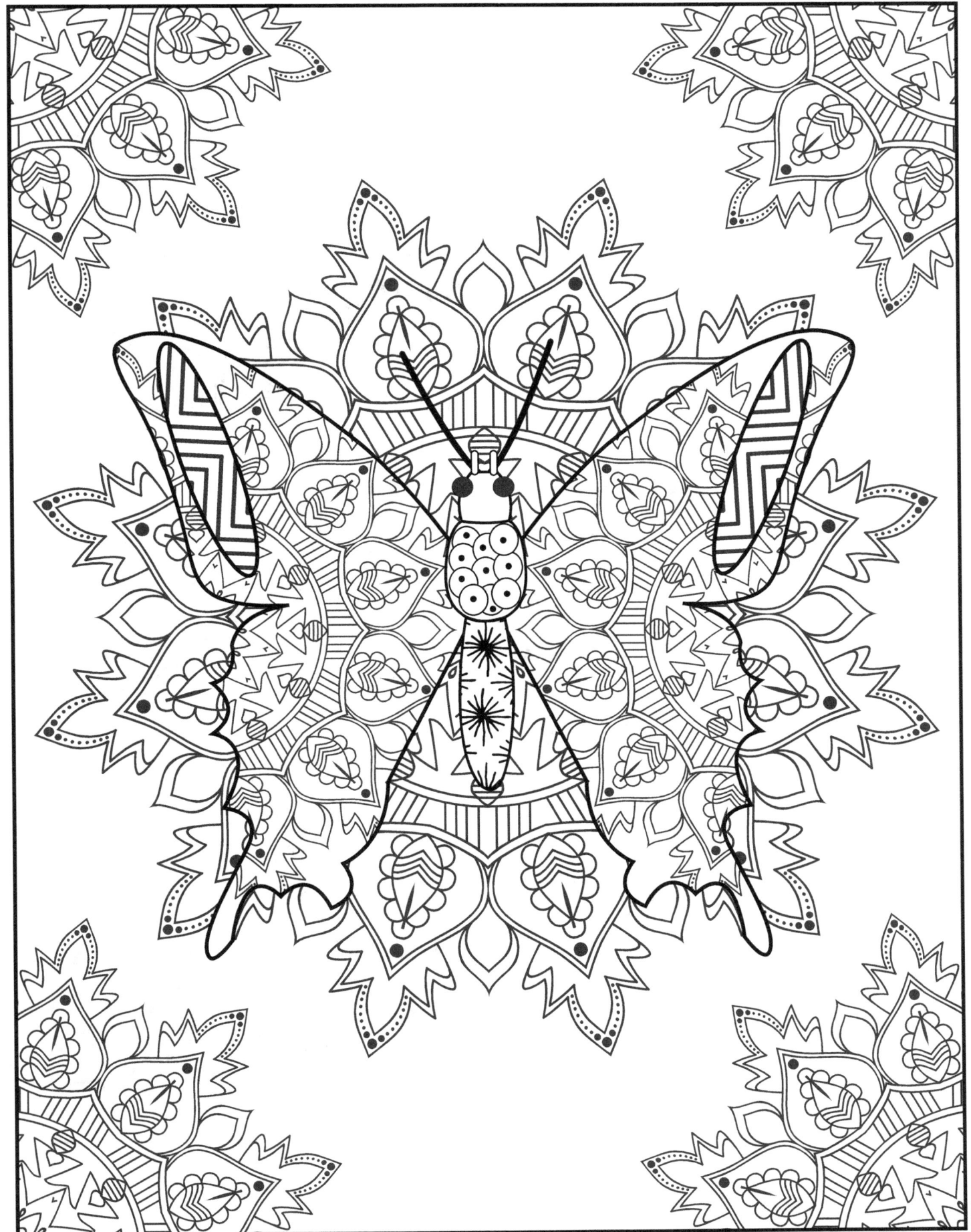

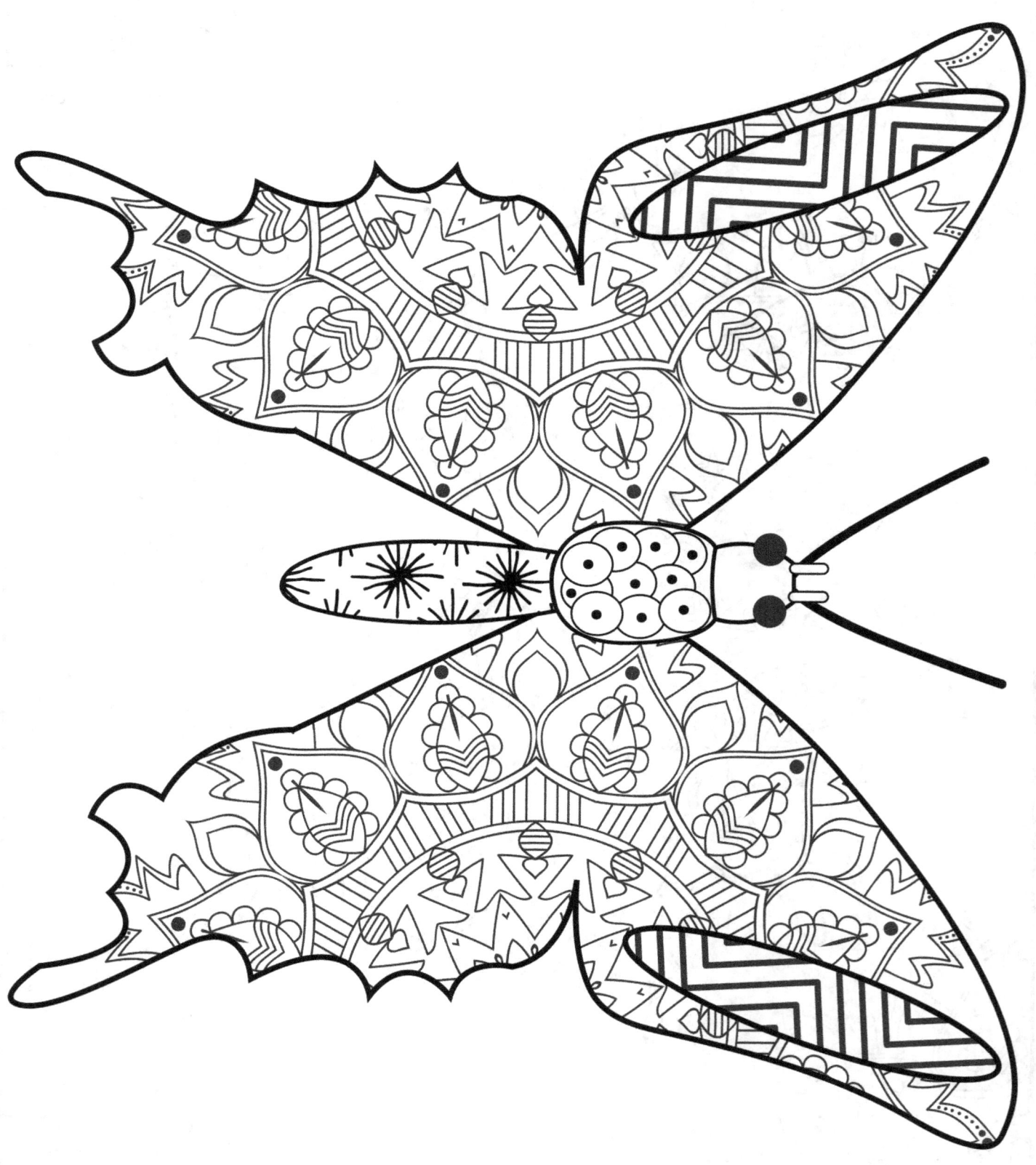

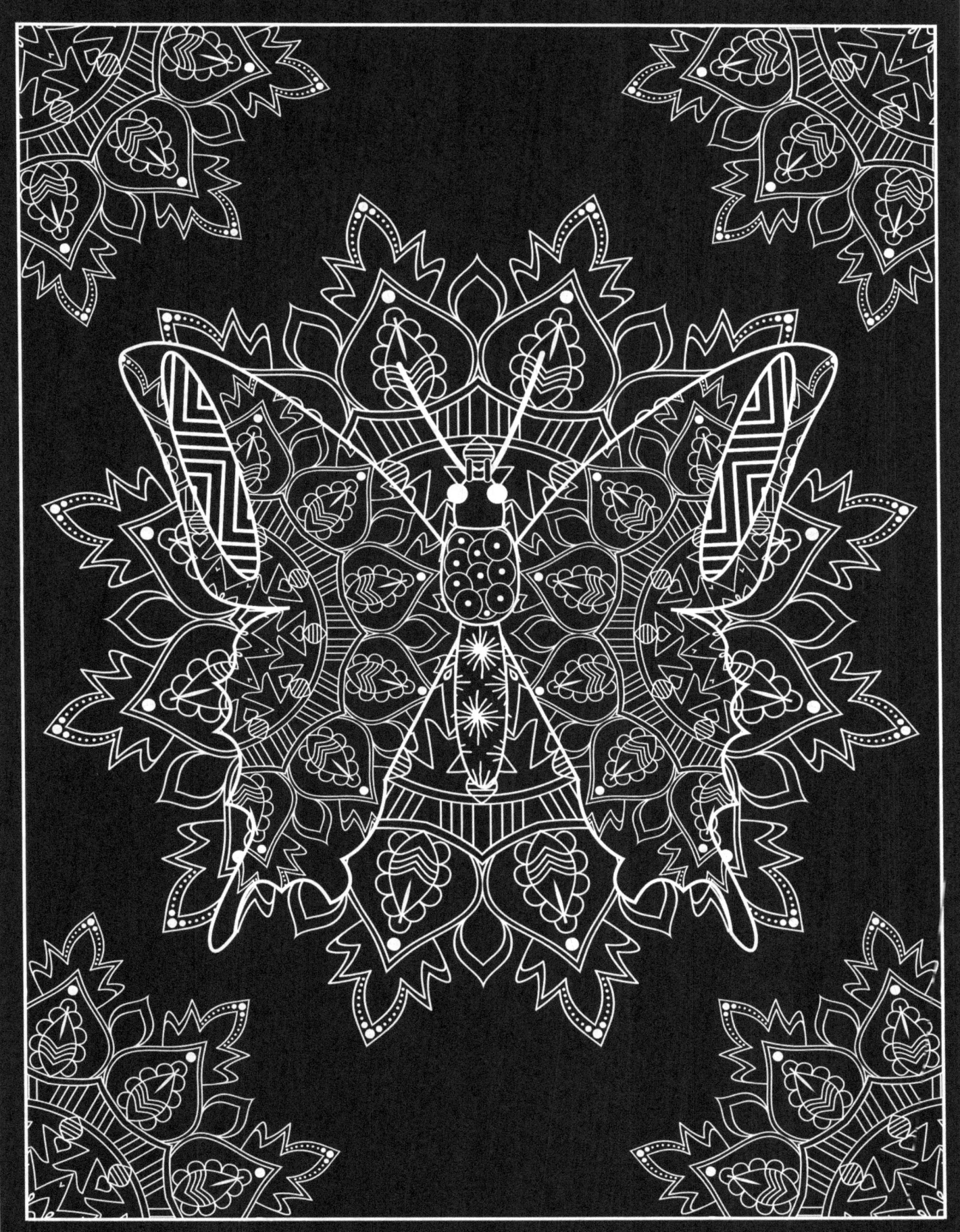

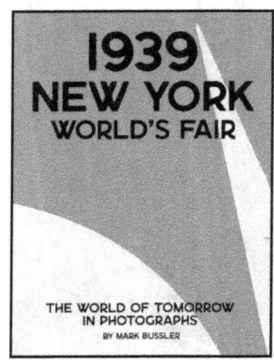

1939 New York World's Fair: The World of Tomorrow in Photographs

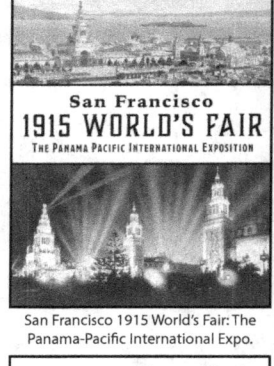

San Francisco 1915 World's Fair: The Panama-Pacific International Expo.

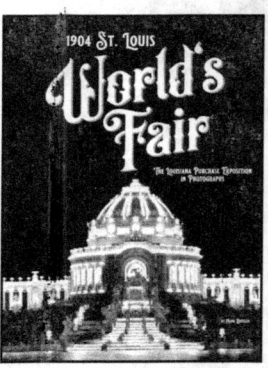

1904 St. Louis World's Fair: The Louisiana Purchase Exposition in Photographs

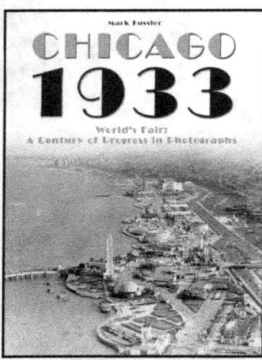

Chicago 1933 World's Fair: A Century of Progress in Photographs

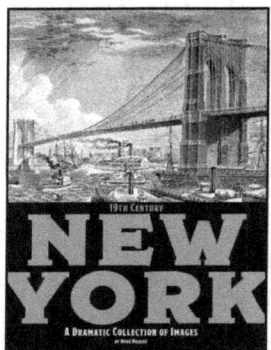

19th Century New York: A Dramatic Collection of Images

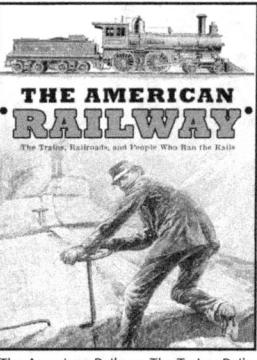

The American Railway: The Trains, Railroads, and People Who Ran the Rails

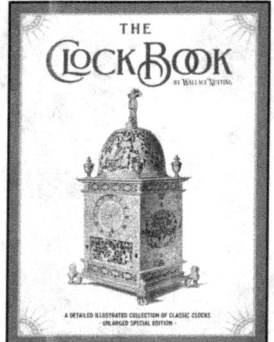

The Clock Book: A Detailed Illustrated Collection of Classic Clocks

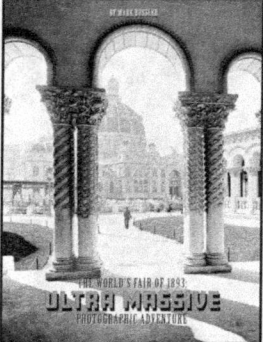

The World's Fair of 1893 Ultra Massive Photographic Adventure Vol. 1

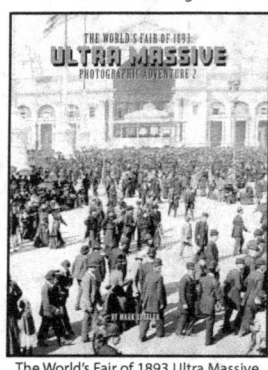

The World's Fair of 1893 Ultra Massive Photographic Adventure Vol. 2

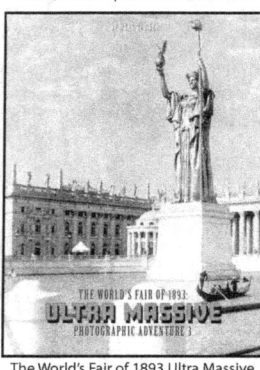

The World's Fair of 1893 Ultra Massive Photographic Adventure Vol. 3

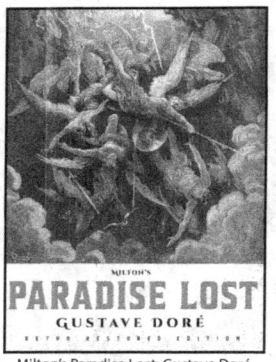

Milton's Paradise Lost: Gustave Doré Retro Restored Edition

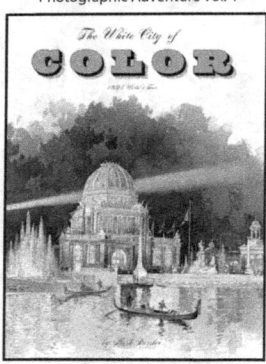

The White City of Color: 1893 World's Fair

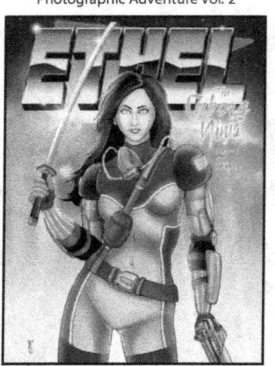

Ethel the Cyborg Ninja Book 1

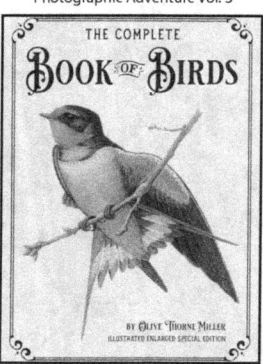

The Complete Book of Birds: Illustrated Enlarged Special Edition

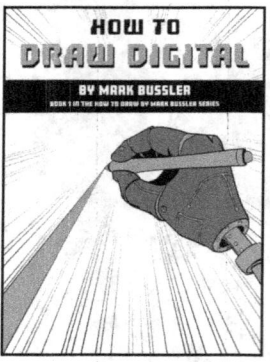

How To Draw Digital by Mark Bussler

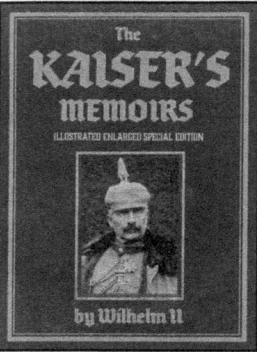

The Kaiser's Memoirs: Illustrated Enlarged Special Edition

## View our complete catalog at:
## www.CGRpublishing.com

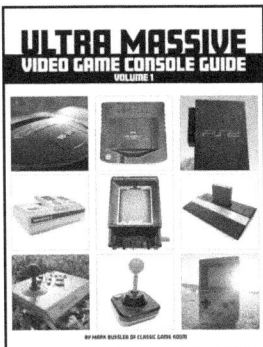

Ultra Massive Video Game Console
Guide Volume 1

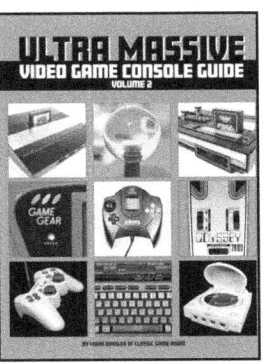

Ultra Massive Video Game Console
Guide Volume 2

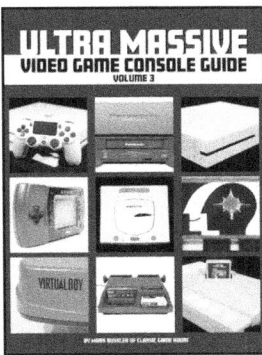

Ultra Massive Video Game Console
Guide Volume 3

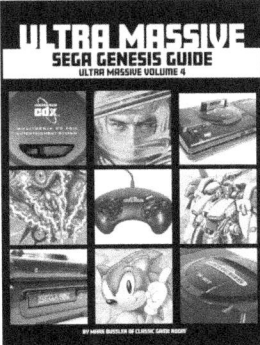

Ultra Massive Sega Genesis Guide

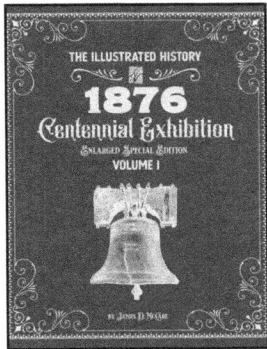

The Illustrated History of the 1876
Centennial Exhibition Volume 1

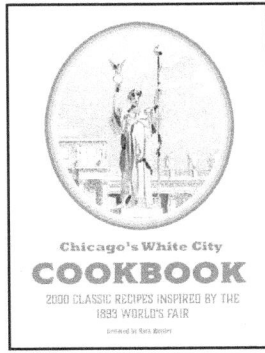

Chicago's White City Cookbook

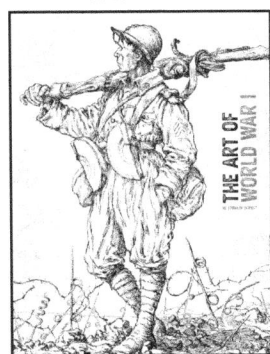

The Art of World War 1

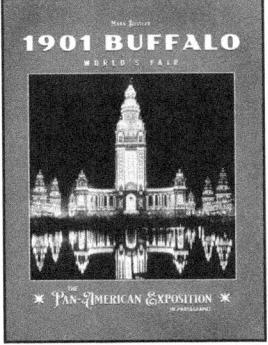

1901 Buffalo World's Fair: The Pan-
American Exposition in Photographs

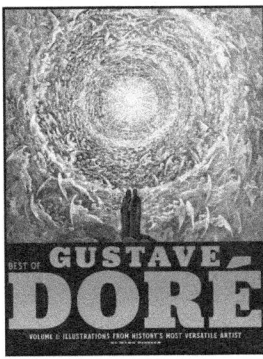

Best of Gustave Doré Volume 1

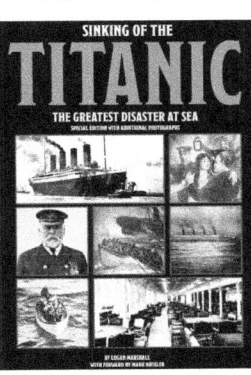

Sinking of the Titanic: The Greatest
Disaster at Sea

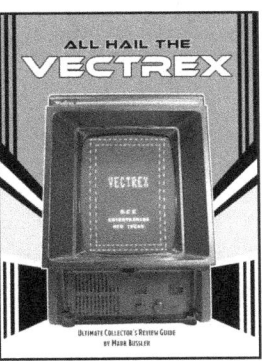

All Hail the Vectrex
Ultimate Collector's Guide

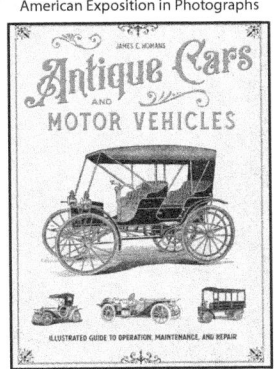

Antique Cars and Motor Vehicles:
Illustrated Guide...

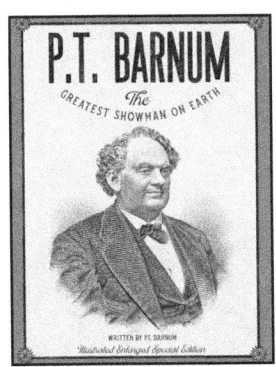

P.T. Barnum The Greatest Showman
on Earth

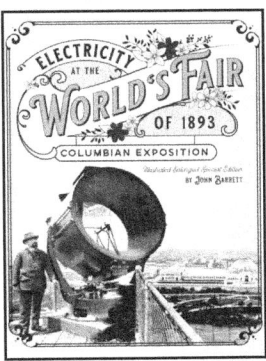

Electricity at the World's Fair of 1893
Columbian Exposition

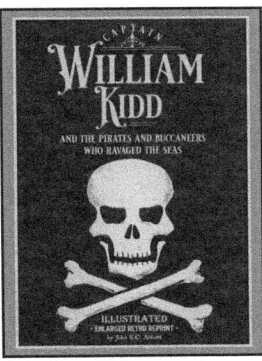

Captain William Kidd and the Pirates
and Buccaneers Who Ravaged the Seas

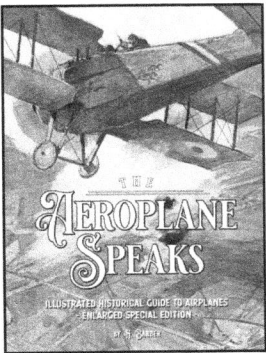

The Aeroplane Speaks: Illustrated
Historical Guide to Airplanes

- MAILING LIST -
JOIN FOR EXCLUSIVE OFFERS & MORE

**www.CGRpublishing.com/subscribe**